THE ENGLISH EDITOR TO THE READER.

——◆——

THIS book of Père Grou is the work of a master of
the spiritual life who speaks in a clear and decisive
manner, as only those can who are thoroughly
acquainted with their subject.   But it should be
understood by those who read it that it is not intended for beginners, but for such as have made some
sort of progress in a knowledge of the spiritual life.
For much that he says is put so tersely that those
whose knowledge of the subject is not within measur-
able relativity to that of the writer may easily miss
the full sense of his words, and thus be led to look
on some parts and passages as unreal or unmeaning,
or at least exaggerated.

Writing for the French public at the time he did,
there would be more likelihood of there being a good
number of people who would be fitted to understand
his work, and less likelihood of its falling into the
hands of those who would misread it.

J. G. W.

CONTENTS.

APPENDIX.

SHORT ACCOUNT OF THE ABBÉ GROU.

———•———

OUR readers will perhaps not be displeased if we give here a short account of the author of this excellent work, extracted from a longer notice which appeared in " *L'Ami de la Religion*." [1]

John Grou, born in the diocese of Boulogne, on, the 24th of November 1731, entered the College of the Jesuits when very young, and was admitted to their noviciate at the age of fifteen ; he made his first vows at the age of seventeen, and was afterwards employed in teaching, according to the custom of the Society. In this employment his taste for literature was developed. He was particularly fond of Plato and Cicero, in whose writings he found, with a great wealth of style, finer thoughts and a purer code of morals than in the generality of the ancient authors. The first fruit of his labours in Greek philosophy was the *Republic* of Plato, translated into French in two duodecimo volumes. This translation

---

[1] Vol. xxxii., p. 65 *et. seq.*

was followed by another, of the *Laws*, by the same author, and later on by that of the *Dialogues*.

Father Grou lived for several years at Pont-à-Mousson, and it was there that he made his final vows, at a time when the Jesuits were already suppressed in France. After the death of Stanislas they were also banished from Lorraine. Father Grou came to Paris, where he took the name of Leclaire. At Paris he led a very retired life, dividing his time between his studies and his religious duties. At first Monsieur de Beaumont, the Archbishop of Paris, employed him to write upon subjects relating to religion; the Archbishop also granted him for some time a pension, which eventually ceased. A holy nun of the Visitation, whose acquaintance he made through one of his brother priests, and who was believed to be favoured with special graces, induced him to enter upon the way of perfection and a life of prayer. He gave to literary work all the time which was left to him after fulfilling his spiritual exercises and the cares of his ministry. The result of this laborious life was the composition of several books upon matters of piety. His first work of this kind was "*La Morale Tirée des Confessions de Saint Augustine.*" Paris 1766, 2 vols. 12mo. The author's design was to contrast the morals of Christianity with the systems of unbelievers, drawing his principles from the writings

of Saint Augustine. This work was succeeded by
"*Les Caractères de la Vraie Dévotion*" (Marks of True
Devotion), Paris 1788, 18mo. In this the author
defined what true devotion is, and also its motives,
its object, and its means. This volume was quickly
followed by the "*Maximes Spirituelles, avec des
Explications*" (Spiritual Maxims Explained), Paris
1789, 12mo.

About the same time he also composed these little
pious treatises which we have now given to the
public, and had them copied for the use of a devout
lady of high rank whose director he then was.
These manuscripts, which consisted of nine small
12mo. volumes, have thus been preserved. He had
also undertaken a great work which had cost him
fourteen years of research and trouble. Before leaving France he confided the manuscripts of this work
to a lady, who was arrested during the Reign of
Terror, and whose servants committed them to the
flames, fearing they might compromise their mistress.

The life of Father Grou was upright and peaceful;
he was much esteemed, enjoyed a pension from the
king, and did great good by his advice and his writings.
When the Revolution broke out he at first wished
to remain concealed in Paris, and there to exercise
his ministry in secret; but the nun of whom we have
already spoken persuaded him to seek refuge in

England.   He followed her advice, and was invited
by one of his former brothers in religion, who was
then chaplain to an English Catholic in good position,
Mr. Thomas Weld, to come and stay with him.
Taking up his abode in the castle, Father Grou
became the director of the whole family.   His gentleness, his wisdom, his experience in the ways of the
spiritual life, were most useful to the persons who
gave him their confidence.   It was then that he
learnt that his great work, the fruit of so many years
of labour, had been burnt at Paris.   He bore this loss
with much calmness, and said simply, "*If God had
wished to derive any glory from this work, He would have
preserved it.*"   He observed, as much as possible, the
rule of the Jesuits ; rose every day at four o'clock in
the morning, without light or fire, made an hour's
meditation, said his office, and prepared for Mass,
which he never failed to celebrate every day until
attacked by his last illness.   He practised the
strictest poverty, having nothing whatever of his own,
and asking with the greatest simplicity for books or
clothes when he needed them.   What was most
remarkable in him was his lively faith, and the constant tranquillity of his soul, his great humility,
modesty, and zeal.   In 1796 he had printed in
London, the "*Meditations, en forme de Retraite, sur
l'Amour de Dieu*" (Meditations, in the form of a

Retreat, upon the Love of God), and also a little treatise upon the resignation of one's self to God— "*Don de Soi-même à Dieu.*" Some theologians imagined these works contained ideas favourable to Quietism ; but a French bishop, after examining them, pronounced them to be perfectly sound, and free from any taint of the kind. There was another work of his published in London, called the "*School of Christ;*" but it has not yet appeared in French.

The Supplement to the Library of Jesuit Writers, published at Rome in 1816, mentions also, as written by Father Grou, "*La Science du Crucifix,*" Paris, chez Aufroy ; and "*La Science Pratique du Crucifix dans l'usage des Sacrements de Pénitence et de Eucharistie*" (Practical Science of the Crucifix in the use of the Sacraments of Penance and the Holy Eucharist), as a continuation of the preceding.

Two years before his death, he had a very painful attack of asthma. Some time after, he was seized with apoplexy, and dropsy then declared itself; his legs swelled to an enormous size, he could not remain in bed, and passed the last ten months of his life in an arm-chair. He continued to the very end to hear the confessions of the pious family with whom he lived. Holy Communion was brought to him twice in the week. When he felt his end approaching, he asked for the last Sacraments, and received them with full consciousness and great devotion.   A short time before he breathed his last, holding his crucifix in his hands, he exclaimed, *"O my God! how sweet it is to die in Thine arms!"*

His death took place on the 13th of December 1803 : he was seventy-two years of age.

His manuscripts, which were numerous, were given up to his former companions; and by them was printed in 1815 *"L'Interieur de Jesus et de Marie"* (The Inner Life of Jesus and Mary), two volumes 12mo.   This esteemed work has been reprinted several times since.

MANUAL FOR INTERIOR SOULS.

I.

ON TRUE AND SOLID DEVOTION.

THE word *devotion*, which is derived from the Latin,
answers to that of devotedness,—a *vowing* of oneself, a consecration of one's self. A devout person
is, then, a person devoted to God, consecrated to God.
There is no stronger expression than that of *devotion*
to mark that disposition of the soul which is ready
to do everything and to suffer everything for Him to
whom she is devoted.

The devotion to creatures (I mean, of course, that
which is lawful and allowed by God) has necessarily
its limits. The devotion to God has none, and can
have none. As soon as the least reserve, the least
exception, intrudes there, it is no longer devotion.
True and solid devotion is, then, that disposition of
the heart by which we are ready to do and to suffer,
without exception or reserve, everything which comes
from God's good pleasure, everything which is the
Will of God. And this disposition is the most
excellent of all the gifts of the Holy Spirit. We
cannot ask for it too often or too earnestly ; and

A

we must never flatter ourselves that we have it in
its perfection, because it can always go on increasing,
either in itself or in its effects.

We see, by this definition, that devotion is something most interior, and which has to do with the
inmost life of the soul, for it affects that within us
which is most spiritual; that is to say, our understanding and our will. Devotion consists, then, neither
in reasoning, nor in imagination, nor in anything
that is sensible. We are not devout just because we
are able to reason well about the things of God, nor
because we have grand ideas or fine imaginations
about spiritual matters, nor because we are sometimes affected to tears.

Again, devotion is not a thing which passes, which
comes and goes, as it were, but it is something
habitual, fixed, permanent, which extends over every
instant of life and regulates all our conduct.

The principle of devotion is, that God being the
one source and the one author of holiness, the
reasonable creature ought to depend on Him in everything, and be absolutely governed by the Spirit of
God. She must be always attached to God in the
depths of her soul, always attentive to His voice
within her, always faithful to accomplish what He
asks of her each moment.

It is, then, impossible to be truly devout unless we
are interior, given to recollection, accustomed to retire
within ourselves, or rather never to go out of ourselves, to possess our soul in peace.

Whoever gives himself up to his senses, to his
imagination, to his passions, I do not say in criminal

things, but even in those which are not bad in themselves, will never be devout ; for the first effect of
devotion is to bring into captivity the senses, the
imagination, and the passions, and to prevent the
will from ever being led away by them.

He who is curious, impulsive, delighting to interest
himself in exterior things, and to mix himself up
with the affairs of others ; he who is never willingly
alone ; he who is critical, speaking ill of his neighbour, satirical, irritable, contemptuous, haughty, ready
to take offence at anything which wounds his self-
love ; he who is obstinate, believing only in his own
opinions, or he who is a slave to human respect and
to public opinion to such an extent that he is in
consequence weak, inconstant, always changing his
principles and his conduct, will never be devout in
the sense I mean.

The true devout man is a man of prayer, whose
sole delight is to be with God, and to speak with
Him, and who scarcely ever loses his sense of the
presence of God. Not that he is always thinking of
God—for that is impossible here below—but because
he is always united to God in his heart, and is guided
in everything by His Spirit. To pray, he has no
need of a book, or of a method, or of great efforts of
the head or even of the will. He has only to retire
quietly into himself ; there he finds God, there he
finds peace, sometimes a peace full of joy, sometimes
a peace in spite of dryness,—but always a deep and
real peace. He prefers the prayer in which he gives
much to God, and in which he suffers, the prayer in
which self-love is undermined gradually, until it can

find nothing to feed upon ; in short, a simple prayer, denuded of all images or of perceptible feelings, and of all those things which the soul can remark or experience in other kinds of prayer.

The true devout man seeks not himself or his own gratification in the service of God, and he endeavours to practise this maxim of the " Imitation of Christ : " Wherever you find self, renounce self.

The truly devout man studies to fulfil perfectly all the duties of his state, and all his really necessary duties of kindness and courtesy to society. He is faithful to his devotional exercises, but he is not a slave to them ; he interrupts them, he suspends them, he even gives them up altogether for a time, when any reason of necessity or of simple charity requires it. Provided he does not do his own will, he is always certain of doing the Will of God.

The truly devout man does not run about seeking for good works, but he waits until the occasion of doing good presents itself to him. He does what in him lies to ensure success ; but he leaves the care of the success to God. He prefers those good works which are obscure and done in secret to those which are brilliant and gain general admiration ; but he does not shrink from these latter ones when they are for the glory of God and the edification of his neighbour. The truly devout man does not burden himself with a great quantity of vocal prayers and practices which do not leave him time to breathe. He always preserves his liberty of spirit ; he is neither scrupulous nor uneasy about himself; he goes on with simplicity and confidence.

He has made a determination, once for all, to refuse nothing to God, to grant nothing to self-love, and
never to commit a voluntary fault ; but he does not
perplex himself ; he goes on courageously ; he is not
too particular. If he falls into a fault, he does not
agitate himself ; he humbles himself at the sight of
his own weakness ; he raises himself up, and thinks
no more about it.

He is not astonished at his weaknesses, at his falls
or his imperfections ; he is never discouraged. He
knows that he can do nothing, but that God can do
everything. He does not rely upon his own good
thoughts and resolutions, but simply upon the grace
and the goodness of God. If he were to fall a hundred
times a day, he would not despair, but he would
stretch out his hands lovingly to God, and beg of
Him to lift him up and to take pity on him.

The truly devout man has a horror of evil, but he
has a still greater love of good. He thinks more
about practising virtue than about avoiding vice. He
is generous, large-hearted, and courageous ; and when
there is a question of exposing himself to danger
for God's sake, he does not fear wounds. In one
word, he loves better to do what is good, even at the
risk of falling into some imperfection, than to omit it,
through fear of the danger of sinning.

No one is so amiable in the ordinary intercourse
of life as a really devout man. He is simple, straightforward, open as the day, unpretentious, gentle,
solid, and true ; his conversation is pleasing and interesting ; he can enter into all innocent amusements ;
and he carries his condescending kindness and charity

as far as possible, short of what is wrong. Whatever
some persons may say, true devotion is never a
melancholy thing, either for itself or for others. How
should the man who continually enjoys the truest
happiness, the only happiness, be ever sad ? It is
the inordinate passions of human nature which are
sad,—avarice, ambition, love which is not sanctified
by God and has not God for its chief end. And it
is to divert themselves from the trouble and uneasiness which these passions cause the heart that men
plunge themselves recklessly into pleasures and excesses, which they vary continually, but which weary
the soul, without ever satisfying it.

Whoever really and in sincerity gives himself up
to the service of God will experience the truth of that
sentence : " *To serve God, is to reign,*" even if it be in
poverty, in humiliations, and in suffering. All those
who in this world seek their happiness in something
that is not God, all, without exception, will verify the
saying of Saint Augustine : " *The heart of man is made
for God alone, and is never at peace until it rests in
God.*" " Thou hast made us for Thyself, and our
heart findeth no rest until it reposeth in Thee."

II.

THE IDEAL OF TRUE VIRTUE.

THERE are very few Christians, even amongst those
who are specially consecrated to God, who have a
right idea of what true virtue is. Almost all of them

imagine it to consist in a certain routine of piety, and in fidelity to certain exterior practices. If with this they have at intervals some emotion of sensible devotion, without taking care to discern whether these emotions come from God or from their own efforts, they at once conclude that they are really virtuous.

Nevertheless, they are subject to a thousand faults and imperfections, of which they take no heed themselves, and which any one else would try in vain to make them conscious of. They are narrow-minded, scrupulously exact in their practices of devotion, full of esteem for themselves, extremely sensitive and touchy, obstinate in holding their own opinions, puffed up with self-love, constrained and affected in their manners ; nothing true, nothing simple, nothing natural about them. In their own hearts they prefer themselves to all others, and often they despise, they condemn, they persecute really holy persons, and true piety, of which they know nothing. Nothing is more common in Christianity than this false and pharisaical virtue. Those who are really good have no greater enemies ; and if we wish to describe them in a few words we may say, it was pretended holy persons who crucified Jesus Christ, and they still crucify Him every day in His most perfect imitators. As soon as any one really gives himself to God and begins to lead an inner life, he is sure to draw upon himself, first of all jealousy and criticism, and then persecutions and calumnies of every kind, from these devout Pharisees.

If we wish to understand what true virtue is, we must contemplate it in our Lord and Saviour Jesus Christ : He is our one great Example ; He gave

Himself to us for that reason; He was made Man
that holiness might be sensible and palpable to us.
All sanctity which is not formed and modelled on
His sanctity is false; it is displeasing to God; it may
perhaps deceive men, but it is useless for Heaven.
Let us, then, make Jesus Christ our study; and that
we may know Him thoroughly, and express His life
in ourselves, let us continually ask Him for light and
grace.   Jesus Christ sought Himself in nothing; never
had He in view His own interests, either temporal or
spiritual; never did He perform one single action
for the sake of pleasing men, neither did He ever
abstain from any good action for fear of displeasing
them.   God alone, God's glory and His Will, was the
sole object of His thoughts and feelings, the sole rule
of His conduct.   He sacrificed all, without reserve, to
the interests of His Father.

Jesus Christ made piety to consist in our interior
dispositions, the religion of the heart; not in vain
and fleeting feelings, but in sincere and efficacious
resolutions, always followed by execution; a disposition of an entire devotion to God, a continual annihilation of self, and a boundless charity towards others.
Every instant of His life was consecrated to the accomplishment of these three dispositions.   He neglected
no observance of any point of the law; but, at the
same time, He declared, both by word and example,
that this observance was only of value when it pro-
ceeded from an inner principle of love, and that the
practice of the letter of the law alone, without the
interior spirit, made slaves, and not children of God.

Jesus Christ always looked upon this present life

as passing away; as a pilgrimage, a time of trial, simply designed to test our love for God. The things which are eternal were His constant occupation. He gave to nature what was absolutely necessary, without going beyond. Although He possessed nothing, and was always dependent on Providence for His simple bodily wants, He was never uneasy about the morrow, and His delight was to experience the effects of poverty.

Jesus Christ embraced by His own free choice that which men accept with the greatest difficulty, and to which they only submit from necessity. He did not absolutely condemn riches, but He preferred poverty. He did not condemn the rank and marks of honour which God Himself has established amongst men, but He taught us that an obscure condition, bereft of every kind of consideration, is more pleasing to God, and more favourable to salvation; and that to think one's self better than others because one is born great, noble, or powerful, or in a position of authority, is an error and the source of countless sins. With the exception of the simple natural pleasure which the Creator has attached to certain actions, and the use of which is limited by the severest rules, He has absolutely scorned every other kind of pleasure, especially those which men seek with the greatest eagerness, and as far as He Himself was concerned, He renounced even the most innocent pleasure. Hard work, apostolic labours, prayer, and the instruction of His disciples and the multitude filled up every moment of His life.

Jesus Christ was simplicity itself; always the

same, without any affectation in His speech or actions. He taught, with the authority of Godmade Man, the most sublime truths, and things which had before been unknown. But He propounded His doctrine in a simple, familiar manner, without any pomp of human eloquence, and so that all minds could under· stand Him. His miracles, divine in themselves, are still more divine from the way in which He wrought them. He wished that the account of the evangelists should agree with the perfect simplicity of His own life. It is impossible to give in a more simple manner than they have done the account of a life, and of words and actions, which bear on them the very impress of Divinity. ·

Jesus Christ had a most tender compassion for sinners who were sincerely humble and repentant for their sins. "*I came for sinners*," He said, "*and not for the just*," *who trust in their own justice.* The publican who stood afar off, Mary Magdalen, the woman taken in adultery, the Samaritan woman at the well of Jacob, were all treated by Him with a kindness and tenderness which astonishes us. But the pride of the Pharisees, their hypocrisy, their avarice, these were the objects of His most severe censure and malediction. The sins of the mind and the spirit, just the sins to which the falsely devout are more subject than any others, are those which He condemned with the greatest severity, because they are a sign of more blindness of the mind and more corruption of the heart.

Jesus Christ bore with a never-failing gentleness the faults and the roughness of His disciples. According to our way of thinking, what must He not have suffered at having to live with men so imperfect and so ignorant of the things of God? Intercourse with our neighbour is perhaps one of the most difficult things in this life; even the saints have felt how much it cost them. And the nearer they are to God, the more need they have of condescension, to lower themselves to others, as it were, to unbend, to conceal and excuse in others a thousand faults which they see and feel more keenly than any one else. And this is a point upon which their practice must be continual, and it all depends upon how they acquit themselves with regard to it as to whether they will make virtue amiable or displeasing to others.

Jesus Christ suffered every kind of persecution at the hands of His enemies, but He never gave way. He only opposed to them His innocence and virtue, and He always confounded them by His spotless life. When the hour came that He allowed Himself to fall into their hands, He permitted their evil passions to act, and looked upon them as instruments of Divine justice. He kept silence when He saw them so obstinate in their malice; He sought not to justify Himself, although it would have been so easy; He allowed Himself to be condemned; He allowed them to enjoy their imaginary triumph; He pardoned them, He prayed for them, He shed His blood for them. This is the most sublime and the most difficult height of perfection.

Whoever aspires to true sanctity, and to be guided in everything by the Spirit of God, must expect to suffer from the tongues of men, to bear their calumnies, and sometimes their persecutions. In this, above all things, we must take Jesus Christ as our model; we must suffer, for His sake, as much as we can, in the interests of truth; our only answer to calumny must be the innocence of our life; we must keep silence when it is not absolutely necessary to speak; we must leave the care of our justification to God, if He sees fit to justify us; we must stifle in our heart every feeling of resentment and bitterness; we must try to soften our enemies by every kind of charitable actions; we must pray to God for their pardon; and we must try to see, in all they make us suffer, only the accomplishment of God's designs upon us.

And when virtue can thus sustain itself in contempt, in opprobrium, in ill-treatment, then we may look upon it as perfected, as consummate virtue. Therefore God generally reserves this trial to the last. Blessed are those who pass through it! When Jesus Christ comes in His glory, they will have a share in it proportionate to their share in His humiliations. To desire such a state as this, to accept it when it is offered to us, to bear it patiently and with joy when we find ourselves in it, this can only be the effect of grace, and of an extraordinary grace. As for us, let us rest content in our lowliness; let us never think we can attain of ourselves to anything so high; and let us only ask of God that human respect may never cause us to abandon His interests.

III.

ON THE MEANS OF ATTAINING TRUE AND SOLID VIRTUE.

THE first means of attaining virtue, which seems the most easy, and is in reality the most difficult, is to *will* it ; but with a sincere, entire, efficacious, and constant will. And oh how rare is this *good will !* We imagine we will a thing, but in truth and reality we do not will it at all. We may have desires, longings, purposes, wishes ; but that is not having a strong and determined will. We wish to be devout, but in our own way up to a certain point, and provided it does not cost us too much. We wish, and we are contented with wishing. We do not carry our wishes into practice ; we are discouraged as soon as it is necessary to put our hand to the work, to overcome obstacles or set them aside, to fight against our faults, to struggle with nature and all its evil propensities. We wish to-day perhaps ; we begin bravely, but alas ! our energies are soon relaxed. We undertake, and then we give up. We do not wish to see that everything depends upon perseverance.

Let us ask God to grant us this *good will ;* let us ask Him for it every day ; and let us try to merit, by our fidelity to the grace of to-day, to obtain it again on the next day.

The second means is to regulate the employment of each day, and to be exact in observing what we

have prescribed for ourselves.   We must not burden
ourselves too much at first.   It is better to add to
our exercises imperceptibly and by degrees.   We must
take into consideration our health, our age, our state
of life, and the duties it imposes upon us ; for that
devotion which is prejudicial to the duties of our state
is a misplaced and misunderstood devotion.

The third means is to try and realise always the
presence of God.   To attain this, we must convince
ourselves of what is of faith, viz., that God dwells
in the inmost heart of man ; that we shall find Him
within ourselves, if we will only enter in and seek
Him there ; that He is in our heart, to inspire us with
holy thoughts, and with good desires, which incline
us to what is right, and draw us away from all that
is evil.   What is called the voice of conscience is in
reality the voice of God Himself, who thus warns us,
reproves us, enlightens and directs us.   The great
thing is always to be attentive and faithful to this
voice within us.   It is not in dissipation, nor in the
agitation and tumult of the world, that we shall hear
it ; but in solitude, in peace, in the silence of our
passions and imaginations.   The greatest step towards
perfection which a soul can make, is to keep herself
habitually in such a state that she can always hear
the voice of God, when He speaks to her ; to endeavour to possess herself in peace, to avoid everything that may distract her, everything that makes
her uneasy, everything to which she is inordinately
attached.   All this must be for a long time the subject of a particular examination of conscience and a
continual struggle.

The fourth means is to give specially to God a certain time in the day, when we can occupy ourselves with Him alone, and with the thought of His presence ; when we can speak to Him, not with our lips, but in the depths of our heart, and listen to what He has to say to us. This is what is called mental prayer. To accustom ourselves to this, we may, in the beginning, make use of the book of the " Imitation of Christ," making a pause at each verse, meditating, and trying to understand the doctrine it contains. At first we may give to this exercise a quarter of an hour in the morning, and the same time in the evening ; but we should gradually accustom ourselves to spend at least half-an-hour every morning in this manner. When we begin to take a delight in this holy exercise, and can carry it on without a book, we may from time to time keep ourselves peacefully in the simple presence of God, recollected in Him, and begging of Him to act upon our soul, and to do with it according to His good pleasure It is a great error to consider as idleness or waste of time the moments which we pass thus, keeping ourselves recollected and attentive before God, whether He pleases or not to make us sensible of His action on our soul.

The fifth means of acquiring true and solid virtue is frequently to approach the sacraments, which are the principal sources of grace. We must not make a torment of confession ; that would be quite against the intention of God ; neither must we make of it a mere matter of routine, and a kind of formula of accusation of ourselves, as so many people do who go frequently to confession. The things of which persons

who are striving after perfection ought chiefly to
accuse themselves, are the lights they have resisted,
the feelings of self-love to which they have yielded,
everything that they have wrongly said, or done, or
omitted, with reflection and with deliberate purpose.
A communion is always well made when we come
from it with renewed courage and a fresh resolution
to be more faithful to God than ever. We must not
think, that to make a good confession and communion
we must necessarily make use of all the acts in detail
which are given to us in books. That is a good
method for young people, whose imagination is generally quick and lively, or for those who communicate
seldom, or for those who have no idea of recollection.
But when we have once entered resolutely on the
way of prayer, we need no longer go for help to
books, either to hear Mass or to approach the
sacraments.

The sixth means is spiritual reading. And we
must be very careful in the choice of books. As a
rule, we should prefer to all others those which touch
the heart and carry with them a certain unction
which is not to be mistaken. Rodriguez is excellent
for beginners. For those who are more advanced,
the "Imitation of Christ," the writings of Father Surin,
Saint Francis de Sales, the Psalms and the New Testament, the "Lives of the Saints," &c. Our spiritual
reading should be half a prayer; that is to say, that
in reading we should listen for the voice of God, and
stop to meditate when we feel ourselves touched by
what we read. We ought to read with a view to
practise what we read; and as everything does not

suit everybody, we should seek what is most in accordance with our own needs, and follow its teachings faithfully, always taking care not to multiply our practices of devotion too much, for that is fatal to liberty of spirit, which we should always try to preserve.

The seventh means is the mortification of the heart. Everything within us is opposed to our supernatural good; everything draws us towards the slavery of the senses and of self-love. We must struggle continually against ourselves, and wage a constant war against our own inclinations, either in resistng impressions from without or fighting with those from within. We cannot watch too much over our own heart, and all that passes there. This is painful in the beginning; but it becomes easy as we grow accustomed to retiring into ourselves and keeping ourselves in the presence of God.

The eighth means is devotion to the Blessed Virgin. Let us ask through her of Jesus Christ the grace and help we need so much, and she will most certainly obtain them for us. Above all things, when we are tempted to disgust, to weariness, to discouragement, to a feeling that we would like to give up trying to be good altogether, let us fly to her with a holy confidence that she can and will help us.

Also, we cannot have too much devotion to our Guardian Angel. He never leaves us; he is given to us, to guide us in the way of holiness. Let us speak to him in all our doubts, in all our difficulties, and let us often ask him to watch over us.

Finally, the most important point is to have a good

guide, a director well versed in the ways of God, and
who is himself led by the Spirit of God.   These good
directors have always been very rare, and to-day they
are more so than ever.   Nevertheless, we may be
quite sure that those good souls who wish to go
straight to God will always find a man who can
conduct them thither.   The good providence of God
is, in a manner, obliged to send them one, and He will
never fail to do so, if they ask Him for it.   We might
almost say that it is always the fault of the souls
themselves if they have not the director God wishes
them to have.   Let them, then, pray earnestly that
they may find him to whom they ought to confide the
care of their perfection ; and when they do find him,
let them open their heart to him without reserve, let
them listen to him with docility, let them follow his
advice, as if God Himself spoke to them through his
mouth.   A soul in good dispositions and well guided
can never fail to attain sanctity.

IV.

ON THE NEW LIFE IN JESUS CHRIST.

THE Apostle St. Paul, in several of his letters, told
the first Christians that, by their baptism, they were
dead and buried with Jesus Christ; that when they
came from the baptismal font they were risen with
Him, and obliged to lead a new life, formed on
the model of His glorious Resurrection.   And this,
following the example of St. Paul, is what is

preached to all the faithful on the great Feast of Easter.

As I am now writing for souls not merely dead to sin, but determined to lead a new life entirely dependent on grace, I will propose to them the Resurrection of our Saviour, not only as a model, but as the very end of that life of entire sanctity which they have embraced; and I will say to them, that to rise again like Jesus Christ they must die, as He did. Now, the life of Jesus Christ was a continual death; 1 mean a mystical death, the last act and consummation of which was His actual death on the cross.

Thus, the new life which they must lead in Jesus Christ is nothing else than a continual death to themselves; they must be dead to the least sins and the slightest imperfections; dead to the world and all exterior things; dead to the senses and all immoderate care of the body; dead to their natural character and natural defects; dead to their own will; dead to the esteem and love of themselves; dead to spiritual consolations, dead to any support of feeling of assurance with regard to the state of their souls; in one word, dead to everything of their own, even in the things which concern their sanctity. It is by these different degrees of death that the mystical life of Jesus Christ is established within us; and when the final blow of death has been borne, Jesus Christ raises us up again, and communicates to us the qualities of His glorified life, even here below, at least as to our soul, and as much as our soul is capable of it in this world. Let us consider in a few words these different degrees of death.

We must be dead to the slightest sins and the
least imperfections.   The first resolution to be made
by a soul which wishes to belong to God alone is,
never to commit any fault purposely or with deliberation ; never to act in anything whatsoever against his
conscience ; never to refuse anything to God; never
to say, "It is such a *little* thing ; God will take no
notice of such a trifle."   This resolution is essential,
and must be maintained with an inviolable fidelity.
It is not that we shall be able to escape altogether
from faults of inadvertence, of impulse, and of weakness ; but these faults will not hinder us in the
way of perfection, because they are not intentional
or foreseen.

We must be dead to the world and to all exterior
things ; that is to say, we must no longer love the
world or seek it ; we must only grant to the world
what we cannot refuse it, on account of the duties
of our state, and what God Himself wishes that we
should grant to it ; we may even go so far as to suffer
and groan in our heart over the indispensable intercourse which we must have with the world ; we must
no longer respect it, or care for its judgments, or fear
its contempt, its mockery, or its persecutions ; never
be ashamed before the world of our religious duties
or the practice of the Gospel ; never turn away from
anything which God and our own conscience dictate
to us, for fear of what the world may think or say of
it.   In an age so corrupt as ours there are many
battles to fight, many obstacles to overcome, many
customs to despise, many prejudices to trample under
foot, in order to triumph completely over human re-

spect. This is one of the subjects of a particular examination of conscience, upon which we must be most strict with ourselves, and never allow ourselves any latitude.

We must be dead to the senses and the immoderate care of the body. We must be on our guard against sloth, the love of our own comfort, and sensuality in all its forms; we must give to our body only what is necessary, in the way of food, sleep, and clothing; we must mortify it from time to time by privations; and if our health permits, and God inspires us with the thought, and our director finds it good for us, we may even afflict our body with some exterior penances. We must above all things watch carefully over our eyes and ears, and avoid as far as possible everything that affects us very strongly.

We must be dead, as to our natural character and our natural defects. And it is not a slight thing to reform our character in such a manner that we only preserve what is good and succeed in correcting what is defective. Even many Saints whom the Church venerates have not been entirely dead to themselves in this matter. All have not been like Saint Augustine and Saint Francis de Sales, in whom natural character was completely conquered and brought into submission to Divine grace. The great means to attain this, without too much study or constraint, is to watch carefully over the heart, to restrain its first motions, neither to act nor speak through ill-humour or satire or impetuosity, and to keep ourselves always in peace and self-possession.

Why should we not do for God, and with the assistance of His grace, what so many worldly people do
for their own interest and their own fortune?

We must be dead to our own will and the
promptings of our own spirit. This point is of
great extent and most difficult of practice. At first,
and in ordinary things, we must take care to submit
our mind and our will to reason; not to allow ourselves to be led away by caprice or fantastic imaginations; not to be obstinate about our own opinions, but
to be ready to listen to those of others, and to yield
to them if we find them good; to follow the advice
and the wishes of others in indifferent things. As to
what regards our spiritual conduct, to receive simply
from God just what He gives us, and to remain where
He places us, without desiring anything else; not to
judge with our own judgment, either of our state of
life or of the operations of grace, to practise, with
regard to our director, obedience of judgment and of
will; to repress the activity of our mind, and to keep
that, as well as our will, in entire dependence upon
God; not to reflect upon ourselves; not to reason
upon things beyond our understanding, but to allow
ourselves to be guided by a divine instinct, far superior
to our own reasoning and intelligence; in our reading,
to seek nothing through curiosity, but simply what
will feed our heart; not making great efforts to understand and to fathom everything we find in spiritual
books, which is a dangerous thing, and might result
in filling us with false ideas, in making us presumptuous, and in exposing us to delusions. Let us
believe that God will give us, just in the right

measure, whatever light is necessary for us; and let us not try to go beyond, but let us receive the spiritual light He does give us, very humbly, and apply ourselves at once to put it in practice.

As a general rule, let us always try to keep our mind and heart "empty and pure," that God may place there what He wishes and do with us as He pleases.

We must be dead to the esteem and love of ourselves. This death, as we see, is always tending to affect something even more interior and closer to ourselves; for if there is one thing more than another most deeply rooted in us, it is pride and self-love. These are the greatest enemies God can have, and consequently nothing can harm us more. God Himself will attack them and pursue them relentlessly in a soul which has really given itself to Him. Such a soul has only to let God do what He will with it, and co-operate with Him when the occasion comes.

We must be dead to spiritual consolations. A time will come when God Himself will wean the soul from them. Then comes the darkness; the soul has no longer any taste for anything : everything weighs upon her; everything wearies her; everything tries her ; she feels no longer the presence of God within her ; she may really be in peace, but she does not perceive it ; she believes herself to have lost the favour of God; and all is desolation. Now is the time for that soul to be generous; she must freely consent to these privations, she must seek herself in nothing, she must love God with a pure love, and serve Him for His own sake alone, and at whatever

cost. Then, naturally, such a service of God is hard
to human nature; nature cries out, complains, is
angry, is in despair. We must let her cry, and
be more faithful than ever; we must drag the
victim to the sacrifice, without any regard for natural
repugnance.

We must be dead to any support or feeling of
assurance with regard to the state of our souls. As
long as the soul, in the midst of all her temptations
and trials, can still find some support in the depths
of conscience, some comfort in the director; as long
as she does not feel utterly abandoned by God, it is
comparatively easy for her to bear the greatest trials;
but when she sees herself suspended, as it were, hell
beneath her feet, nothing to support her, and every
instant ready to fall into that terrible gulf; in a word,
when she feels that God has forsaken her, that she
is lost without hope, and when nothing is able to
persuade her to the contrary, and everything helps
to confirm this dreadful fear, it is then that her
agony becomes extreme; it is then she has need of
heroic courage to persevere, and to resign herself to
whatever it shall please God to ordain for her, for
all eternity.

We must be dead to everything of our own, even
in the things which concern our sanctity. The soul
begins to appropriate to herself the gifts of God, the
virtues with which He has enriched her, and to feel
a certain complacency in her purity and sanctity. In
a moment God despoils her of all; not in reality, but
in appearance, and reduces her to an entire poverty
and nakedness; she sees in herself neither gifts

nor virtues, nor anything supernatural. She knows
neither what she is, nor what she has been, nor what
she will become. Her sins, her nothingness, her
reprobation : this is all she sees in herself, and of
which she counts herself worthy. This is the end
and consummation of the mystical death in Jesus
Christ. The resurrection and the glorified state come
afterwards. Let us leave to God His own secrets,
and let us say no more on such a subject.

V.

ON THE VIOLENCE WE MUST USE TOWARDS OURSELVES.

"*From the days of John the Baptist, even until now,*"
said our Lord and Saviour Jesus Christ, "*the kingdom of Heaven suffereth violence, and the violent take it
by force.*"

If, in one sense, Jesus Christ has rendered the way
to Heaven more easy, by the abundant outpouring of
His grace, and by the spirit of love with which He
has replenished His disciples ; on the other hand, He
has made this way even more strait, because He came
to fulfil the law in its *perfection*, and He requires
from His followers more than God required formerly
under the law of nature and the law of Moses.
Thus, from the moment when John the Baptist announced the coming of the Saviour, the kingdom of
Heaven is only to be obtained through the violence
we do to ourselves ; we must seize it, and carry it,

as it were, by assault. This saying is hard to nature, because it is against nature herself that we must wage war, and this resistance must sometimes be "unto blood," without truce or repose. If the service of God consisted only in a certain routine of external devotion, compatible with a life of ease and comfort, with all the allurements of self-love, and with a secret complacency in ourselves and all we do, the number of saints—that is to say, of true Christians, true lovers of the Gospel—would not be so rare, and our condition would be in every respect happier than that of the Jews, to whom God prescribed so many exterior practices from which the law of grace has delivered us.

But for these exterior practices Jesus Christ has substituted interior ones, which are incomparably more difficult and painful. *He came not,* He said, *" to bring peace, but a sword."* He puts this sword in the hands of His servants, and He wishes that they should make use of it against themselves, in that circumcision of the heart which mortifies without pity all the inclinations of corrupt nature, even to finally putting it to death, and leaving in the heart, thus mortified, no single trace of the old Adam.

Again I say, how hard, how difficult to bear this ! So long as it is only a question of saying certain pre-scribed prayers, of visiting the churches, of practising works of charity, plenty of people can be found to embrace this kind of devotion. A director who requires no more than this is eagerly listened to: he is a man of God: he is a saint. But if he begins to speak of correcting certain defects, of overcoming human respect, of reforming natural character, of keeping a check on natural inclinations and feelings, and of following in everything the leading of grace, he is no longer listened to ; he exaggerates ; he goes further than is necessary.

It is nevertheless certain that the true spirit of Christianity consists in this : that a real Christian should look upon himself as his greatest enemy : that he should wage continual war against himself; that he should spare himself in nothing, and count all his progress by the victories he gains over himself.

When we begin to give ourselves entirely to God, He treats us at first with great kindness, to win us to Himself; He fills the soul with an ineffable peace and joy; He makes us take a delight in solitude, in recollection, in all our religious duties ; He makes the practice of virtue easy to us ; nothing is a trouble to us, we think we are capable of everything.

But as soon as He is once certain of a soul, immediately He begins to enlighten her as to her defects ; He raises by degrees the veil which concealed them from her, and He inspires her with a firm will to overcome them. From that moment such a soul turns against herself; she undertakes the conquest of self-love ; she pursues it relentlessly wherever she perceives it ; and when she is thoroughly illuminated by the Divine light, where does she *not* perceive it ? She sees in herself nothing but misery, imperfection, and sin ; self-seeking and attachment to her own will; her very devotion appears to her full of defects. She once thought she loved God, and now she finds that this love was nothing but another form of self-seeking;

that she has appropriated to herself the gifts of God; that she has served Him only for selfish ends; that she has thought highly of herself and despised others whom she considers not to have received the same graces as herself.

God shows her all this gradually; for if He were to show it to her all at once she could not bear it, and would fall into despair. But the little He does show her is sufficient to convince her that she has not even *begun* to enter upon the way of perfection, and that she has many and many a hard battle to fight before she can arrive at the end of it.

If the soul is courageous and faithful, what does she do then? She humbles herself, without despairing; she places all her confidence in God; she implores His assistance in the war she is going to undertake. Then she fills her mind and heart with this maxim from the book of the " Imitation of Christ :" " *You will make no progress except in so far as you do violence to yourself;* " a maxim which contains the purest spirit of the Gospel, and which all the Saints have followed.

After their example, she also declares war against nature, against her own mind and heart, against her natural character and disposition; and in order that she may not be carried away by imagination or an indiscreet zeal, she begs of God that He will Himself direct her in this war, that He will enlighten her as to the enemies against whom she ought to fight, that He will pass over nothing, but will warn her of all that goes on within her, that she may regulate all by the help of His grace. She forms the generous resolution of restraining herself in everything, and of allowing nothing in herself which could wound the infinite sanctity of God.

Now she is a true soldier of Jesus Christ ; now she is enrolled under His banner. Until now God has only been preparing and disposing her for this great grace ; but from this moment she is clothed with the armour of faith, and enters in good earnest upon the field of battle.

How long shall this conflict last ?

It shall last as long as there is *one* enemy to conquer, as long as nature shall preserve one spark of life, as long as the old Adam is not utterly destroyed.

A good Christian never lays down his arms, and all is not finished for him even when he has fought till his strength is exhausted. What do I mean to express by this ? What can remain for him to do when he is worn-out by his own victories, and when he has carried his violence against himself as far as it can possibly go ? There remains nothing for him to *do*, but there remains for him to *suffer* the action of God, Who henceforth will do alone what is beyond the strength of man.

Sanctity is begun by our own efforts, sustained and assisted by Divine grace : it is finished and perfected solely by the Divine operation. Man raises the edifice as high as he can, but because there is a great deal that is human in this edifice, God destroys all the work of man, and substitutes for it His own work ; and the creature has nothing else to do but to allow the Creator to act as He pleases. The creature acts no more, but he suffers, because God is acting upon him ; he no longer uses violence towards himself, but he suffers it; and this purely passive state is immeasurably more painful. As long as the soul is acting there is always the consciousness of strength, and that consciousness is sustaining. Also, in the consciousness of strength there is always a little self-love, and the soul can scarcely help attributing to herself some share in the victory, since she has indeed contributed to it.

But when God acts alone, every faculty of action is taken from the soul. She sees perfectly what God is doing in her, but she cannot second Him; and it is no trouble to her now to attribute nothing to herself, because she sees plainly that she has no part in it. Besides, all the work of God then consists in destroying, in overturning, in despoiling the soul, and reducing her to a perfect emptiness and nakedness; and He demands of her no other correspondence than that she should patiently allow herself to be despoiled of all the gifts, all the graces, all the virtues with which God had adorned her, and which she had appropriated to herself.

Oh! what a great and difficult work is this total destruction, this annihilation of the creature! What a warfare to sustain for so many long years! And then, when we think all is finished, to have to bear new and far more terrible blows from the Hand of God Himself, Who acts upon His creature as the sovereign Master, and exercises upon her all the authority she freely gave Him by renouncing her liberty to Him! What courage is necessary to undertake and bring to a final conclusion the war against ourselves! But what a far greater courage is necessary to bear the war which God Himself wages against us, and to allow ourselves to be crushed under the blows of His all-powerful Hand!

O my God! now I begin to understand what that violence is which he whom You call to the perfection of Your Gospel must do to himself, and must experience. But thanks be to Your infinite Mercy, this sight does not frighten me. If I relied on myself, I should give up all, because I feel that I am capable of nothing. But I rely upon You *alone*, and "I can do all things through Him that strengtheneth me." You have begun the work; and my ardent hope is, that You will continue it and finish it. I wish to have no other part in it than to co-operate with You as much as I am able, and then to leave You to do with me as You will.

VI.

ON THE WAY OF THE CROSS.

"*IF any man will come after Me, let him deny himself, and take up his cross daily and follow Me,*" said our Lord and Saviour Jesus Christ.

The cross is the summary of the Gospel and the standard of the Christian. Through the cross, Jesus Christ repaired the glory of His Father, appeased His anger, amd reconciled Him with the world. But the cross which our Lord bore for us, and by which He redeemed us, does not dispense us from bearing our own cross; on the contrary, it is for us an indispensable engagement to walk in the footsteps of our

Divine Master.   His cross has sanctified our cross ;
His cross has given the value to ours, and makes it
worthy of an eternal reward !   Without the cross of
Jesus Christ, all our sorrows, all our sufferings, could
never have satisfied God for the least sin, and
Heaven would always have been closed against us.
We know this well enough ; but what we do not
know, or rather what we cannot make up our minds
to practise, is, that to make the cross of Jesus Christ
our true Salvation we must deny ourselves, we must
die to ourselves, and this not once, or twice, but
every day, and continually.   If we do not do this we
are not true Christians : Jesus Christ will not acknowledge us : He will renounce us.   His own words are
quite clear on this point.   Whether we will love God,
or whether we will love ourselves : we have to decide :
there must be no hesitation.

Let us see, then, in what consists this necessity of
bearing our cross, and if it is really as hard as it
seems at first sight to human nature.

The necessity of carrying our cross consists first
and principally in avoiding sin and all occasions of
sin.   This is quite just : every Christian will agree
to it : but it is a thing which extends very far in
practice.   Sin has its attractions ; it has its temporal
advantages ; the occasions of sin are frequent and
even daily ; the temptations are very great, and most
Christians, who find themselves incessantly exposed
to these temptations, must do themselves a continual
violence, that they may not yield.

This necessity consists, in the second place, in
mortifying our passions, in moderating our desires,

in keeping our flesh subject to the spirit, in watching over our senses, in guarding carefully all the avenues of our heart : for the source of sin is in ourselves and in our own evil inclinations. We are naturally inclined to evil; we are not ignorant of this, and a sad experience teaches us, that without a continual vigilance our falls are inevitable.

This necessity consists, in the third place, in separating our mind and heart from all terrestrial, carnal, and temporal objects, that we may occupy our thoughts and affections only with celestial, spiritual, and eternal things ; and to do this, we must struggle incessantly against the weight of our corrupt nature, which is always· drawing us towards the earth. If we watch over ourselves, we shall constantly surprise in ourselves thoughts and desires which attach us to the earth, like animals, and which bring us back incessantly to the needs and the well-being and the comfort of our bodies, and the means of procuring them. That which is physical occupies us far more than that which is moral, unless we make continual efforts to raise ourselves, as it were, above ourselves.

This necessity of carrying our cross consists, in the fourth place, in receiving patiently, as from the hand of God, all the adversities which happen to us, whether they come from natural causes, or from the malice of men, or through our own fault. These crosses from the hand of God are very frequent; the more He loves us, the more crosses He will send us, because they tend to detach us from earth and to attach us to Him ; and they are more especially

c

calculated to sanctify us, because they are not our
own choice, and for that reason are more mortifying.

This necessity consists, in the fifth place, in embracing willingly all the trials and sufferings of which
the spiritual life is one continual tissue; this is a
cioss which belongs especially to those interior souls
who have made a resolution to walk in the footsteps
of Jesus Christ. Our Divine Saviour, in accepting
them for His spouses, lays upon them His cross, the
very same cross which He bore for them : a cross
formed of two branches, which are humiliations and
sufferings both interior and exterior; a cross which
the devil, and men, and God Himself will agree in
laying upon them; a most intimate cross, which will
penetrate to the very depths of the soul; a cross
beside which all the preceding crosses are absolutely
nothing; a cross, in fact, which ends in the total
extinction of self-love and the voluntary sacrifice of
our dearest interests.

This last cross is the portion of only a small number of favoured souls; it is not a cross of necessity,
but a cross of love; and for that reason it is much
heavier, because the motive of love is immeasurably
stronger than that of duty. To this cross we may
associate all those which the soul voluntarily embraces,
as austerities and penances, the vows of religion, and
the religious state itself.

These are some of the crosses which enter more or
less into the life of every Christian, and from which
the wicked are not exempt any more than the good;
for they are not less exposed than the good to all the
crosses of Providence, without speaking of those par-

ticular punishments which belong to them especially, and which are the consequence of their passions and crimes.

Let us now examine if this necessity of bearing our cross is as hard as it appears to human nature. And upon this subject, I shall first lay down as a general rule, that there is not, and never can be, upon this earth any real happiness but by the way of the cross. I say that it costs us far more to be lost than to be saved ; that the wicked have in one sense, even in this world, far more to suffer than the good, because they suffer without consolation and without hope ; that they are in a continual trouble and agitation, never daring to look within, or to reflect ; never at peace, always condemned by the secret reproach of their conscience. If there were only this single reason for carrying one's cross as a Christian, viz., that by so doing we escape the remorse which tears the libertine and the unbeliever, we should need no more to defend the doctrine of the Gospel and exculpate it from unnecessary harshness. But let us consider again all these different kinds of crosses, and let us see the consolations which grace attaches to them.

The first cross, then, consists in avoiding sin and all the occasions of sin. This is painful to nature, and often costs us many sacrifices. But does it cost nothing to our reason and our conscience to offend God ? Do we not pay dearly for a moment of unholy pleasure, followed by inevitable regrets, as long as we have a vestige of religious feeling remaining ? And, on the contrary, what peace is so sweet as the peace of a good conscience ? Is it not preferable to a moment of madness ? What a joy to overcome ourselves, and to resist a temptation instead of yielding to it! With what confidence and gladness we then draw near to God, and unite ourselves with Him by prayer and the holy sacraments ; whilst the guilty man dares not appear before Him, and all the duties of piety are for him a constraint and a punishment !

The second cross consists in the mortification of the passions. But is it not more painful to become the slaves of our passions than to overcome them ? Are not all the passions in themselves, tyrants and executioners ? Do they not excite in the soul an insatiable hunger ? We may appease this hunger for a time; but does it not come back again with renewed vehemence ? The ambitious man, the avaricious man, the voluptuous man,—even if nothing opposes their desires, which scarcely ever happens,— are they happy ? Can they be happy ? Are not the consequences of many passions frightful, even according to the judgment of the world ? Compare in any manner you like, either by the light of reason or of religion, the state of a man who is a complete slave to his passions with that of a man who wages war with them, and ends by becoming their master, and you must confess that the Gospel, in ordering this war, has in view our happiness even in this world.

The third cross is the violent separation of the soul from herself; that is to say, the separation of the higher and spiritual part of the soul from that which is low and animal. This separation is very painful, because the body is incessantly trying to draw the soul down to its own level. But is there anything more humiliating than this miserable body? Is it ever content? As fast as we grant it one thing, does it not demand another? And this continual care of the body, this constant attention to its wants, this anxiety to avoid everything that may hurt it, is it not a real torment? On the other hand, is there any exercise of authority more worthy of a man, and more agreeable to him, than that of mastering his body, of forcing it to be content with what is necessary, of hardening it to endure labour and suffering; of taking no notice of the importunities of the body, but instead, to be able to give all his attention to those higher things which the duties of religion, of his position, and of society impose upon him?

The crosses from the hand of Providence, which are the fourth kind, are inevitable. The wicked are not less exposed to these than the good. But by their resignation, their patience, and submission to the Will of God good Christians sweeten all that is bitter in these inevitable crosses; and their religion furnishes them with motives for bearing them in peace, and even joyfully. It is not so with those who are in rebellion against God, who give way to sadness, depression, and despair, and who make their crosses infinitely heavier by the bad disposition with which they receive them.

Finally, those spiritual crosses which come only from God, to prove and try those who love Him, and which, as I have said before, are crosses of pure love, these are the delight of the favoured souls who bear them. They accept these crosses of their own free-will and choice; far from asking to be delivered, they

beg of God incessantly to add to them, crying out
with a great Saint: " *Yet more, Lord ; yet more :* " they
wish to die fastened to the cross, like their Lord and
Saviour.   These crosses, which are the most terrible
of all, are also those which are borne with the most
courage, with the most love, with the deepest interior
peace, with the greatest strength and support from
above ; and they lead in another life, and sometimes
even in this, to an ineffable and inexpressible happiness.   In this matter, which is above our comprehension, we must believe the Saints of God, on their own
experience.   Now, the Saints have no two languages
on this subject : they are unanimous ; and we cannot
suspect that they have all conspired to deceive us.

It is, then, true, unmistakably true, that even the
present and temporal happiness of the Christian consists solely in the cross; and that, on the contrary,
those who fly from the cross, and seek only what will
content nature, find neither happiness nor peace, but
only disappointment in this life, and eternal misery in
the next.

VII.

ON THE TRUE LIBERTY OF THE CHILDREN OF GOD.

IT is a thing which sounds like a paradox, but which
is nevertheless true, with a most exact truth, that of
all the persons who serve God, those are the *most*
free, indeed it might be said the *only* really free, who
allow themselves to be guided entirely and in every-

thing by the Spirit of God, and whom St. Paul calls, for that reason, the children of God. "*Those*," he says, "*who are led by the Spirit of God are the children of God.*"

Worldly people who live according to their desires, and who restrain themselves in nothing, appear free, but they are not really so. They soon become mere slaves to their passions, which tyrannise over them with the utmost violence. This is a truth which they are themselves obliged to confess; and even if they did not, their conduct expresses it sufficiently; for there is no man who gives himself up entirely to his passions whom those passions do not lead much farther than he ever intended to go, whom they do not hold enchained, as it were, and whom they do not force at last to do what in his heart he condemns: such is the terrible empire of an evil habit.

Most of those who are sincerely Christians, and yet who are lax and remiss in the practice of their religion, are not free either. The occasions of sin draw them away; they yield to the least temptation; human respect holds them in subjection; they wish to do good, and yet allow a thousand obstacles to stand in their way; they detest sin, and yet they have not the courage to put it away from them. Now, certainly, this is not freedom, not to be able to do the good they wish to do, and to be forced to do the evil they detest. Devout persons, also, who are led by their own spirit are not free either. They think they are, because they make their own plans of devotion and follow a certain routine, from which they never deviate. But in reality they are the slaves of their own imagination; full of inconstancy, of uneasiness, of peculiarities, and of caprices; always seeking for sensible devotion, and when they find it not, which very often happens, then they are discontented with God and with themselves. More than this, they are generally scrupulous and undecided, constantly experiencing in themselves an agitation, which they know not how to quiet. Self-love rules them, and they are no less the absolute slaves of it than worldlings are of their passions.

We must then say, either that there is no true liberty in the service of God, which would be an error, and a kind of blasphemy; or that this liberty is the portion of those only who give themselves to God with their whole heart, and who resign themselves to follow in everything the leadings of Divine grace. But, you will say, how can a man be free and yet subject in everything to the Spirit of God? Are these not contradictory ideas? Not at all. The perfect liberty of the reasonable creature consists in this subjection, and the more complete the subjection, the greater the freedom.

To understand this truth thoroughly we must remark, in the first place, that liberty is the chief perfection of man, and that this perfection is the more excellent in him in proportion as he uses his liberty in conformity to reason and the designs of God; for liberty without this rule degenerates simply into vice and licentiousness.

We must remark, in the second place, that true liberty does not consist in the power of doing evil. This power is a defect inherent in the creature, who is essentially fallible, because drawn from nothingness. But such a power is so little an appendage of true liberty, that God, Who is free above all things, is in a state of absolute impossibility of doing evil. It would follow, then, that man was more free than God if liberty consisted in the power of giving oneself up to good or evil.

Now, man has this unfortunate power, and it is in him a radical imperfection, which may lead him to his eternal ruin. What must he do, then, to correct this imperfection of his liberty, and to approach as near as possible to the liberty of God? He must implore of God to direct him in the choice of his actions; to make him listen for the voice of Divine grace within him; to help him to follow it, and to abandon himself to it. By doing this he comes to wish what God wishes; he does what God inspires him to do; he protects himself against all bad use of his liberty; he raises himself, as far as he can, towards the perfection of the Divine liberty; the liberty of God becomes, in some sort, his own, because he acts no longer according to his own desire, but solely as he is guided by the Will of God. Thus, by his perfect subjection to God he is as free as he can possibly be.

But, you will say, this subjection is a great constraint. And why is it such a constraint? It is because of our natural inclination to evil, of our bad habits, of that spirit of independence and pride which caused the fall of the angels and of the first man. What is it that feels this constraint so much? Is it the reason of man? Is it his conscience? No; it is his corrupt nature, it is his passions. Human reason, which is an outflow and a spark of Divine reason, will never complain of the necessity it is under of submitting and conforming to that Divine reason : conscience, that instinct of right, which God Himself has implanted in our hearts, will never murmur against this subjection, which is its primary law, and will never give the odious name of constraint to the wise rule which is its faithful guide.

The constraint is only for our mad passions, for our pride, for our self-love : it is a salutary check, it is a yoke of sweetness and happiness, to our reason enlightened by faith.

Besides, this constraint only lasts until our evil passions are exterminated, our self-love conquered, our pride trampled under foot ; it only lasts until our bad inclinations are changed, by custom and perseverance, into a real inclination towards all that is good, and until the voice of grace is stronger than the voice of nature. This happy moment will come when we have for some time made generous efforts against ourselves, and when, by the assistance of grace, we have acquired some command over our senses, over our imagination, and over those first ill-regulated impulses which often carry us away in spite of ourselves.

Then we begin to feel independent of all that is not of God; then we begin to taste, in all its sweetness, the true liberty of the children of God. Then we begin to pity the miserable slaves of the world, and to congratulate ourselves on having escaped their chains. Tranquil upon the shore, we see them tossed about on the waves of that sea of iniquity, troubled by a thousand contrary winds, always on the point of being engulfed by the tempest. We enjoy a profound calm; we are masters of our own actions, because what we wish to do, we do. No object of ambition, of avarice, or of unholy pleasure can tempt us; no human respect keeps us back; the judgments of men, their criticism, their raillery, their contempt, have no longer any effect upon us, and can no more have power to turn us from the right path. Adversities, sufferings, humiliations, crosses of every kind, can no longer frighten us, nor have we any dread of them.

In one word, we have been lifted above the world and its errors, its attractions and its terrors. If this is not to be " free indeed," what is freedom ?

More than this : we are free with regard to ourselves; we rely no longer on our own imagination and on the inconstancy of our will ; we are firm and unshaken in our resolutions, fixed in our ideas, decided in our principles, consistent in all our actions. The Spirit of God, which we faithfully follow, communicates something of His own immutability to the creature, who by itself is so changeable; and in the midst of all the interior conflicts to which we may be exposed the will remains firm as a rock. This is a matter of experience on which those who are led by another way are incapable of judging. But those persons who have really and truly given themselves entirely to God, even those who are only beginners, are astonished at the difference they find in themselves, between what they are and what they were formerly. This difference is exactly like the difference there is between a calm and peaceful sea, which is, in a measure, mistress even of the very movement of its waves, and a raging sea, tossed into fury by every wind. What liberty can be greater than this entire possession of ourselves, this empire over every movement of our soul, from which scarcely ever escapes, even for one short moment, any indeliberate impulse !

Is there anything beyond ? Does the liberty of the children of God extend any farther ? Yes. They are free, with regard to God Himself. I mean to say, that whatever is the conduct of God towards them ; whether He tries them, or whether He consoles them ; whether He draws near to them, or whether He appears to abandon them, the real fixed state of their souls is always the same. They are raised above all the vicissitudes of the spiritual life ; the surface of their soul may be troubled, but the inner depths enjoy the greatest peace. Their liberty with regard to God consists in this : that, willing everything that God wills, without inclining to one side or the other, without any thought of their own interest, they have given their consent beforehand to all that can happen to them ; they have lost their choice in that of God ; they have freely accepted everything that comes to them from Him ; in such a manner, and so completely, that they can always say, that in whatever state they may be, they are not there against their will, but that they are perfectly content, and have all that they wish for.

Yes : even if they are surrounded and weighed down with crosses ; if they are submerged in an ocean of sorrow; if the devil, and man, and God Himself seem to be fighting against them; if they are absolutely without support, either exterior or interior; still, they are in peace, their joy is perfect and over-abundant, according to the expression of the Apostle; and they take a pleasure in their state, so that they would not change it for any other, nor would they allow themselves to take any steps to go out of it.

This, and even greater still, is the liberty of the children of God. Nothing in this world can possibly happen to them against their will; they desire nothing; they regret nothing; nothing troubles them; nothing affects them. Compare this state, I do not say merely with worldlings, in their false joys, in their annoyances, in their projects, their fears, and their hopes, but compare it with the state of ordinary good people, whose self-love will never allow them to taste what true peace is, and you will agree that there is no sacrifice we ought not to be ready to make in order to attain to a state so blessed and so high.

VIII.

ON THE STRENGTH WE HAVE OF OURSELVES, AND OF OUR STRENGTH IN GOD

St Paul said: "*When I am weak, then I am strong.*" That is to say, when I have a clear conviction of my weakness, when I know it thoroughly by my own experience, when, seeing that of myself I can do nothing, I humble myself and put all my trust in God, it is then that I am strong with the strength of God, Who delights in making His power shine forth through the weakness of His creature ; it is then that *I can do all things, through Him that strengtheneth me.*

No less true is it, that when we are strong with our own strength, then we are really weak. That is to say, when we think ourselves strong, when we take to ourselves the credit of this strength, when we presume upon it, when we are proud of it, and think ourselves capable of doing everything and suffering everything, it is then that we are really weak, because God takes away His strength from His presumptuous creature, and abandons her to herself.

Strength in ourselves is, then, a real weakness, and even an extreme weakness ; it is an inevitable cause of falls, and almost always of the most humiliating falls. On the contrary, weakness in ourselves, if it is accompanied by humility and trust in God, is a real strength, an all-powerful strength, even the strength of God Himself. But why does God wish us to be penetrated by this conviction of our own weakness ? It is that He may make His strength shine forth in us. It is because He wishes that all the good in us should be attributed to Him alone ; it is because He wishes to be recognised as the sole Author and the sole Finisher of all human sanctity ; it is because He cannot endure—in the order of grace above all things —that the creature should think she can of herself do the least thing, or that she should depend on herself, on her own resolutions, her own courage, or her own dispositions.

The great secret of the conduct of God towards

a soul which He wishes to sanctify is, then, to take
from that soul every kind of confidence in herself;
and to do this, He begins by delivering her up, as it
were, to all her misery. He allows every arrangement she makes by her own judgment to deceive all
her hopes; He allows all her ideas and projects to
fail; He allows her understanding to lead her astray,
her judgment to deceive her; He allows her foresight
to be in vain, her will to be feeble; He allows her
to fall at every step. He wishes to teach her never
to rely upon herself in anything, but to rely only
upon Him.

When we begin to serve God, when we experience
the sensible effects of grace, when our mind is illuminated by a great light and our will is transported
by holy emotions, it is quite natural that we should
think we are capable of doing everything and suffering everything for God; we cannot imagine that
we could ever refuse Him anything, or even that
we could hesitate ever so little in the most difficult
things. Sometimes, even, we go so far as to ask for
great crosses or great humiliations, persuaded that
we are quite strong enough to bear them. When a
soul is upright and simple, this kind of presumption,
born of the intense realisation we have of the strength
of grace, only comes from want of experience, and
does not displease God, provided it is not accompanied
by a great opinion of ourselves and a vain feeling of
complacency in ourselves.

But God is not slow in curing the soul of this
good opinion of herself. He has only to withdraw
His sensible grace, to leave the soul to herself, to

expose her to a very light temptation : at once she feels disgust and repugnance ; she sees everywhere obstacles and difficulties ; she succumbs to the smallest temptations : a look, a gesture, a word, throws her off her guard : she who thought herself superior to the greatest dangers. Now she passes to the opposite extreme : she fears everything ; she despairs of everything ; she thinks she can never overcome herself in anything ; she is tempted to abandon everything. In fact, she would give up all, if God did not quickly come to her assistance. God continues this method with regard to the soul until, by reiterated experiences, He has well convinced her of her own nothingness, of her utter incapacity of all good, and of the absolute necessity there is for her to lean upon Him alone.

To this end, He allows temptations to come upon her, so that a hundred times she sees herself ready to yield, if God did not come to her assistance, when there is no other resource ; He allows the revolt of passions which, she thought, were for ever extinguished, and which suddenly rise up with an extreme violence, obscuring the reason and bringing the soul to the very brink of ruin ; He expressly allows her to fall into every kind of human weakness, on purpose to humble her ; He allows strange repugnances and difficulties in the practice of virtue ; a strong aversion for prayer and the other exercises of piety : in one word, He gives that soul a clear vision of her own natural malignity and aversion for good. God employs all these means to annihilate the soul in her own eyes, to inspire her with hatred

and horror for herself, to convince her that there is
no crime too horrible for her to be guilty of, and not
the least good action, not the least effort, not the
faintest good desire, nor the smallest good thought
which she is capable of producing by herself. When
at last, after many blows, many falls, many miseries,
the soul is finally reduced to such a state that she
relies no longer on herself in the smallest thing,
then God clothes her by degrees with His own
strength, always making her feel that this strength
is not in herself, but comes simply from above.
And when she has this real strength, she can undertake all, she can bear all : sufferings, humiliations
of every kind, labours and troubles for the glory of
God and the good of others ; she succeeds in everything ; no difficulty stops her, no obstacle resists
her, no danger frightens her ; because it is no longer
herself, it is God Who is acting and suffering in
her. Not only does she give God all the glory, but
she recognises and knows by experience that He
alone does all, and can do all, and that she is nothing
but a feeble instrument in His hands, to be moved
by His Will, or rather that she is an abyss of
nothingness which He deigns to employ for the
execution of His designs. It is thus that St. Paul,
after having related all the great things he had done
and suffered for the Gospel, adds with the most
intense conviction : "*Nevertheless, I am nothing; it
was not I, but the grace of God, which is in me.*"

Such a soul renders to God all the glory He
expects from her, and reserves absolutely nothing for
herself, because she looks upon herself as she really

D

is, and that is nothingness ; thus she glorifies God in
two ways, by all she does and suffers for Him, and
by this interior disposition of annihilation.   Oh, how
dead we must be to ourselves, through how many
trials must we have passed, to attain to this !   But
then, when we have attained it, our life is one long
canticle of praise ; God Himself is praised and glorified in such a soul : all there is for Him ; there is no
self left.

But what must we do to succeed in being thus strong
with the strength of God ?   Of course, the determination must be firm and unshaken to refuse nothing
to God, and to do nothing deliberate which may displease Him.   When this foundation is well laid, I
say that we must humble ourselves for our faults, but
never allow them to trouble us, looking upon them as a
proof of our own weakness, and drawing from them
the fruit God wishes us to draw from them, which is
never to trust in ourselves, but always and only in
Him.   Then we must not think too much of the good
sentiments which come to us in certain times of fervour, nor must we think ourselves better and stronger
than we really are because of these passing emotions ;
the only time to judge ourselves rightly is when
sensible grace is withdrawn from us.   Also, we must
never be discouraged by the sight of our own misery,
nor must we say : " No, I can never do or suffer such
and such a thing ; " but, while we confess that we of
ourselves are incapable of the least effort of virtue, let
us always say : " God is all-powerful ; as long as I lean
only on Him, He will make easy and possible for me
those things which seem beyond my strength."   We

must say to God, like Saint Augustine : *"Give what Thou commandest, and command what Thou pleasest."* We must not be astonished at any disinclination we feel in ourselves, but we must incessantly ask of God the grace to raise us above it ; and when we have overcome ourselves in anything, we must not take the credit of the victory to ourselves, but thank God for it.

Finally, we must be neither presumptuous nor cowardly : two faults which arise, one from trusting too much in ourselves ; the other from not trusting enough in God. Cowardice comes from a want of faith : presumption from an insufficient knowledge of ourselves. The remedy for both these faults is simply to look upon God as the one and only source of strength. How can we be presumptuous if we are convinced that our strength comes from elsewhere ? How can we be cowardly if we believe, as we ought to believe, that our strength is the very strength of the Almighty ?

IX.

ON THE CONDUCT OF GOD TOWARDS THE SOUL.

" Behold, I stand at the door and knock. If any man shall hear My voice, and shall open to Me the door, I will come in unto him, and sup with him, and he with Me :" the words of our Lord Jesus Christ, in the Apocalypse (chap. iii. 20).

Whilst we are in this world, the sole desire of God is to enter into our hearts, and reign there ; not for His own happiness—what need has He of us to make Him happy ?—but only for our happiness, not simply in eternity, but even in this life : for it is quite certain, to reason, to faith, and to experience, that there is no happiness for man but in God.   And to bring this happiness to us what does God do ?   He stands constantly at the door of our hearts : He knocks there by the light of grace, by good inspirations, by remorse and sorrow for sin, in order that He may draw us to seek good and to fly from evil. If we were attentive to His voice, if we often entered into our hearts, we should notice that He is always knocking there, and that when we do not hear Him it is because we do not put ourselves into a state to hear Him.   He knocks there, without wearying, for many long years, or rather, we may say, for the whole of our life.   His patience in waiting for us is inconceivable ; He bears our contempt, our resistance, our obstinacy, with a goodness and a perseverance beyond expression.

Bring back, O my Lord and my Love, to my memory the time when You began to knock at the door of my heart, and the time when my heart began to resist You !   Bring back to my memory all Your loving invitations and all my resistances !   Alas ! they are both innumerable.   Did one day pass, in all those long years, in which You did not call me, not once, but many times ?   Did one day pass without my rejecting Your call over and over again ?   What an excess of goodness on Your part !   What an excess of ingratitude on mine !   Ah ! Lord, this double view pierces me and confounds me ; it excites in me the most lively horror of myself, and a boundless gratitude for Your benefits. How many sins! what an abuse of Your grace! What an ineffable patience on Your part, in bearing with me, in waiting for me,—You, Who, immediately after my first sin, could have thrust me down to hell! How many souls are there, and will be there for ever, who have offended you less than I! Why am I not there, as they are? That is the secret of Your justice and of Your mercy! I shall bless it, I shall eternally sing this mercy, while a crowd of souls less guilty than I am will be for ever the victims of Your avenging justice!

When, after He has knocked at the door for a long time, more or less, any one at last opens it, God enters; He takes possession of that heart; there He establishes His kingdom; He will never go away again, unless He is wilfully driven away. He enters there with eagerness, with a joy which nothing can equal! He enters there with all the treasures of His grace, determined to communicate them without measure to that soul, if she is as faithful as He is liberal. He pardons, He forgets all the past. The soul, surprised at such generous treatment, almost herself forgets that she has so long and so often offended Him; and if she does remember it, it is a memory which has no bitterness, and which is produced by love and gratitude. In such a soul that remembrance flows like a river of peace, an interior peace, a delicious peace which is above all mere feeling, a *deep* peace which passes understanding.

If all souls do not experience what I have just said, it is because they return to God rather by a feel-

ing of fear than by the way of pure love ; it is because
they give themselves to Him only half-heartedly and
with reserve ; it is because their fidelity does not
respond to His benefits.   Therefore, for the most
part, they fall back again into their sins, and their
life is only one continual succession of falls and of
repentance.   But as for those souls who give themselves to God entirely, who open to Him their whole
heart, and who are more touched by His love than
the thought of their own interest, those souls taste,
even from the first moment of their return to Him,
how good God is, and what a welcome He gives to
the sinner who in all sincerity returns to Him.

Ah ! Lord of my soul ! this is what I have had the
happiness of experiencing, and never will I forget it.
Yes; from the moment that I gave myself entirely to
You, You have blotted out all my iniquities ; You
have washed my soul in the Blood of Your Divine
Son ; You have enlightened my mind with a heavenly
light ; You have poured into my breast a ravishing
peace ; I have known, I have felt, how sweet it is to
belong to You alone, and how all that is not You
is worthy of the utmost contempt.   Every day You
load me with new favours ; every day You unite me
more closely to Yourself, and You detach me more
and more from creatures and from myself.   Give me,
then, fidelity, O my God ; give me generosity.   May
I look upon it as the greatest of misfortunes to refuse
You anything, or even to hesitate for a moment to
grant You *all.*   Whatever You ask from me, is it not
my good alone You consider ?   And what other
happiness can I find than in sacrificing all to You,

without reserve? Life of love, life of renunciation, life of sacrifice, now I begin to understand all your value; I begin to understand that the true and holy use of my liberty can only, and must only, consist in sacrificing myself and allowing myself to be sacrificed by Your Hand.

This peace which the soul tastes in the beginning of its course is nothing in comparison with the deeper peace which Jesus Christ promises to her, even in his life, if she continues to be faithful and generous. The end of the spiritual life is immediate, close, entire union with God. It is more than union; it is transformation; it is *oneness;* it is a symbol of the adorable unity which exists between the Three Divine Persons. Jesus Christ expressly says so, in the last prayer which He addressed to His Father for His elect: *"That they may be one in us,"* He says, *"as Thou, Father, art in Me, and I in Thee.* And in the Apocalypse, to express the intimate familiarity of this union between God and the soul: *"I will sup,"* He says, *"with Him, and He with Me."* There shall be a kind of equality between that soul and Me; My table shall be his, and his shall be Mine; our food shall be the same. And what food! That by which God Himself sustains Himself. God will pass into His creature, and the creature will pass into God; they shall have one same Life, and one same principle of life.

This is what is promised, even here, to the soul that loves and resigns herself; this she can begin to enjoy, even here, under the veil of faith. But these are things upon which we must keep silence. They ·

are too high and too deep for human language.   This
Divine communication is such, that even the soul to
whom it is granted cannot express it, and feels that
it is beyond knowledge, and beyond conception !

But to be one with Jesus Christ in His state of glory
we must first have been one with Him in His humiliations and sufferings ; we must have been altogether
dead to self, and to self-love in all its forms.   It is
to bring about this perfect purification of the soul,
that Gods allows her to pass through all these trials :
trials which are necessary, because only by them
can she possibly be entirely freed from herself; trials
which are painful, but in which God Himself sustains
her, and in which the soul has nothing to do but to
abandon herself entirely to God, and allow Him to
do all He pleases ; trials which give more glory to
God and are more profitable to the soul than all the
good works and holy actions of the longest life.

Ah ! my God and my All, if I love myself, and if
I love You more than myself, can I draw back, and
refuse to give myself up to the accomplishment of
Your designs for me, however hard they may be to
human nature ?   Hitherto You have done everything
for me ; You have loved me even when I was offending You.   Now that I am Your very own, and that
I wish to be so for ever, with my whole heart, must
You not love me incomparably more ?

What have I, then, to fear from Your love, and why
should I shrink from being its victim ?   Even if this
love destroys and consumes me, it is only that I may
be renewed and may live in You.   I give myself up,
then ; I abandon myself without reserve to all it may

please You to do with me. I accept entirely and
most willingly all the crosses which Your goodness
has destined for me; I embrace them, and cherish
them, from this moment, as the most precious favours
I can receive from You, and I will never desire to be
released from them, unless it is Your Holy Will, until
I breathe out my last sigh.

So be it.

X.

ON THE FEAR OF GOD.

St. John says : "*Perfect love casteth out fear.*"

There is no doubt that God wishes to be feared ;
and it is not in vain that Holy Scripture declares in
many places that He is terrible in His judgments,
and that St. Paul says that it is dreadful to fall into
the Hands of the living God : it is quite true that
the fear of the Lord is the "*beginning of wisdom ;*"
but it is only the beginning of it : *love* is its progress
and its consummation. Fear is a gift of the Holy
Ghost : but it is a gift by which He wishes to prepare us for more excellent gifts. It is useful and
even necessary to have this feeling of fear, and to
be penetrated by it, not only in our soul, but in
our flesh. But we must not stop there : we must
aspire to that perfect love which casts out fear, or
rather, which so purifies and ennobles it, that it is
changed into quite another sort of fear, the daughter
of pure love.

If we have to rise from the state of sin, let us

give ourselves up to all the terror of the judgments
of God; let us fear His inexorable justice; let us
dread His eternal vengeance. Let us permit this
feeling to act with all its strength, and let us take
care not to attempt to weaken it; it is the Holy
Ghost Himself Who places it in our hearts, to lead
us to a true conversion.

After our conversion, let this fear still sustain us
in the practice of penance; let the thought of the
fires of hell, which we have so often deserved, still
animate our courage, render us holy enemies of our
own selves, and make us embrace generously all that
is painful to human nature, in a life of Christian
mortification.

Let us still fear the constant occasions of sin
to which we are exposed, considering our extreme
weakness and the dominating strength of evil habits.
Let us oppose to the attractions of sinful pleasure,
to the suggestions of the devil, or to our own violent
passions, that wholesome fear of the Divine justice,
and its terrible threats against sinners who relapse
into their former faults, after having received the
pardon of them. Fear is a counterpoise as necessary to those happy souls who have preserved their
innocence as to reconciled sinners; both need it, in
thousands of dangerous occasions, to preserve them
from sin.

But, after all, the motive of fear is not that which
should predominate in the life of a Christian; that
is not the Will of God; He deserves to be served
for a higher motive, and the human heart is made to
be guided by love. Love is the only feeling really

worthy of God ; He has made it the first and greatest
of His commandments. He deserves this feeling on
our part on account of His infinite perfections, the
benefits with which He has loaded us, in the order
of nature and grace, and the eternal happiness which
He has promised us, which is to be the reward of
our love. And also this feeling is the only one which
can really change our hearts, which can really turn
them towards God, and inspire them with dissatisfac-
tion for creatures ; which can really soften us, enlarge
our hearts, raise us up, and make us capable of doing
and suffering all things for God's sake.

Two things are commanded to the Christian : to
avoid evil, and to do good. Fear can make us avoid
evil ; but it cannot lead us to the practice of good.
Love, on the contrary, can perfectly produce both
effects ; it can efficaciously draw us away from evil,
and even from the appearance of evil ; it can lead
us to good, and to the most perfect good, in spite of
all difficulties and all sacrifices, however painful to
nature.

Fear, which has only an eye to our own interests,
is not generous ; it goes no farther than to those
things which are of obligation, and even then thinks
it is doing a great deal in accomplishing so much.

It is not so with love. Love is always in advance
of and above what it gives ; so that it counts as
nothing all it has hitherto done when it can see its
way to do something more. All the refinements
of devotion, the listening for the least indication of
the Will of the Beloved, and the instant accomplishment of it, when known—all these things are familiar

to love, and to love only : fear has not even an idea
of them. When, then, God begins to fill our hearts
with His Divine love, when we feel that we do love
Him, and that our greatest desire is to give Him a
proof of it, we must give ourselves up entirely to
this feeling, we must nourish it with the utmost care,
and we must avoid everything which could weaken
it. God Himself then takes pleasure in manifesting
Himself to the soul in all His beauty; He grants to
the soul such a lively sense of His goodness and
tenderness, that she is almost astonished that He
must also be feared; she can approach Him with the
greatest confidence; she speaks to Him Who is her
All with a holy familiarity, and all her language is
love; the terrible truths of religion affect her no
longer, she scarcely ever thinks of them; fear has
given place to something infinitely sweeter, and she
experiences with rapture the truth of what Saint
John says : *" Perfect love casts out fear."* Yet she
still fears; but with a sweet fear, which belongs
only to the children of a loving Father. It is no
longer because of the awful judgments of God that
she fears to offend Him, but because He is her
Father, because she loves Him so much, because He
is infinitely perfect, and sin displeases Him above
all things. She learns to have a horror, not only
of mortal sin, but of the smallest venial sin, of the
least fault, and she would never, willingly and with
deliberation, commit one. She knows that sin is
the evil of God, and to do the least evil to God,
Who is her only love, appears to her greater than
any other evil, whatever it may be. Now, what a

strength does this filial, loving fear give her to fight against and resist all temptations! With what a constant and vigilant attention it inspires her! What precautions it suggests to her to avoid everything that could possibly displease Him Whom she loves so. well! How easily she forces her way through all obstacles, breaks all ties, which would hold her back, triumphs over the world and its false pleasures, over the flesh, with all its seductions, over the devil and all his temptations! What a joy for that soul to find herself freed from all that held her captive, and to be able to love, with all the intensity of her affection, Him Who alone deserves to be loved! The fear of slaves, the fear which freezes the heart, and narrows and constrains it, can never produce effects like these.

If the fear of displeasing the Beloved can thus draw away the soul from all evil, the desire of pleasing Him can excite her to the practice of every good which He expects from her. She seeks out occasions of pleasing Him, but always quietly and peacefully, only desiring to do His Will; she joyfully seizes all those that are presented to her: labours, sufferings, sacrifices, cost her nothing. Provided only she can please God, she is content; and her greatest grief would be to have to reproach herself with any negligence or cowardice in this respect. As she knows that the greatest enemy God can have is herself, her corrupt nature, her self-love,—she hates herself, as God hates all that is corrupt in her; she struggles against herself, will not live at peace with one bad inclination, mortifies herself in everything; and because

she feels that of herself she cannot thoroughly succeed
in overcoming nature, she offers herself to God in all
simplicity, that He may strike where He will, destroy
what He will, and do with her just as it pleases Him.

This is what perfect love does : when love takes
entire possession of a heart, it is fear that first intro-
duced it there ; but once entered into possession, love
banishes fear and reigns alone.   And, in truth, these
two sentiments are incompatible.   Love, which only
looks to God, renounces all self-interest; and, on the
contrary, self-interest is the only thing which influences fear, the only motive of its actions.   Love does
not serve God because He is terrible, but because
He is good ; love does not fear Him as a Master, but
loves Him as a Father; it is not the thought of reward or punishment which influences love; it is the
thought of God alone, *in* Himself, and *for* Himself;
not for His gifts, not for His rewards ; simply *God
alone.*

When, then, a soul which has given herself to God,
without reserve, loving Him truly above all things,
is nevertheless vividly impressed with the terror of
His judgments, if this feeling comes from God, it is a
trial and a heavy cross, and she must bear it with
love and patience ; if it is an effect of the imagination,
she must not pay any attention to it, and must avoid
all reflections that encourage it ; if it comes from the
devil, who in this way tries to tempt her to despair,
she must raise up her confidence in God, she must
cast herself in His arms, she must abandon herself
entirely to Him, begging of Him to draw glory to
Himself from this temptation, and make it serve only

for the triumph of His love. For God only permits such a temptation, to draw the soul nearer to Himself, to make her love Him more purely and entirely, to detach her more completely from all remains of self-interest, and to force her to renounce herself in all that is most precious to her. If she will generously make this sacrifice, at once she is in peace; the devil departs, and loses all power over her; the reign of love is established and confirmed in her.

It is thus that fear, even when it comes as a trial and a temptation, can only end, according to the designs of God, in perfect love. Let us try, with the help of Divine grace, to make this use of it.

XI.

ON HOLINESS.

"*Be ye holy, because I am holy,*" God said to the children of Israel.

"*Be ye perfect, as your Father in heaven is perfect,*" Jesus Christ said to His disciples.

These words show us that God is at once the motive and the model of our holiness. If we really understand these words, they will teach us more than the wisest and most enlightened philosophers could do. But we shall never understand them, except by the favour of the Divine illumination, and practice will disclose the meaning of them to us far better than speculation.

"*Be ye holy,*" says the Lord God, "*because I am holy.*" Now, what is holiness in God? It is the love of order. God loves order essentially; He cannot approve of anything, excuse anything, suffer anything to go unpunished, which is contrary to it.

He can permit disorder in His creature, bear with it for a time, forgive it freely, if the creature repudiates and amends it; but essentially He hates it, He pursues it, and He punishes it wherever He sees it, when the moment for His justice is come and the time for mercy is past. And why is this? It is because He is holy. He cannot help, if we may dare so to speak, He cannot help insisting on the love of order in His free and intelligent creature; neither can He leave that creature without a recompense if His law of order is observed. He will exercise that creature for a time, afflict him, put him to many trials; He may even appear to abandon him, to be the more sure of his virtue; but if the creature does not swerve from the path of order, if he perseveres constantly therein, God must and will reward him, God must and will make him happy, *because* of His own holiness.

This essential holiness of God is incontestably the first and greatest motive for our own holiness. We are obliged to love order, because God loves it; our reason and our liberty were only given to us for that reason, that we might understand what order is; liberty, that we might freely submit ourselves to it.

In proportion as we are reasonable creatures, we are made in the likeness of God. God has a knowledge of Himself, God loves Himself as the source of all sanctity, as sanctity itself. We, who are made in His image, must know Him, love Him, obey Him, and imitate Him in this respect. It is not sufficient for us to be made in His image by our spiritual nature, and endowed with intelligence and liberty ; we must be so also by our free-will and our choice. I ought to wish to be holy, I ought to labour with all my strength to attain holiness, I ought to reject with horror everything which is contrary to holiness, because God is holy, because I have had the privilege of being created in His image, and therefore His holiness is to be the measure of mine.

How shall I ever dare to draw near to God if I am not holy, or at least if I do not aspire to become so ? I was created to have an intimate union with Him, a close communication ; a communion of gratitude, for I have received all from Him ; a communion of prayer, for I need His help continually ; a communion of hope, for I expect every good thing from Him ; a communion of love, for He is my sovereign Good, and I can find no happiness but in Him. But what will become of this close communion with God if I give up holiness ? It will be absolutely broken. In proportion as I draw away from holiness I shall draw away from God, and He, on His side, will draw away from me. I shall no longer be able to bear the sight of Him ; and He will cast me from His presence ; He will hate me, He will forsake me, He will condemn me : I shall be eternally separated from Him.

And this is not all. God has drawn me towards Him by His grace, still closer than I am to Him by the order of nature ; He has raised me to a supernatural state ; He has destined me to see Him face to face and to enjoy His own happiness for ever and ever. Has He not, then, still more right to say to

E

me, "*Be holy, because I am holy*"?   Can I dare to aspire to the eternal enjoyment of an infinitely holy God, can I dare to hope to be closely united to Him, and to share His beatitude, if I am not holy, and even holy with a spotless holiness?   What, then, should be my constant and only occupation here below?   Should it not be a continual striving to purify myself more and more, to destroy in myself everything that is opposed to holiness, and to acquire all those virtues which can make me pleasing to God?   And as I can never succeed in attaining this perfect purity by my own strength, what can I do better than to give myself up entirely to God, that He Himself may sanctify me, and make me all He wishes me to be, that so I may be worthy to stand in His presence?

What!   I am eternally to possess Him Who is holy by His very essence, Him Whose holiness is the admiration, the joy, the happiness of the blessed spirits; I am destined one day to exclaim with them for ever, "*Holy, Holy, Holy, Lord God Almighty;*" and yet I am not to labour with all my might to become holy, I am not to employ for that every moment of my life!   Why, then, am I upon the earth?   What other object is worthy of my desire?

Is there still a more powerful motive yet?

Yes.   God says to us, "*Be ye holy, because I am holy,*—because I Myself have united your nature to My own, that I might sanctify it."   The Christian is not simply a man; through Jesus Christ, he is made a partaker of the Divine nature; he has become by adoption the son of God the Father, and the brother of the Incarnate Word.   Not his soul only, but even his body takes part in this adoption. His very members are the members of Jesus Christ; it is Saint Paul who tells us so. Far more do his soul and all his faculties belong to Jesus Christ. How holy, then, should a Christian be, holy in body and soul, he who is incorporated with the Divine nature! O my God! if only we were penetrated with this truth, as we ought to be, what would be our ardour, our thirst for holiness! I am not surprised now that the Apostles gave no other title than that of "*saints*" to the first Christians, and this was the custom in the Church for a long time. To-day, would it not be indeed a mockery to give such a title to the generality of Christians? Are they not for the most part in their practice, and many of them in their principles, not saints, but enemies of sanctity? What a frightful change in the aspect of Christianity!

But what is the holiness which is proposed to Christians as a model? No other than that of God Himself: "*Be ye therefore perfect, as your Father in heaven is perfect:*" it is our Lord and Saviour Jesus Christ, it is God made Man, to teach us the way of holiness, Who addresses these words to us. What do they really mean? Can we, in very deed, be holy as God is holy? No; it is impossible for us to be holy as He is, or even to approach His infinite perfection. But whatever may be our holiness, it must be moulded upon His, which is the only source and the only pattern of all holiness.

And because our eyes are too weak to contemplate holiness, such as it is in God Himself, and because we should be incapable of applying it as a rule for

our own conduct, God was made Man, He lived with
men, He conversed with them, He instructed them by
His discourse, by His example, by His whole life,
and gave them, in our nature united to His, a model
of holiness which they can understand and imitate.
It is, then, no longer a question of saying, "Who
shall ascend up to heaven, there to understand, by
the contemplation of God Himself, what is the true
character of holiness?" Holiness in a human person
has come down to earth; holiness was revealed in
mortal flesh; holiness spoke and acted as a Man;
nothing remains for us but to study the Spirit of
Jesus Christ, to conform ourselves to His maxims,
to walk in His footsteps. If we do this we shall
become perfect, as our Father in heaven is perfect.

But Jesus Christ is not only the model of our
holiness; He is its principle, and its first efficient
cause. We can do nothing without His grace; and
this grace must act upon our liberty to the utmost of
its power if we would become holy as He is. He
offers this grace to us continually, and He has promised
to increase it in proportion as we correspond with it.
But our good use of His grace depends even more
upon Him than upon ourselves; and if we well
understand our own interests, the wisest and safest
plan we can adopt is to give and consecrate to Him
our liberty; to beg of Him to dispose of it as His own,
and to assure Him that we wish only to act under
His direction and only to be guided by His inspiration. Happy are those who give themselves to Him
like this, and who never take back their gift! Their
holiness will be the work of Jesus Christ; they will

have no other part in it than that of allowing Him to do with them according to His good pleasure, of never resisting Him, and of dying to their own heart, their own spirit, their own will, that they may live with the true life of Jesus Christ.

XII.

ON COMMERCE: AS A FIGURE OF THE SPIRITUAL LIFE.

THE spiritual life is nothing else than a sort of commerce, an exchange between God and the soul. God gives that He may receive, and receives that He may give : so it is with the soul. God gives first; and He also gives last. He presents the soul with His grace, in time; He gives the soul His glory for ever, in eternity. This grace and this glory are a direct communication, more or less perfect, from God Himself.

The soul, on her part, also gives herself to God; she sacrifices to Him her tastes, her inclinations, her will, her own interest; in one word, she gives herself entirely to God, that He may dispose of her every moment according to His good pleasure. This is what she does, or at least what she ought to do, in this life. In the other life she can do nothing, she is no longer free ; she does not give herself, she is enraptured and carried away : she belongs no more to herself, but to the sovereign Good who possesses her, and whom she possesses. Oh! most blessed and glorious possession ! Who shall speak of it !

Therefore, between God and the soul there is no
question of free exchange, except during this life.
Let us now see what, on the part of God, are the
laws of this holy commerce, and what are the laws
which the soul on her part must observe, that she
may respond to the ineffable goodness of God.

The first law.   God always makes the first advance ;
He must always do this in everything.   " *Who has
given to thee first ?* " exclaims Saint Paul.   This is easily
to be perceived in the order of nature, where we derive
our being from God every moment of our lives, and
with our being that which tends to its preservation.

The same thing is no less true in the supernatural
order : everything there begins by grace, either justi-
fying grace or actual grace, which is a gift of God,
a free and purely gratuitous gift, which it is impossible for us to merit.   If, after having lost the grace
of our baptism, we regain it by penance, it is God
Who makes the first advance to recall us to Himself;
for when we are once separated from Him by sin, we
can never of ourselves draw near to Him again.   If
we preserve the grace of our baptism, it is simply by
virtue of the actual graces which we receive every
moment.   It is an article of faith, that for every
supernatural act we must receive a special grace,
which goes before and accompanies that action ; and
God will never refuse us such a grace, unless it is to
punish us for infidelity to and neglect of graces He
has given us before.   Thus, it remains an incontest-
able truth, that God begins everything in us, and this
ought to be so, since He is always and in every case
the source of all good.

Hence the law as regards the creature here can only be a law of correspondence and of fidelity. God goes before: the creature must follow; God gives: she must carefully preserve; God graciously deigns to ask something of His creature: she must generously grant all He asks of her. How could a just exchange and commerce take place if she received all without giving anything in return, or if she did not give in proportion as she receives? There is also a law of gratitude on the part of the creature, gratitude to the God Whose benefits prevent and follow her incessantly; and a gratitude full of humility, because she sees plainly that she deserves nothing, and that by her constant falls she is even more worthy to be abandoned entirely than to be sought after and assisted by grace.

The second law. The gifts of God are perfectly disinterested; He has nothing to gain for Himself in all His goodness to us. If He requires a return on our part, it is not for His own advantage, it is for ours. The good use which we shall make of His grace is not even the motive which induces Him to grant it to us. How many graces has He given us which we have neglected and abused, and He foresaw that we should abuse them! This foresight of our unfaithfulness did not arrest the course of His benefits. What goodness! What disinterestedness!

The soul can never respond to this law, except very imperfectly. Because it is impossible for her *not* to gain in what she gives to God: therefore she ought not to and cannot entirely renounce her own interest. All that she can do, in proportion as grace solicits her, is not to dwell too much on her own interest; never to bargain with God; never to think she is doing too much; never to refuse anything to God under a pretext that she is not obliged to do it, and that He does not absolutely require it; not to be too much attached to His gifts, or to regret them too much when He chooses to take them away, but to be always generous and faithful when God sees fit to try her love; and finally, in great temptations and desolations, when she thinks herself hopelessly lost, to continue patiently to serve God, and to do those things which she knows are pleasing to Him.

By this disinterestedness she imitates, in some slight degree, that of God; she loves Him, she serves Him; she gives to Him, for His own sake alone, without seeking herself at all; and this is what gives most glory to God, of all the service which His creature can render to Him; this is what He will reward above all things with an infinite liberality.

But He often conceals from the soul the sight or thought of this reward, that He may purify her motives and increase her merit. This is an admirable artifice of Divine love of which few indeed know the secret.

The third law. The gifts of God are "*without repentance.*" It is Holy Scripture which tells us so. He never regrets, He never takes back what He has once given; He does not even reproach the soul for the gift if she abuses it; He simply reproaches her for the abuse she has made of His gift, and is ready to load her with still greater benefits, if she will only return to Him in sincerity. See how He treated David, how He treated Saint

Peter, and many others, after their conversion ! See
what a welcome this good Father gives to the prodigal son on his return : how He restores all to
him, and even adds new favours ! The just themselves might almost be jealous of the tender and kind
treatment He shows to penitent sinners.

This is the great law for the creature. Sunk as
she is in self-love, low, mean, and interested, when
God does not pay her as she expects for sacrifices,
often very insignificant and light, when she does
not immediately see in her hands the recompense
for her good works, she dares to complain that God
is not faithful; she regrets what she has given to
Him ; she even goes so far sometimes as to reproach
Him. Ah! what an indignity ! Where should
we be if God treated us like this, if He withdrew
His grace when we did not respond to it, or if He
refused it to us because He foresaw how we should
abuse it ? Let us give, like Him, without ever
repenting of it ; let us give, without ever thinking
afterwards of what we have given ; let us forget what
we have given already, and only think of what still
remains for us to give ; let us regret that we cannot
give more ; let us not be content until we have given
all, entirely and without reserve. What does it
matter to us whether God appears to accept our
gifts or not ? What does it matter to us if He
seems to make no account of them, and after all our
sacrifices only treats us with more severity ? Is
that what we are to consider ? No. There is only
one thing to consider. Does He wish us to make
such and such a sacrifice ? Does He deserve it ?

Yes, undoubtedly. If it is so, all is said for a generous soul.

The fourth law. God never forsakes, if He is not forsaken. He is the first to give, but He is not the first to withdraw. On the contrary, He long seeks after the creature who has forsaken Him. His patience is never weary ; and so long as a spark of life remains to the greatest sinner, God will always leave him sufficient grace to return to Himself. What faithfulness !

This is the most beautiful model for the soul which has given herself to God. God will never forsake me ; then I will never forsake Him. I am sure of Him ; then I ought to neglect nothing, that He may be sure of me. Alas ! I find nothing to be sure of in myself; I cannot answer for myself for one single instant. Nothing is more inconstant or weaker than my will. To-day I protest to God that I will always be faithful to Him ; to-morrow perhaps I shall deny Him. This is what should keep me in a continual distrust of myself, this is what should make me resolve once for all to give into God's keeping this liberty, which I am liable to abuse at any moment. This is what should make me inviolably faithful to His least grace. If I neglect one, voluntarily and with deliberation, what have I not to fear, from God, and from myself?—from God, Who may grow cold towards me, and Who may take away from me all His graces, in order to punish me ; from myself, who may become still weaker, still more ready to fall ? Ah ! Lord, I hope that Your good- ness will pardon all my faults of weakness, of inadvertence, of first impulse; but I beseech of You never to allow me to commit a fault, deliberately and with purpose to offend You ; never wilfully to resist one single grace ; never to refuse what you ask of me, whatever it may be.   I have all to fear from myself; and for this reason, fully and with my whole heart, I place my liberty in Your hands, that You may govern and dispose of me in all things.   The crowning grace of all graces is a constant fidelity ; I implore it of You, O my God ! and whatever it may cost me to obtain it, I shall never think I have bought it too dearly.   So may I observe exactly all the laws of the holy commerce which is between You and me, as You observe so strictly those which Your infinite goodness has imposed upon Yourself!   This is all I beg of You, and I leave my future, without fear, to Your infinite mercy !

XIII.

HOW GOD IS ALL, AND THE CREATURE IS NOTHING.

HE who has well embraced these two ideas can understand the spiritual life, in all its extent ; for the sole end of the spiritual life is to give to God and the creature their just due ; all to God, all without reserve : nothing to the creature, absolutely nothing. He who acts in all things conformably to these two ideas will be really humble and perfectly in subjection to grace.   As soon as we begin to give ourselves to God, we begin also to understand how God is all

and how we ourselves are nothing : I do not mean
by this understanding a knowledge which is purely
speculative and without effect, such as any one may
have who reflects on what God and what he himself
is ; I mean a practical knowledge, which effectually
influences our conduct, both interior and exterior.
The effect of this knowledge is to empty us by degrees
of ourselves, to take from us all that we have usurped,
and to reduce us at last to what we really are, that
is to say, to nothing ; at the same time, to fill us
with God, in such a manner that He is entirely in us
and we are entirely in Him.   As long as we think
ourselves to be something, when we are nothing ; as
long as we look to our own interest in anything ;
as long as we look to ourselves as our final end in
any thing whatsoever, so long we do not really consider ourselves as pure nothingness, nor God as the
sole end from Whom proceed all things, and to Whom
all things must return.

God is all, in the order of nature   Everything else
was nothing until God gave it existence : now existence, simple being, is a gift without which no other
possession is possible.

Therefore I am nothing of myself, and I owe to
God alone all that I am ; my understanding, my
memory, my will, as well as the power to exercise
these faculties, all is a gift from God.   If I appropriate these gifts to myself, if I am proud of them, if
I prefer myself to those who are, or whom I suppose
to be less gifted than myself, I steal from God what
is His own, I do not comprehend my own nothingness, I commit an injustice towards those to whom I

prefer myself, because I am nothing, as they are ; and, by my pride, I begin even to be less than nothing ; I begin to be the object of the hatred of God, Who cannot bear that what is really nothing should dare to attribute to itself any good.

"*What have you ?*" Saint Paul says, "*that you have not received ? And if you have received it, why should you glorify yourselves as if you had not received it ?*"

Not only is God all in the order of nature, but He has made all for Himself; all that exists belongs solely to Him ; He is the only and necessary end of all things. In one sense, it is true that this world was made for man, and for his use, during this life ; but the intention of God is that man should use for Him and for His glory all the creatures which he may lawfully use ; that man is to glorify God through other creatures, because man alone is gifted with intelligence and free-will, and he should make use of these only in accordance with the Will of God.

This is, then, the commandment : man, being alone capable of glorifying God by his reasonable service, must refer all to God: his being, all his powers, all his free actions ; he must submit in all things to the sovereignty of God ; and because God has made him the master and ruler of other creatures, he must look upon those creatures as so many benefits from God, and use them only for the glory of his Benefactor. If man does not obey this commandment, if he looks upon himself in anything as independent, as master of his own will ; if, without regard to the supreme sovereignty of God, he acts or thinks as he chooses ; if he makes use of creatures otherwise than as God wishes and permits; if he attaches himself to them inordinately, and makes of them his only happiness and his final end he is a rebel, a traitor, a most ungrateful servant, a usurper of what belongs to God.

God is all, in the order of grace, and here man is, if we can say so, even more completely nothing than in the order of nature.

Now, what is the order of grace? It is an order by which the intelligent creature, who is nothing of himself, is destined to the eternal possession of God, Who in Himself is all. And this destiny is so sublime, so immeasurably above the natural capacity of the creature, that there is less distance from absolute nothingness to his simple actual existence in this life than there is from his simple actual existence in this life to a destiny so supernatural.

This destiny is, then, a pure grace of the Creator, but a grace so excellent, so sublime, that God Himself, God as He is, could do nothing greater for man. So that it is principally in the order of grace that man must look upon God as all, and upon himself as nothing.

God is all in the order of grace: 1st, Because He alone has given or could give to us the knowledge of the excellence of our destiny. Man never would have had, and never could have had, the least idea of it by himself.

2nd, Because God alone could indicate to us, and has indicated to us, the necessary means to attain to this supernatural end. Religion, the worship of God, His sacraments, His precepts, all this is absolutely of Divine institution. Human reason, left to itself, could never have known these means, any more than it could have had any authority to establish them.

3rd, Because man, if he is not assisted by a heavenly light, which makes things clear to his mind, and by a good inspiration acting on his will, can never form one holy thought, one good desire, or perform one action which is worthy of eternal life. His free-will needs to be continually prevented and assisted by grace. The very consent which he gives to the promptings of grace is a grace in itself, and God has more part in it than he has himself. His will is excited to good, his actions are made good and meritorious, by the help of God alone and entirely ; his only merit consists in faithfully and constantly co-operating with God, and even this is not a merit, for it is simply what he ought to do.

This is how man would stand with regard to grace, this is what would be his dependence upon it, even if he had never sinned. But since original sin has entered into the world, this dependence is much greater. The natural corruption of man inclines him to what is evil, and inspires him with a secret aversion to what is good. His passions overpower and obscure his reason ; his ignorance and weakness are extreme. He needs a far stronger grace, if he would do what is right, and persevere in it; and he owes this grace to the pure goodness and mercy of Jesus Christ, Who in His own nature repaired our human nature, fallen through the sin of Adam.

But if to original sin, which has already so weakened him, a man has added frequently and during a long course of years an innumerable number of actual sins ; if he has contracted terrible habits of sin, which have made evil natural to him, and apparently necessary, that man is no longer a simple nothing in the order of grace : he is a formal opposition to it : he resists grace, so to speak, with all his strength, and God must actually struggle with him to make him good. It is then indeed that God is all, as regards the sanctification of that man, who is not only nothing in His sight, but who has opposed Him to the utmost of his power.

And this is what we have nearly all done : for how few are those who have preserved the innocence of their baptism ! And this is what we may become again at any moment. How ? By one single wilful infidelity, one single resistance to grace. Yes ; when God has sought after a soul, loaded it with the gifts of His grace, drawn it back from its wanderings, and led it safely into the path of His pure love, then one deliberate fault, one formal and obstinate refusal to do something which God requires, may have the most terrible consequences, and may cause its eternal ruin. And what kind of deliberate faults ? One simple thought of self-complacency and pride, wilfully indulged; one deliberate yielding to pride, when thinking of the graces we have received, or of what we have done for God; one feeling of contempt for our neighbour, or preferring of ourselves to him. Such faults may lead us, by degrees, into a state far more dangerous than that from which God once rescued us. Alas ! alas ! who would not be seized with a holy terror at the sight of this abyss into which sin has plunged him, and into which it may plunge him again at any moment! Who can think anything of himself when he considers what he has been, what he would be now, if God had not come to his assistance, and what he certainly may become at any moment if he withdraws himself from the protection of God, to lean on his own strength?

O my God, and my All! be all for me, all in the order of nature, all in the order of grace! Teach me to sacrifice all to You, to attribute to You alone any good I may be able to do, and to expect everything from You! Teach me to look upon myself as absolute nothingness from beginning to end, as disposed to evil by my will, as incapable of doing the least good of myself, and as capable of the greatest sins, if for one instant I turn away from You!

Destroy in me that love of self which sin has planted there, and reduce me to that blessed state of annihilation which has no life but in You, which is no longer able to oppose any obstacle to Your designs, and which renders to You all the homage and glory which is possible from the utter nothingness of Your creature! Amen.

XIV.

ON WHAT GOD ASKS OF US, AND WHAT WE MUST ASK OF GOD.

It is very important, it is even absolutely necessary, in the spiritual life, that we should be able to distinguish clearly, with regard to our interior dispositions,

F

between what God actually asks of us and what we ought to ask of God—or rather between what He has a right to expect from us, and what He wishes us to expect from Him.

For the want of a clear discernment in these two things, we often fall into very trying doubts and perplexities about our state; we are discontented with ourselves when there is no occasion to be so, or we are delighted with ourselves, and think God is delighted with us, when He is not; we complain of the designs of Providence, and murmur against them unjustly; and in the end we commit many real faults and expose ourselves to the danger of giving up everything. Let us then try, by the light of truth, to distinguish between these two different things, and to fix each one clearly in our minds, that we may be able to make of them afterwards the rule of our judgments and the guide of our conduct.

God only asks from us what it depends upon ourselves to give. This principle is self-evident. Now, only one single thing depends upon us, and that is, the good use of our liberty, according to the actual measure of grace which is enlightening our mind and exciting our will.

God then asks of us, in the first place, a constant attention to what is passing in our own hearts, and to His Voice which will speak to us there. This constant attention is not so difficult as we might think, if once we love God sincerely and are determined to please Him in all things.

He asks of us that we shall never give ourselves up to anything which can distract us from this attention, whether it be exterior amusememt, or curiosity, or undue attachment to any object, or useless thoughts, or voluntary trouble and agitation of mind, from any cause whatever; He also asks that when we notice that anything in particular has the power to distract us from this attention to the voice of grace, we shall at once give up that thing and put it away from us. But we must not imagine that either the duties of our state of life, or domestic troubles, or the ordinary events of every day, or the courtesy we owe to society, can of themselves injure this interior recollection; we can preserve it in the midst of all these things. And, besides, after one has used a little violence towards one's self for a time, this recollection becomes so natural that one scarcely perceives it, and seldom or ever loses it.

God asks of us a full, perfect, and faithful correspondence to grace, in all circumstances in which we may find ourselves. The grace of beginners is not the same as that of those who are more advanced, and the grace of those who are advanced is not the same as that of those who are consummated in the way of perfection. A disposition which is good in a beginner is not so in one who is more advanced; such and such a practice is proper for one state, and would not be so for another. We must, then, understand how to take them up and leave them, following the instinct of grace, and not to attach ourselves to any one of them with any kind of obstinacy. Still less must we desire to raise ourselves above our present state, until God Himself raises us; nor must we undertake or wish for what is beyond our strength, or imagine we can do what we admire in the saints, or think we may allow ourselves certain liberties which God grants only to those souls who have passed through every sort of trial.

God asks of us, that when we have once given ourselves to Him, we shall never take ourselves away from Him ; that we shall never act on our own responsibility, but always consult Him in everything, and also those guides whom He has given us to direct us, especially when we wish to do anything extraordinary : He asks that we shall remain passive and submissive to His will in any state in which it pleases Him to place us ; that we shall never do anything of ourselves to go out of this state, on the pretext that it is too painful for human nature, and that we cannot bear it any longer. We must not ask Him to deliver us from a temptation, or a humiliation, or an interior trial, if He wills that we should be tempted, or humiliated, or tried, for our greater purification ; but we must ask of Him the courage and strength to bear it to the end.

What God asks of us, above all things, is the entire resignation and abandonment of ourselves to Him—a resignation of all without exception and for ever. But as this abandonment has its degrees, and goes on increasing, until in the end we lose ourselves utterly in Him, we have simply to keep ourselves in a general disposition to sacrifice to Him each thing as He asks it of us ; and when the occasion presents itself, to make the actual sacrifice. There is, then, no necessity to anticipate anything, or to imagine ourselves in circumstances where, perhaps, we shall never be, or to exhaust our strength beforehand by wondering if we could bear such and such a trial. All this is useless, and even dangerous : useless, because we never can foresee the future, or form a just idea of any situation, whether interior or exterior, in which we may be placed ; and dangerous, because by such thoughts we expose ourselves to presumption or to discouragement. Entire resignation of self leaves to God the care of the future, and only occupies itself with the present moment.

God does *not* ask of us either sensible devotion or those great lights and fine sentiments on which self-love feeds but too much. These graces depend on Him alone : He gives them and takes them away when He pleases. There is, then, no necessity for being desolate and miserable if we have no sensible devotion at prayer or Holy Communion, if we are dry, stupid, heavy, incapable of any pious feeling. Still less must we think that prayer and communion made like this is worth nothing. Self-love might so judge, but God judges differently.

God does not ask that we keep our imagination captive in such a manner that we are absolutely masters of our thoughts. This does not depend upon us ; but it does depend upon us never wilfully to dwell on thoughts that disturb our peace, to despise them, not to allow them to trouble and torment us, and in this, as in all else, to be guided by the decisions of our director. It does not depend upon us, either, to be free from temptations against purity, against faith or hope. These are temptations which God may permit for our greater advancement. We may ask submissively, as St. Paul did, to be delivered from them; but if God answers us, as He answered St. Paul, "*My grace is sufficient for thee,*" we must bear these temptations with humility, and fight against them as well as we can, using the means prescribed by obedience.

In all those events which depend upon Providence or the will of others God asks of us entire submission, and that we should try to draw from them as much profit as possible, both for His glory and our own sanctification, being persuaded, as St. Paul says, that "all things work together for good to them that love God."

With regard to all our undertakings, even the most holy, in which we are engaged by the Will of God, He only asks of us our faithful labour, our careful application, and the employment of the means in our power; but He does not ask of us *success:* that depends on Him alone; and He sometimes permits, for our greater good, that the success should not be according to our hopes and intentions.

This is in some slight degree, and briefly, what God asks of us, and what depends on the good use of our free will. As to what we must ask of God, it is quite certain that we are not fit judges as to what is best for us, or what would harm us, and we cannot do better than leave it entirely to God. Our best plan is, then, to keep in general to what the law teaches us we must necessarily ask for, and to observe a holy indifference with regard to all those things which are not absolutely necessary to our perfection.

One thing we must ask is, that we may know God, and know ourselves; what He is, and what we are;

what He has done for us, and what we have done
against Him; what He deserves, and what He has a
right to require of us; the value of His grace, and
the importance of making good use of it.

We must ask for a perfect and entire trust in Him,
a trust which will reach so far as to make us say
with holy Job, "*Though He slay me, yet will I trust
in Him.*"

We must ask that we may love and serve God, at
the expense of any sacrifice of ourselves, without
the slightest regard for our own interest, solely for
His glory and the accomplishment of His good
pleasure.

We must ask for the spirit of faith, which will
raise us above all testimony, above all assurance,
above all reason; that is to say, our faith will rest,
not on human testimony, not on any mere feeling of
assurance, not on mere reason, but simply and solely
on the Will of God, as revealed to His Church; and
this bare and simple faith will sustain us in the most
obscure darkness, in the deprivation of all sensible
support, and will keep us in a profound peace, though
we may feel as if suspended between heaven and
hell.

We must ask for a spirit of blind obedience, which
will make us die to our own judgment and our own
will, which will make us act against what appears to
be reason and our own natural aversions, which will
neither allow us to reflect or to reason, because it is
certain that the ways of God are above all our thoughts
and contrary to all our natural inclinations, and that we
shall never advance in the way of perfection until

we cast ourselves blindly and without reserve into
what may appear to us at first as an abyss, unfathom-
able and without resource.

XV.

ON THE EMPLOYMENT OF TIME.

THE greater number of mankind employ their time
badly ; many others are perfectly embarrassed by
their time, and do not know how to employ it, or
rather, how to lose it ; their sole object is to fritter
it away, to pass it agreeably to themselves, or at
least without feeling themselves wearied and bored.

Do they ever succeed in this ? No. Experience
teaches us that those people who are most greedy for
pleasure are soon satiated with it, and that disgust,
weariness, and idleness soon render them unbearable,
even to themselves. But unfortunately, when they
have acquired this experience, it is very rarely that
they profit by it : the bad habits are formed ; it would
cost too much to adopt good ones : they continue
to live as they have lived, although they no longer
flatter themselves with the hope of the happiness
they once confidently expected. Woe to those who
abuse and misuse their time ! One day they will
regret to have acted so, but then their regrets will be
in vain.

Let us now propose for Christians and interior
souls some salutary and useful reflections.

What is *time*, with regard to myself ? It is my

present and actual existence. Past time, or my past existence, is no longer anything, as far as I am concerned; I can neither recall it, nor change anything in it. The time to come, or my future existence, has not yet arrived, and perhaps never will arrive. It does not depend upon me; I cannot count upon it; and the most powerful monarch in the world cannot make sure of one single instant of life. No one is ignorant of these two simple truths, but very few draw from them the conclusions they ought to draw.

It is true and certain that I have only belonging to me the present moment, which cannot be divided, which nothing can fix, not even thought, and which is passing away with a rapidity which nothing can equal.

This present moment, or this actual existence, from whom do I hold it? From God. It is He Who called me from nothing into being, twenty, thirty, forty years ago, more or less: it is He Who has preserved my existence from one instant to another, and Who is preserving it at this present moment. Will He preserve it for me in the moment which shall immediately follow this one? I do not know; and nothing in the world can give me the assurance of it.

Why has time been given to me? That by it I may merit a happy eternity. I shall live for ever: faith teaches me this: my reason even assures me of another life: the desire of immortality is implanted in the depths of my heart; and this desire, which God Himself has planted there, can never be frustrated of its object. I am, then, born for eternity; but this eternity will be happy or wretched; and that is

according to the use I make of time.   If I sincerely
repent of the bad use of time I have made in the
past, if I am beginning to make a good use of it, if
I persevere in this good use until the moment comes
when time shall cease for me, then I shall be eternally
happy.   If I have made a bad use of time in the
past, if I am still doing so, if I continue to do so,
and death surprises me in this state, I shall be eternally miserable.

My fate for all eternity depends, then, upon the
use I make of time; and since neither the past nor
the future are in my own power, it is quite true to
say that my eternity depends always upon the present
moment.   Now, at this present moment, what is my
state?   Should I like to die just as I am now?
Should I dare to run the risk of my eternity just as
I am now?   If I should not, am I not a fool to remain in the state in which I am, to count upon the
future, when I am not sure of the moment which
shall follow this one, when perhaps between me and
eternity there is only one instant of time?

All the events of life, except sin, can contribute to
my happy eternity.   It is sin alone which can make
me lose it.   And what is sin?   It is the result of
a moment's determination.   As soon as the deliberate
intention of mortal sin is formed by my will, whether
the exterior act follows or not, if I die in that state I
am lost for ever, and without resource; and I have no
assurance that I shall not die as soon as this deliberate intention to sin is formed in my heart.   What
folly, then, to consent to that which can ruin me for
ever, at the very moment I give the consent of my

will, even before I have passed to the exterior act of sin !

All the other evils which may happen to us in time are only evils belonging to time itself, and they are evils which may be converted into blessings for all eternity, if we will accept them all as a Christian should, and make a holy use of them. We need not fear them so much, and we need not torment ourselves so much to avoid them or to remedy them. Sin alone is the evil which lasts for all eternity; it is an evil which we can never be sure of remedying when once we have committed it; it is an evil which can only be cured by repentance, but by a repentance which perhaps may never be in our power, and which certainly will not be, unless God Himself, by granting us more time, gives us, through His infinite goodness alone, the grace of conversion.

From these deep and serious reflections it is easy for me to conclude what sort of employment I ought to make of time : 1st, Never to do anything which may expose me to the danger of forfeiting my happy eternity; 2nd, To make of each moment the use which God wishes me to make of it, that by it I may merit that happy eternity ; 3rd, Never to put off to a moment which perhaps may never come to me what I can and ought to do at the present moment; 4th, Never to give to any frivolous amusement, still less to any dangerous amusement, to any useless occupation, or to simple idleness, the time whose moments are so precious; 5th, and finally, To be convinced that a life which may finish at any moment, and which has only been given to me that by it I

may merit eternal happiness, ought to be a very
serious life, a life divided between the duties I owe
to God, to my state, and to society; a life in which
I do not seek for any other rest and recreation than
what God Himself allows and authorises, so that this
very rest and innocent enjoyment may be another
means towards gaining that blessed eternity. What
a reform there would be in the world, and what a
difference, if every one would be guided by these solid
truths, upon which depend our greatest and only
real interest! These rules are for the generality of
Christians.

But with regard to interior souls there is more
than this. They must never look upon time as a
thing they may dispose of as they will; they must
never think they are masters of one single instant.
Since they have given themselves entirely to God,
their liberty and the use they ought to make of it
belong solely to Him, at every instant of their lives.
It is for Him to inspire them from one moment to
another as to what they have to do, for Him to
regulate all their interior dispositions, their exterior
acts, and even their innocent amusements. He has become the Master of all that, by the gift they have made
Him of themselves. They would take back that gift
if they were to make one step, if they were to speak
one word, of themselves, without consulting Him.

There is no longer any constraint for them in this;
on the contrary, God treats them as His own children; and as long as He knows that their hearts are
His alone, He allows them to enjoy a sweet liberty
which mere servants know not of.

The only use which these souls should make of time is to be attentive each moment to what God asks of them, and faithful to accomplish it. With the exception of this attention and this fidelity, which soon become a habit with them, they are free from all other care whatsoever : and God, Who is the sole Master of their time, disposes of it Himself just as He pleases. There is no longer any necessity for them to trouble themselves about what employment God wishes them to undertake ; there is no need for them to form plans for the future ; God will provide for that ; He will not suffer them to be idle for a moment ; He will arrange everything ; He will direct everything ; and even if He gives them no exterior occupation, He will keep them interiorly occupied with Himself. Even if a spiritual life had no other advantage than this, that it keeps us in perfect repose as to the employment of our time, and gives us a calm assurance that all our moments are employed according to the Will of God, that alone is an inestimable advantage, which we can never buy too dearly.

The sole object of the interior soul is to glorify God, to love God ; to glorify Him by all her actions, and by all her sufferings, which come to her through His choice, and in which she has nothing to do but patiently to submit ; to love Him, not by formal acts or by effusions of sensible devotion, but by being effectually and continually devoted to Him, and by an entire resignation of her own will to His.

This, from one moment to another, and without any interruption, is the constant occupation of that

favoured soul.   Her exterior situation may change ;
she may pass from repose to action, from health to
sickness ; she may experience every sort of vicissitude
from within and without.   In this, as all others are,
she is subject to the changes of time.   But the depths
of her heart are changeless as God Himself, and fixed
in a constant peace, except that her union with God
goes on increasing, and becomes closer and closer, as
time goes on.   In this respect time has almost ceased
to exist for her ; she is almost transported to eternity.
Yes ; from the moment that she gave herself entirely
to God, so long as she does not take back that gift, so
long as she remains in that state of simple dependence
on God's Will, and never swerves from that dependence
by any deliberate act, she participates in the depths
of her being in the very being of God, because she is
every moment just what He wishes her to be.   She
works and acts as a creature ; but God works and
acts with her as a Creator ; and as this Divine action
is continual, and as she is always submissive to it,
she is, notwithstanding occasional miseries and weakness, already on this earth in a peace which is almost
like that of the blessed in heaven ; and the changes
of time no longer affect her, more than they affect
God, because they are incapable of altering the fixed
disposition of her heart.

Happy are those who understand this ; happier
still are those who faithfully practise it !

XVI.

ON THE BLINDNESS OF MAN.

Our Lord Jesus Christ said, "*For judgment I am come into this world; that they that see not might see: and that they who see might be made blind.*" Our Saviour uttered these words with relation to the man who was born blind, and to whom He granted sight of the soul, after having restored to him the sight of the body, in the presence of the Pharisees, whom this miracle ought to have enlightened, and who were only made blinder than ever by it. The hidden meaning of this sentence of our Lord and Saviour Jesus Christ is very deep, and is meant for us all: let us try to penetrate it, by the help of His grace.

We are all born blind as a deplorable consequence of original sin. We neither know God nor ourselves. We are in a profound ignorance as to our destination; that it to say, as to the one thing which is indisputably the most important of all, or rather, the one thing which alone is truly interesting to us. We neither know in what true happiness consists, nor what steps we must take to attain it. This ignorance is a fact to which the whole universe bears witness. We have only to remember what was the state of the world before the coming of Jesus Christ, and what is still the state of the nations to whom He is unknown. But this ignorance is not the greatest evil. We are blind, and we do not know that we are blind. Born with this disease, we think ourselves in perfect health ; and we should never have known anything about our blindness if God-made Man had not come to deliver us from it.

The greatest of all evils is to think that we see when we do not see. This was the evil of the pretended wise men of paganism, and of the proud Pharisees of Judaism.

Now, although Christianity has enlightened us in some degree on essential matters, it has not entirely done away with our blindness. As long as our trust in our own spirit, as long as our self-love reigns in us, so long we are blind in many respects, both as regards God and ourselves. As regards God : we understand nothing of His ways ; we entertain quite false ideas as to holiness ; we know not in what true virtue consists. As regards ourselves : the real main-spring of our dispositions is unknown to us ; we can see the faults of others clearly enough, but our own faults are hidden from us ; our judgment, in all that regards ourselves, is nothing but a delusion. ·And as this blindness affects the soul, the soul is not conscious of it, and cannot be ; for how can she see by her own light that which she sees not ?

This evil is very great, but it is not without remedy ; it is not hopeless. The Divine light can disperse this blindness easily, when it is not volun-tary. But how can the Divine light disperse a blind-ness to which we will not acknowledge ? How can it enlighten those proud souls who think they see everything, and who reject it because they imagine they have no need of it ? What means can it take to penetrate those perverse spirits, led away by a thousand prejudices, obstinate in not seeing what it tries to show them, and determined to see things only in a false light which they have created for themselves ? This is a very common disease with pious persons ; and because the root of it is pride, it opposes to Divine grace an obstacle which humility only can overcome, and which humility even does not always overcome.

Jesus Christ is the Light of the world : He came to cure our blindness. But in doing this He exercises a kind of judgment which is full of goodness for some, and of justice for others. He gives sight to those who see not, and He blinds those who see. What do these words mean ? Do they mean that amongst men, before our Lord enlightens them, there are some who see, and others who do not see ? No : all are equally blind. But some, enlightened by grace as to their sad state, acknowledge humbly that they are blind ; they implore our dear Lord earnestly and with importunity for their cure ; and to them He will give sight, and He will never cease to grant them that sight as long as they make a good use of the light He has granted them, and allow themselves to be entirely guided by it. Others will not confess that they are blind, and these He will leave in their blindness, until it becomes incurable. Either they attribute to themselves the light they receive from Him, and appropriate it as if it came from themselves, and so, as a punishment, He takes it away from them ; or they make a bad use of the light He gives them ; they neglect its warnings ; they fear it and

G

fly from it; and so most justly do they deserve that He should deprive them of it.

Now, to which of these classes do we belong, and do we wish to belong? Unhappy shall we be if we cleave to the leadings of our own self-will, if we use our own judgment with regard to the ways of God, and act in all things as our own spirit prompts us! God will leave us to ourselves! And what can happen to a blind man who attempts to guide himself but to fall over a precipice! Unhappy also shall we be if we regard as our own the light which God sends us, if we look upon it as our own property, if we are vain of it, if we make use of it only to nourish our pride and presumption! The jealousy of God will never pardon us such a theft; He will take away that light from us; He will never suffer us to usurp His gifts. And finally, unhappy shall we be if we do not draw from the light we receive all the profit which God intends we should draw from it, if we fear to be enlightened as to what He asks of us, because we cannot make up our minds to grant Him *all!* He will give to others the light He intended for us; and instead of advancing in the way of perfection, we shall fall back.

Let us then imitate the poor blind man in the Gospel: let us be fully convinced that we are always enveloped in darkness, and that of ourselves we have no power to free ourselves from it. Let us say continually to Jesus Christ: "*Lord, that I may see!*" Give me light, either by your own voice in my soul, or by the voice of him whom You wish to be my guide. If we have to consider anything, let us fear to decide

of ourselves; let us fear to act through a natural
instinct, through a movement of passion, through prejudice, or human respect; but let us humbly ask of
God that He will enlighten us, that He will show
us the truth, and give us the strength and courage
to follow it. Let us keep our soul in a state of continual dependence upon the Divine light, and let us
feel convinced that if God's light leaves us for a
single instant, we shall make a false step.

This is not all. Let us give thanks to God for all
the light He gives us, acknowledging that it is from
Him alone that we receive it. Let us never rely
upon our own judgment, or upon the penetration of
our own mind. The things of God can only be
understood by the spirit of God. He takes pleasure
in enlightening simple souls, who are convinced of
their own ignorance, and who attribute nothing to
themselves; who judge nothing by their own judgment, and who give to God the sole glory of all they
know and experience, recognising Him as the Source
of all good. O! if we could know how dangerous
it is to follow the leading of our own spirit, how
much God wishes to humble it, to cast it down, to
annihilate it, we should never rest until we had
trampled it under foot; we should sacrifice it with
the greatest joy; we should think ourselves happy
if we could foresee nothing, reflect on nothing, not
say a single word, nor have a single thought, nor form
a single judgment of ourselves, but in all these things
depend entirely upon the Divine guidance; we should
endeavour always to keep in our souls a sort of
empty space, as it were, for God to fill it as He

pleases, and we should carefully suppress every
thought which we feel to be our own! Happy is
that state of prayer, happy is the entire state of that
soul in which the human spirit acts no longer; it is
a proof that God has taken entire possession of it,
and that He wishes to be the sole Master there. Let
us not complain if this state is somewhat painful to
human nature. It may be a kind of blindness, but
it is a blindness which is produced by the very
splendour of the Divine light. We may not be able
to see anything distinctly; but by virtue of that same
light, when it is necessary, and God wishes us to see,
we shall see well enough, we shall know what we
have to do. And what can we need more? Is not
the repose of our spirit in God far preferable to any
exercise of it independent of God?

Finally, let us make use of the light which God
gives us, either to know our own misery, and so
humble us, or to discern what God wishes us to do,
and practise it, or to show us our faults, and help us
to correct them. Let us not be afraid of the sight
God gives us, because it shows us what perhaps we
would rather not see, or nerves us to do what our
cowardice shrinks from. Let us not hate the mirror
which shows us our own ugliness; let us love the
truth which reproves us; and let us believe that
after the knowledge of God there is nothing so useful for us as the true knowledge of ourselves. More
than this, let us be persuaded that we shall only be
raised to the true knowledge of God in proportion as
we know and feel our own nothingness. These are
the two abysses which " *call to each other* " according

to the expression of Holy Scripture. And blind as we are with regard to these two things, which nevertheless comprise everything for us, let us say with Saint Augustine, "Let me know Thee, Lord, and let me know myself!"

XVII.

ON THE WEAKNESS AND CORRUPTION OF THE HUMAN HEART.

WE have been considering how blind is the natural understanding of man ; and now we will see also how his heart is naturally weak and corrupted. When I say weak, I mean when there is a question of doing good ; his heart is only too strong when there is a question of doing evil.

This will of man, which God created upright and pure, has been corrupted by original sin, and we are all born in this unfortunate and hereditary corruption. The order of creation has been reversed. Once the heart of man had a natural inclination to love God above all things. But since sin entered into the world, all our love is bestowed upon ourselves, and we love nothing but as it affects ourselves. Again, if this love of ourselves was reasonable, if we really understood our true interests, this very love would lead us quickly to God, our first beginning and our last end. But it is not reason, it is not our true interests, that regulate our self-love. This love is unreasonable, because it makes us our own end, and our own centre : it is contrary to our true interests, because it only looks to a present and temporary good, to a sensible advantage, and entirely loses sight of a divine and spiritual good, of supernatural and eternal advantages.

Hence it happens that from our earliest childhood we seek after earthly things with the whole strength of our souls ; that we only look for happiness in the enjoyment of them ; that the necessities and pleasures of our body occupy and enslave us ; and that our soul, buried, so to speak, in matter and material things, either cannot rise at all, or only rises with the greatest difficulty towards spiritual things.

From this comes that terrible concupiscence, the source of almost all our sins. The saints knew this, and groaned over it, because they felt how humiliating it is for them, to how many temptations it exposes them, and how contrary it is to the primitive order, which made the soul subject to God, and the body to the soul. But the greater number of men, and even of Christians, instead of deploring this cruel malady, cherish it, take a pride in themselves for it, and would even think themselves unfortunate if they were not subject to it. For the man without passions seems to them a being without emotion and without life. And the man who fights against his passions, instead of yielding, passes, in their eyes, for a fool, and an enemy of his own happiness.

This is the cause of that frightful difficulty which we find in understanding, in appreciating, and in practising Christian morality, the end and aim of which is to destroy in us the reign of concupiscence. And if Christian morality seems to us beautiful, and reasonable, and worthy of the dignity of man, we must not think that we so regard it by our natural and human light. Never could it appear so to us if we were not enlightened by the rays of Divine grace. But from clearly seeing that the teachings of Christian morality are beautiful to the practice of it, how far it is! By the aid of grace we form good resolutions; we promise God that we will be faithful to Him; we think ourselves firm and immovable in virtue; but alas! at the first occasion, the first temptation, we fail; the least difficulty frightens us; the attraction of a sensible and present good makes us forget everything; in a word, we fall at every step; and it is impossible for us to raise ourselves up again by our own strength. What weakness! How humiliating it is!

I do not do the good I wish to do; but the evil I wish not to do, that I do. Again, if I wish to do good, although it may only be a feeble desire, and if I do not wish to do evil, this is all the gift of Divine grace; for the corruption and malice of my will are such, that its first natural movements would draw it away from good, and incline it to evil. We need not watch ourselves for a long time to discover this sad disposition. Our heart is almost always at war with reason. Reason advises us to do such and such a thing; passion advises us the exact contrary. We see, and we approve of, the better part; but we follow the worst. Even a pagan remarked this. This constant fight between reason and the passions keeps the soul in one continual state of agitation.

But this is only the beginning of our malice. Our natural malice is irritated at the forbidding of evil:

it is angry with God, Who is the Author of this prohibition. It exhausts itself in reasonings in subtle
arguments, to persuade itself that such a prohibition
is unjust and tyrannical, and that man has a right
to give himself up, without restraint and without
measure, to the guidance of his passions. Listen to
self-love; self-love wishes to be the master of all, he
pretends that everything belongs to him; he has no
respect for the rights of others. Any resistance that
is opposed to what he desires seems to him an injustice. He envies others for what they have, and he
has not; and not only does he envy them, but he
tries by every means to take away from them what
they have. And it is quite certain that passion would
stop at nothing, if once it were strong enough to tear
down the barriers. It is never the fear of God which
arrests its fury; it is simply the fear of man, and
of human laws: therefore passion will substitute
fraud and deception, as much as it can, for violence.
And the crime is committed in the heart, even if we
are wanting in the courage and the means to carry it
out. Many disorders are committed in the world;
but incomparably more are committed in the secret
of men's hearts, which are never able to be actually
committed for want of occasion and resources. Whoever could look secretly upon all that men desire,
resolve, and execute in the interior of their mind,
would find them a thousand times more wicked than
they appear outwardly.

Not only does the prohibition of evil irritate man;
it is actually an additional attraction to make him
commit evil. The law, far from arresting the will,

only excites it; and the great charm of sin is that it *is* sin. Saint Paul has said it, and daily experience only shows it to us too well: it is quite sufficient for a thing to be forbidden us, to make us instantly desire to do it. A book, a picture, a play, have been forbidden to us; at once our curiosity is aroused, and we have no rest until it is satisfied. What has been hidden from us is the thing of all others we desire to know. What has been refused to us is the thing of all others we desire to have. It seems as if every law, every restraint, were an attempt against our liberty; and as if neither God nor man had any right to control our desires. Can the corruption and malice of our will be carried any further?

The worst of all is that instead of being covered with confusion at all these miseries, we glory in them: instead of condemning them, or at least excusing them, we seek to justify them; we boast of the evil we have done, and even of that which we have not really done; we give ourselves out for more wicked than we really are. The great triumph of libertines, when they are together, is to surpass themselves in this manner. And their only shame is when they see that others have succeeded in carrying their wicked pleasures and debaucheries farther than they themselves have.

If we do not feel ourselves capable of such excesses as these, we know ourselves but very imperfectly. The root of corruption is the same in all hearts; nothing is necessary but to give one's self up freely to any one single passion, and at once the corruption is developed. Let us go a little way into the depths

of our own heart; let us recall what has happened
there in such and such circumstances; let us see
where such a desire, such an inclination, such a feeling would have led us, if education, and fear, and
religion had not restrained us, or if the occasion had
not been wanting. Let us be just to ourselves; and
let us confess in all humility that if God had not
specially watched over us there is no crime, however
terrible, into which our natural corruption might not
have led us. Let us thank God, both for those sins
which He has forgiven us, and for those from which
He has preserved us. And let us say, with Saint
Augustine, that there is no crime which one man has
committed which another man is not capable of, and
which he would not, perhaps, commit, in very deed, if
it were not for the Divine assistance.

The depth of our misery is so great that we
could not possibly bear the full sight of it; and if
God were to allow us to see it as it is, when we
begin to give ourselves to Him, the sight would drive
us to despair : therefore He only shows it to us by
degrees, and with a reserve that is full of wisdom.
But as this knowledge of our true selves is absolutely
necessary for us to make us humble, watchful, and
full of distrust of our own strength and confidence
in God, by degrees, and gradually, as we grow
stronger and advance in virtue, God will show us our
natural corruption and our weakness. And by the
greatness of the evil He will make us judge the price
of the remedy ; He will make us approach that dreadful abyss from which His grace has drawn us back,
and will discover to us all the profoundness of its

depth. Thus He made Saint Teresa see the very place in hell which she would have occupied if He had not called her to Himself by His infinite mercy. And it is thus that the sins we have actually committed, and those we might have committed but for the assistance of His grace, are made to serve as a foundation for our humility and our sanctity.

But God does not stop there with those souls which He designs to call to the highest perfection: He is not contented with giving to them a speculative knowledge of their misery; He will give to them an experimental knowledge. For this He waits until their will is so confirmed and rooted in good that there is no longer any fear that they will actually sin. Then He makes them experience the feeling of their corruption: He permits bad thoughts and evil desires of all kinds to take possession of their minds and their hearts; all their passions seem to be unchained; the devil joins his black suggestions to the inclinations of corrupt nature. These souls, in reality so pure, so full of horror for everything evil, are plunged into evil, and hemmed in by it; they think they have plunged themselves into it, and have surrounded themselves with it, through their own fault; they see themselves covered apparently with the most horrible sins; they imagine they have consented to these sins, when in reality they are farther from them than ever. Their Director, who knows so well what are their real dispositions, cannot succeed in reassuring them. God will keep them in this state until they have acquired a humility proportionate to the high degree of sanctity to which He intends to raise them. The lives of many of the greatest saints show us the truth of this, and mystical writers have given rules for the discernment of this state, and for the conduct of the favoured souls whom God causes to pass through this terrible trial. Saint Paul tells us of himself, that to hinder him from being filled with pride at the greatness of the revelations vouchsafed to him, God gave him a thorn in his flesh, and allowed the angel of Satan to buffet him. And he adds that when he asked and prayed God three times to deliver him from this trial, God answered him : My grace is sufficient for thee : for my strength is made perfect in weakness ; that is to say, that when we feel most deeply our own weakness, it is then that we experience the strength of the Divine grace, and it is then that our virtue is really purified.

XVIII.

ON THE THREE WORDS THAT WERE SAID TO SAINT ARSENIUS—FLY : KEEP SILENCE : REST.

THESE three words, which were spoken by a voice from heaven to Saint Arsenius, contain everything that it is necessary for us to do on our part to correspond with the designs of God for us. We must fly from all that could draw us away from God : we must keep ourselves in a silence both exterior and interior, that we may hear the voice of God : and we must calm all the agitations and anxieties of our mind and heart, that they may be fixed on God alone.

All souls whom God destines for the interior life are not called, as Saint Arsenius was, to fly from the world, and to retire into complete solitude : but all are called upon to use this world as though they used it not, to detach from it their mind and heart, and to have with it only those relations which are indispensable ; in short, in all their intercourse with the world, to avoid everything which could separate them from God.

Now this detachment goes much farther, and is much more difficult than appears at first sight. It is not sufficient to avoid everything which is actual sin, or which leads to actual sin ; we must also avoid all which pleases our senses, curiosity, esteem of ourselves, the desire of being praised, approved, thought much of; all which is capable of distracting us, of drawing our soul towards external things, and taking her out of herself, and of that peaceful centre where God deigns to dwell. We cannot be too careful in this matter, because our exterior relations with the world are one of the principal sources of our faults, and the most ordinary cause of our slight progress in the spiritual life.

That which makes the great difficulty of this perfect detachment is the powerful inclination in our soul to pour itself out upon created things, to allow them to lead it astray, to seek in them its repose, and to attribute to them a reality and a solidity which they have not. This is the sad effect of original sin, even in the most innocent souls ; much more in those who have had the misfortune to have actually offended God.

The next great difficulty comes from the love we
have for ourselves, and the desire we have to be
loved and esteemed by others.   If we wish people to
love us, we must love them, and love what they love.
If we wish to be esteemed by them, we must esteem
them ; we must think, we must speak, we must act
as they do.   This is a law which the world imposes
upon us, a law which self-love persuades us to be a
duty, and to which are sacrificed often the laws of
God, the maxims of the Gospel, and the light of
reason and conscience.

If we associate with the world otherwise than
through necessity and absolute charity, and even
then fortifying ourselves interiorly against its seductions, it is quite impossible for us not to end by conforming to its judgments and opinions, and to its
natural, human, and sensual ideas.   We do this either
to please others, or from human respect, or from
being carried away, almost without our consent ; it
is quite impossible for us not to end by approving or
at least excusing in others those things which God
expressly condemns, because we are afraid of making
ourselves ridiculous if we think differently from other
people, and if we dare to oppose the pure maxims of
the Gospel to the maxims received by the world.

What must we do then to practise this flight from
the world which is so necessary and so recommended
to us ?   We must look upon the world as the greatest
enemy to the Christian faith, and as the most dangerous deceiver, because it always agrees but too well
with the promptings of our own self-love.

We must retire from the world as much as possible;

we must break with all useless ties which have no
other object than amusement; we must speak but
little in company, and not always say what we wish
to say; but when we are obliged to speak, we must
do so plainly, and without human respect, remembering
those words of our Lord Jesus Christ: *"Whoever shall
be ashamed of Me before men, of him will I be ashamed
before my Father in heaven."*

We must *keep silence*, both exteriorly and interiorly.
It is a great mistake to imagine that the practice of
silence is only for those souls consecrated to God in
the life of the cloister: it is necessary for every one
who wishes to lead a really interior life; and it was
not for religious alone that Jesus Christ said that at
the day of judgment we must give an account of every
idle word.

Great freedom of speech is the sure mark of a frivolous and dissipated soul.   I defy any one to come away
from a useless conversation, and to return easily to
a state of recollection, or to pray or make a spiritual
reading, with the peace and calm that are necessary
for drawing any profit from such devout exercises.

But it is not enough to keep silence with others.
We must keep silence with ourselves, we must not
indulge our imagination, we must not be always thinking of what we have said or heard, we must not occupy
ourselves with useless thoughts and reflections upon
the past and the future.   How can God make His
voice heard by a soul so dissipated?   And if she
allows herself thus to roam over all sorts of objects,
how can she recollect herself for prayer?   It is not
a little thing to be able to master our imagination,

to control it, to fix it upon the present, upon what we are actually doing, and not to allow it to pause willingly before that crowd of thoughts which pass continually through our minds. I know that we cannot help having these kind of thoughts; but we can help letting our heart dwell on them, we can despise them, and take no notice of them. We can, when they come from some trouble, from some revolt of self-love, from some inordinate desire, make a sacrifice to God of that trouble, we can subdue that revolt, we can repress that desire. The exercise of interior mortification is an efficacious means, and more than that, it is the *only* means by which we can attain that perfect silence of the soul which disposes us for close communion with God.

Finally, we must fix in God the agitations and anxieties of our mind and heart. It is in vain that we seek for rest outside of God; we can only find it in God, and in God alone. It is not by agitating ourselves, by being very eager, and doing many external acts, that we succeed in resting in God; it is when we give up all agitation, all eagerness, all activity, and allow God to act upon us. God is always in activity, but always at rest. And the soul that is closely united to Him shares in His activity, and in His rest. That soul is always in action, even when she does not perceive it; but she acts always in the greatest peace. She does not fore-run the action of God, but she waits for Him to direct her; she moves under the Divine guidance, like the hand of a child who is learning to write moves under the guidance of his master's hand. If this child did not keep his hand supple and docile, if he wished to form the letters by himself, he would write badly. The child does undoubtedly act in writing, but his action is directed by the action of his master. The repose of the child does not consist in not moving his hand, but in not moving it of himself, and in simply following the guidance of the guiding hand.

So it is with the faithful soul under the immediate action of God : the soul is not idle for a single moment, as those imagine who have no idea whatever of what true rest in God means ; God guides the rudder of that soul, and leads it as He will. It is quite true that the action of God on the soul, as well as the action of the soul herself, is sometimes imperceptible, but it is none the less real : only then it is even more direct, more close, more spiritual. Even in a natural state, how many interior movements are there of which we take no note, and which are nevertheless the motive-principle of our exterior actions? I look, I speak, I walk, I turn away my eyes, I keep silence, I stop, just because I will to do so; and, in a general way, I pay no attention to this constant exercise of my will. It is just the same, and still more so, in the supernatural state. We pray without thinking that we are praying; our heart is united to God, and we are not conscious of this union. Therefore, it must not be said that those whom God raises to the prayer of quiet are doing nothing, and losing their time : they are in reality acting there in a manner which is very real, although very secret, and, besides that, in a manner in which self-love can find nothing

H

to nourish it, or to attract it, or to reassure it.   And
it is in this that the great advantage of this state of
prayer consists ; it is the very death and destruction
of self-love ; it is the soul losing itself entirely in God.
As long as the soul thinks itself conscious of its state,
as long as it knows where it is and how it stands it
is not lost ; it has still something to lean upon.   When
does the soul begin to be lost in God ?   It is when it
feels nothing any more, when it no longer sees anything in itself, when it has even ceased to look within,
or anywhere else, and when, ceasing to reason or reflect, it abandons itself entirely to the guidance of God.
God will lead that soul by degrees in this way of loss,
He will guide it by this prayer which has nothing sensible, until at last, finding no resource, either in itself
or in any man, its trust is established in God alone,
and, like Jesus Christ upon the cross, forsaken by all
men, and apparently by His Father also, that soul can
say, " ' *Father, into Thy hands I commend my spirit :* '
I give myself to Thee, to do as Thou wilt with me, in
time and in eternity."

It is to this great act of resignation, so glorious to
God and so useful to the soul, that the prayer of quiet
leads, when it is well understood and rightly practised.   Of ourselves we cannot enter upon this way
of prayer ; of ourselves we cannot advance in it ; but
when God has raised us to it we must have the
courage to follow it, and to persevere to the end.
This grace is given to very few souls ; and Saint
Teresa complains that so many give up the prayer
of quiet, and go no farther when their prayer ceases
to be sensible and perceptible ; that is to say, just

when it begins to be most profitable to the soul, through the mortification of self-love.

Let us not be of the number of those cowardly and interested souls who only seek themselves in the service of God; let us seek Him for Himself alone, and most surely we shall find Him, and in Him the source of all good.

XIX.

ON FAITHFULNESS IN LITTLE THINGS.

HOLY SCRIPTURE has said on this subject two things which may well convince us of its importance: " *He that despises small things,*" we are told, " *shall fall by little and little.*"

And our Lord Jesus Christ said, " *He that is faithful in that which is least, shall be faithful also in that which is greatest.*"

We see from the first passage that the neglect of little things exposes us infallibly to great falls; and from the second, that fidelity in little things ensures our fidelity in great things, and is consequently a necessary means of mortification. We only need to understand these two thoughts well to be inviolably faithful on the smallest occasion.

To develop this matter a little more, let us remark, in the first place, that, properly speaking, there is nothing either little or great with regard to the things of God. Everything that bears the impress of His Will is great, however small it may be in itself. Thus,

as soon as we are quite sure, by an interior voice, that
God desires some particular thing of us, the infinite
greatness of God does not allow us to regard as small
or indifferent that thing which is the object of His
desire.   On the contrary, however great in itself a
thing may be, were it even the conversion of the whole
world, if God does not require it from us, any idea of
the kind which we might form to ourselves would
have no value in His eyes, and might even displease
Him.   It is only the Will of God which gives any
value to things.

In the same way, with regard to our sanctification,
such and such a thing, which appears to us very
little in itself, may be of so great consequence, that
our perfection, and even our salvation, may depend
upon it.   God attaches His grace to what pleases
Him ; we cannot know of ourselves what may be the
good or evil consequences of any single action which
seems to us of little importance.   Of what grace may
I be deprived if I neglect it ?   What grace may come
to me if I perform it ?   This is just what I do not
know ; and in this uncertainty a constant and exact
fidelity to grace is the only course to pursue.

Now, great things and great occasions of heroic
virtue are rarely presented to us.   But little things
are offered to us every day.   And how shall we ever
prove our love to God if we wait for grand and
brilliant occasions ?   Perhaps one may never come
to us all our life long.   More than this, great things
require great courage.   How can we make sure of
our strength in heroic actions if we have made no
trial of it in small ones ; if we have not striven and

prepared ourselves by degrees for difficult things by the performance of those which are more easy?

Great things, also, cannot be accomplished without great graces on the part of God. But to merit and obtain these great and special graces we must have been faithful to the smaller graces. Humility wishes us to look upon great things as far above us, and that we should never of ourselves aspire to them; humility teaches us to attach ourselves to little things, as being more within our reach. Let us, then, perform our little and every-day actions with fidelity to our ordinary graces, and let us be quite sure that, when God requires greater things from us, He will certainly care to give us the necessary graces.

The desire of doing and suffering great things is very often, indeed almost always, an illusion of self-love and an effect of presumption. I should like to practise great austerities, like such and such a saint; I should like to bear great crosses : this is all pride, all vain-glory. The saints never formed such desires. Now, what happens to us when we do? We try of our own will to perform great austerities; then our fervour cools down, and we give them up; then some very ordinary crosses present themselves to us, and the soul, which thought it could bear such great things, finds it cannot bear the very smallest.

Let us desire nothing, let us choose nothing, let us take things just as God sends them to us, and just when He chooses to send them to us; let us think nothing of our own courage and strength, but believe ourselves inferior to the weakest; and let us be persuaded that if God did not take pity on our weakness, and did not sustain us by His strength, we could not advance a single step. And, as little things are constantly recurring, an exact fidelity to them requires more courage, more generosity, more constancy, than one would think for at first sight. To do it perfectly requires nothing less than consummate virtue; for, indeed, it is a question of dying to one's self at every moment, of following in all things the guidance of Divine grace, of never allowing one's self a thought, or desire, or word, or action which could give the least displeasure to God, and of doing everything, even to the simplest thing, with the perfection which He requires of us ; and all this without any relaxation, without ever granting anything to nature. In very truth, we must confess that in all sanctity there is nothing greater than this constant fidelity, nothing that needs a more sustained effort.

There is much danger of self-love being mixed up with the great things which we do or suffer for God ; there is much danger of our applauding our own courage, taking credit to ourselves for it, preferring ourselves to others. Little things do not expose us to the same danger ; it is easier in them to preserve humility ; in them there is nothing for self-love to fix upon as matter for glorification ; there is no need of comparing ourselves with others and preferring ourselves to them. Therefore, the faithful practice of little things is incomparably safer for us, and far more conducive to our perfection, which consists in dying entirely to ourselves. Little things destroy and consume by degrees our self-love, almost without its perceiving the blows directed against it. These blows are slight; but they are so frequent and so varied, that they have as much effect as the most violent blows.

And if the death of self-love is more gradual, it is none the less sure, for the constant practice of little things reduces it to such a state of weakness that at last it has no power of reviving : therefore, it is gene-rally in this way that God finishes our self-love. Sometimes, in the beginning, He may deal it great blows ; but it is by these quiet and scarcely percep-tible blows that He reduces it to the last extremity. The soul then no longer knows what to do ; God seems to take away everything from her, and to leave her naked and destitute ; she no longer takes pleasure in anything ; she seems scarcely to be doing anything ; she remains in a kind of annihilation, in which God acts so completely and solely in her, that she perceives neither the action of God nor her own.

If the love of God seems to shine with more gene-rosity in great sacrifices, it shows in little sacrifices, continually repeated, more attention and more delicacy. We do not love perfectly when we neglect small occasions of pleasing the one whom we love, and when we do not fear to wound him by trifles. The jealousy of God is infinite ; it extends to everything ; it embraces everything ; and if human love is so ex-acting, so all-absorbing, Divine love is infinitely more so. And every soul that truly loves will try never to give this Divine jealousy any cause of offence. To wound the tender and loving Heart of God in the least thing will be for that soul a crime which will inspire her with the greatest horror. And to refuse anything whatever to God, deliberately and intention-

ally, under the pretext that it is nothing, is to fail in
love in a most essential particular; it is to renounce
our familiarity with God, our close union with Him;
it is to deprive Him of His greatest glory; for it is
in this that He makes His glory to consist, viz., that
His creature shall never look upon anything as small
which can please or displease Him, and that His
creature shall always be disposed to sacrifice everything to His good pleasure. It is quite certain that
we do not begin to love God with a love that is
really worthy of Him until we have entered into
these dispositions.

I am not speaking here of our own interest. But
it is easy to see that a soul which is faithful to its
resolution of pleasing God in the smallest things
will most assuredly gain the Heart of God; that it
will draw to itself all His tenderness, all His favours,
all His graces; that by such a practice it will amass
every moment inconceivable treasures of merit; and
that, in the end, it will be capable of doing for God the
greatest things, if He should call it to perform them.

These are, it seems to me, quite sufficient motives
to make us take at once the great and heroic determination to neglect nothing in the service of God,
but to apply ourselves to please Him in everything,
without distinction of great or small. Let us, then,
make this determination once for all; and let us beg of
God that we may be faithful to it until our last breath.
Nevertheless, we must take care to carry our resolution into execution without too much care or anxiety.
Love wishes for a holy liberty; everything consists
in never losing sight of God, and in doing from one

moment to another just what His grace inspires us to do, and in turning away at once from anything which we know would displease Him.   He will never fail to give us warnings in the interior of our souls whenever we need them.   And when He does not give us such warnings, we may rest assured that there is nothing in what we have said or done that was contrary to His good pleasure.   And if we do not allow anything to draw us from our recollection in Him, we cannot fail to know whether we have received any interior warning or not, and whether we have followed it.   Thus there is never the least occasion for us to torment ourselves unnecessarily.

XX.

ON THE PROFIT WE OUGHT TO DERIVE FROM OUR FAULTS.

THE subject I am now going to treat of is one of the most important in the spiritual life.   It is quite certain that, in the designs of God, the faults into which He permits us to fall ought to serve for our sanctification, and that it only depends upon us to draw this advantage from them.   Nevertheless, it happens, on the contrary, that our faults themselves do us less harm than the bad use we make of them.

What I have to say on this subject has nothing to do with those cowardly and interested souls who use reserve with God, and who only wish to belong

to Him up to a certain point.   They commit deliberately and knowingly a thousand faults, from which it
is impossible they can draw any profit, on account of
the bad dispositions in which they are.   The persons
for whom I write are only those who have made up
their minds never deliberately and with intention to
commit a single fault, and who nevertheless do fall into
many faults, in spite of their good resolutions, through
inadvertence, or on the impulse of the moment, or
through weakness.   To these persons it generally
happens that they are astonished at their faults, that
they are troubled by them, that they are ashamed of
them, and so are angry with themselves and fall into
discouragement.   These are just so many effects of
self-love, effects far more pernicious than the faults
themselves.   We are astonished that we should be
troubled with these constant falls; but we are quite
wrong, and it is a sign that we know nothing whatever about ourselves.   We ought, on the contrary, to
be surprised that we do not fall much oftener, and
into much more grievous faults, and we ought to give
thanks to God for all the falls from which He preserves us.   We are troubled every time we discover
some fault in ourselves; we lose our interior peace;
we are quite agitated, and we occupy ourselves about
this fault for hours, or even for whole days.   Now,
we ought never to be troubled; but when we see
ourselves on the ground, we must raise ourselves up
again quietly; at once we must turn to God with
love and humility and ask His pardon; and then we
must never think about the fault again, until the
time comes to accuse ourselves of it in confession.

And even if in our confession we forget it, there is no occasion to be uneasy on that account.

Or again, we are so ashamed of our faults: we hardly dare to tell them to our confessor. "What will he think of me, after so many promises, after so many good resolutions I have made in his presence?" If you declare your faults to him simply and humbly, he will only think the better of you; if you tell them to him with difficulty and reserve he cannot help taxing you with pride in his own mind. His confidence in you will diminish as he sees that you are not sufficiently open with him.

But the worst of all is this: we are vexed with ourselves; we are angry, as Saint Francis de Sales says, at having been angry; we are impatient at having been impatient. What misery! Ought we not to see that this is pride pure and simple; that we are humiliated at finding ourselves, when put to the proof, less strong and less holy than we thought we were; and that we only aspire to be exempt from faults and imperfections that we may take credit to ourselves for it, and that we may be able to congratulate ourselves on having passed a day or a week without having anything to reproach ourselves with?

Finally, we grow discouraged; we give up, one after the other, all our practices of piety: we give up prayer, we regard perfection as impossible, and we despair of ever attaining it. What is the use, we say, of restraining ourselves, of watching continually over ourselves, of giving ourselves up to recollection and mortification, when we grow no better, when we correct nothing, and are always falling afresh?

Now, this is one of the most subtle snares of the devil. And do you wish to be preserved from it? Then you must never be discouraged, no matter into how many faults you fall; but you must say to yourself, "If I should fall twenty times, a hundred times a day, I will get up again every time, and I will go on my way." What will it matter, after all, how many times you have fallen on the way if you reach your journey's end safely at last? God will not reproach you. Often our very falls come from the rapidity of our course, and because the ardour which impels us scarcely gives us time to take certain precautions. Those timid and over-cautious souls who always wish to see where they are putting their feet, who are always turning out of the way to avoid making a false step, and who are so dreadfully afraid of contracting the least stain will not advance half so fast as the other more generous souls, and death often overtakes them before their course is run. It is not those who commit the fewest faults who are the most holy, but those who have the most courage, the most generosity, the most love, who make the greatest efforts, and who are not afraid of stumbling a little, or even of falling and staining themselves a little, provided they can always advance.

Saint Paul says that "*all things work together for good to them that love God.*" Yes, everything is for their good, even their faults, and sometimes even very grave faults. God permits those very faults, to cure us of vain presumption, to teach us what we really are, and of what we are really capable. David confessed that the adultery and murder of which he was guilty had served to keep him in a continual distrust of himself. "*It is good for me,*" he said to God, "*that You have humbled me; I have been more faithful in keeping Your commandments.*"

The fall of Saint Peter was for him the most useful of lessons, and the humility with which it inspired him disposed him to receive the gifts of the Holy Spirit, to become the Head of the Church, and preserved him from the dangers of so eminent a position. Saint Paul, in the great success of his apostolate, preserved himself from pride and vain-glory by remembering how he had once been a blasphemer and a persecutor of the Church of God. And more than this, a humiliating temptation, from which God would not deliver him, served as a balance to the sublimity of the revelations granted to him.

If God was able to draw such an advantage from even the greatest sins, who can doubt that He will make our daily faults serve for our sanctification? It is a remark which has been made by many masters of the spiritual life, that God often leaves in the most holy souls certain defects, from which, notwithstanding all their efforts, they cannot free themselves entirely, to make them feel their own weakness, and what they would be without His grace; to hinder them from being proud of the favours He grants them, and to dispose them to receive these favours with more humility; in short, to nourish in them a certain disgust with themselves, and so to protect them against all the snares of self-love; to animate their fervour and keep them in a constant state of watchfulness, of trust in God and preserverance in prayer. The child who falls when he has gone a little way from his mother, and wishes to walk alone, returns to her with more affection, to be cured of the hurt he has given himself, and he learns by that fall to leave her no more. The experience of his own weakness, and of the tenderness with which his mother received him, makes him love her more than ever. '

The faults which happen to us often give us occasion for great acts of virtue, which we certainly should not have had the opportunity of practising without them; and God allows these faults with that intention. For instance, He permits a flash of ill-natured sarcasm, an act of rudeness, a lively impatience, that we may at once make an act of humility which abundantly satisfies for our fault and the scandal it may have given.

The fault was committed on the impulse of the moment, but the act of reparation is made with reflection, with an effort over ourselves, with a full and deliberate will. This is an act which pleases God much more than the fault displeased Him.

God also makes use of our faults and apparent imperfections to conceal our sanctity from the eyes of others, and to procure for us humiliations from them.

God is a great and wise Master: let Him do as He likes; He will not fail in His work. Let us make up our minds carefully to avoid everything that can displease Him the least in the world; but if we should fall into any fault, let us be sorry on His account and not on our own; let us love the humiliation into which this fault throws us; let us beg of God to draw from our humiliation His glory: He will do this, and by this means will advance us far more than by a life apparently more regular and holy, but which would destroy our self-love less efficaciously.

When God asks of us to do certain things, let us never draw back on the pretence of fearing the faults we may commit in executing His wishes. It is better to do good, even with imperfection, than to omit it. Sometimes we do not administer a necessary correction because we are afraid of doing it with too much severity; or we avoid associating with certain persons because their faults try us so much, and make us feel so impatient and irritable. But how shall we acquire virtue if we fly from the occasions of practising it? Is not such a flight a greater fault than the faults we fear to fall into?

Let us only take care to have a good intention; then let us go wherever duty calls us, and let us be sure that God is kind enough and indulgent enough to pardon us all the faults to which His faithful service and the desire of pleasing Him may expose us.

XXI.

ON THE DIRECTOR.

WE ought not to draw a distinction between the director and the confessor, any more than we draw a distinction between the physician who cures an illness and him who prescribes a rule for preserving health. The confessor hears the acknowledgment of our sins, and absolves us from the guilt of them ; he tells us what we are to do, that we may avoid sin for the future, and he gives us wholesome advice, that we may advance in virtue. The tribunal of penance, then, includes confession and direction, and it is as essential for it to preserve us from faults as to absolve us for them. Nevertheless, quite as much by the fault of the penitents as of the confessors, there have always been very few confessors who are directors at the same time.

To direct a soul is to lead it in the ways of God, it is to teach the soul to listen for the Divine inspiration, and to respond to it ; it is to suggest to the soul the practice of all the virtues proper for its particular state ; it is not only to preserve that soul in purity and innocence, but to make it advance in perfection : in a word, it is to contribute as much as possibly may be in raising that soul to the degree of sanctity which God has destined for it. It is thus that Pope Saint Gregory thought of direction when he said that the guidance of souls is, of all arts, the most excellent.

In order that direction may be successful, it is clear that certain dispositions are necessary on the part of the confessor, and of the person whom he directs. It is necessary that the confessor should be, as it were, the voice of God, the instrument of Divine grace, the co-operator with the work of the Holy Spirit, and, consequently, that he should be an interior man, a man of prayer, a man well versed in spiritual things, as much by his own experience as by study and reading ; that he should have no purely natural designs, either of vanity or self-interest, but that he should only consider the glory of God and the good of souls; that he should never act according to the leadings of his own spirit, but that he should judge of the things of God by the spirit of God. From all this it is easy to conclude that true directors are very rare.

As to the persons who desire to receive direction, it is evident that they are only fit for it in the same measure as they are docile, obedient, simple, straightforward, upright; resolved not only to avoid sin, but to practise all the good which God requires of them, to correspond faithfully to grace, and to refuse nothing to God, whatever may be the cost to human nature; finally, to die to themselves, that they may live entirely to God: and this can only be attained by the spirit of prayer and interior mortification.

We can judge from this, that if true directors are rare, true spiritual children are none the less so, because there are very few persons who aspire to sanctity through the way of the cross and continually dying to themselves. There are many devout persons, but devout in their own way, guiding themselves according to their own ideas, following a certain routine of exterior practices, but suiting their devotion to their self-love, and not having the least idea of real prayer, of the real mortification of the heart. However this may be, nothing is more important for souls who sincerely wish to give themselves entirely to God, than, 1st, to be thoroughly convinced of the necessity of a director; 2nd, to make a good choice of one; and, 3rd, to make use of him according to the · designs of God, when they have once chosen him.

I

It is necessary to have a director, because the greatest mistake of all is to wish to guide ourselves, and the greatest delusion we can fall into is to think we are in a fit state to guide ourselves. Even the most clever man, and he who is in the best dispositions, is blind as to his interior conduct; and even if he were a saint, and capable of directing others, he is not capable of directing himself; and if he thinks he can, it is through presumption. The first thing God requires of any one who aspires to sanctity is that he should renounce his own spirit, that he should humble himself, and submit to the guidance of those to whom God has intrusted the care of souls. As there are very special graces attached to this spirit of submission and obedience, so there are many manifest dangers to be incurred when we have the pride to think we can judge and govern ourselves. The way of perfection is full of darkness and obscurities, of temptations and precipices; and to wish to walk alone in it is to expose ourselves to our own ruin. Thus there is no medium course: either we must absolutely give up the idea of entering upon the way of perfection, or, if God has called us to it, we must take a director, that is, a guide, to whom we can open our souls entirely, to whom we can give an account of everything, and whom we can obey as if he were God Himself. The important point is to make a good choice of such a guide. And in a choice of such importance, it is God above all Whom we must consult: it is to Him we must pray that we may choose aright. His good providence is engaged to furnish us with all the necessary means for our salvation and sancti-

fication; and as this is one of the most necessary
means, we must believe that He will grant it to us,
if we ask it of Him with simplicity and confidence.
If we are guided by merely human motives in the choice
of a director, if we lean only on our own judgment,
and think we are capable of making such a choice of
ourselves, we expose ourselves to the danger of being
deceived, and we deserve to be deceived. But if we
leave the matter entirely in God's hands, He will
guide us to the director He wishes us to have, either
by a secret instinct, or by the advice of pious persons
whom we can trust. Did He not send Saint Francis
de Sales to Dijon on purpose for Madame de Chantal?
and did she not recognise at once, by certain signs,
that he was the director whom God had destined
for her?

These signs are an inexpressible attraction, which
leads us to give all our confidence to such and such
a priest of God, and which forms a union of grace
between him and us; a peace which takes possession
of our souls when he speaks to us, which reassures
our doubts, dissipates our scruples, and gives us the
calm and joy of the Holy Ghost; a certain ardour,
a strong desire of belonging entirely to God, with
which his words inspire us; in fact, an impression
of respect, of love, of docility and of obedience, which
makes us, as it were, see God in him. These signs
can never deceive upright and pure souls, who seek
only their own spiritual advancement. And I am
quite certain that all those who are deceived when
they seek direction have brought it upon themselves,
through having been influenced by their imagination,

or their self-love, or some other human motives, whatever they may be.

The certainty which God gives us at first of having made a good choice increases from day to day, and we soon have undoubted proofs of this. Nevertheless, if it should happen that we have been deceived, God will never permit a soul that is upright and pure to be long in error: she will soon discover, by one thing or another, that she has made a mistake, and God will guide her elsewhere.

As to the use we are to make of our director, there are many precautions to take and faults to avoid; but we may say, in a general way, that when the director and the person directed are both interior souls, it is very rare that any great imperfections can intrude upon the direction, because both are on their guard that no abuse may spoil such a holy communion of souls.

The first rule is for them not to meet except from necessity, and then to speak only of the things of God.

The second rule is to have a great mutual respect for each other, and always to preserve a certain courtesy and gravity, remembering always that their meetings are in God's interest, and that He is always a third in these kind of conversations.

The third rule is never to conceal anything from the director, under any pretext whatsoever, even if it should be thoughts and suspicions we have had against him. The more the director is forwarding the work of God, the more the soul is tempted with regard to him, through the instigation of the devil,

who will try in every way to withdraw the confidence
of the soul in the director. But we must resist his
suggestions, and make a rule for ourselves to tell
everything, and always to begin with that upon which
we would rather be silent.

The fourth rule is a measureless obedience in all
those things which cost us the most, which are most
repugnant to our own inclinations and ideas, and
never to allow ourselves any formal resistance of the
will, nor even any interior judgment, which is contrary
to the judgment of our director. I have spoken elsewhere of obedience ; so I will only say here that it
cannot be carried too far ; neither can entire trust
and perfect openness.

The fifth rule is in the use of our director, to look
beyond the man, and only to see God in him ; only
to be attached to him for God's sake, and to be
always ready even to give him up if God required it,
and to say with holy Job : "*The Lord gave, and the
Lord hath taken away; blessed be the Name of the Lord.*"
We may be quite sure that, as God gave him to us
for our good, He has taken him away for our greater
good ; and even if He should withdraw from us all
human aid, His goodness alone is able to supply us
abundantly.

"*The just shall live by faith,*" St. Paul says, following
the teaching of the prophet Habacuc. This faith,
which is the very life of the just, is not the faith
that is common to all Christians, by which they
believe the doctrines which God has revealed to His
Church ; but it is an especial and personal faith,
which has for its object the supernatural providence

of God for those souls who have abandoned themselves to Him without reserve, and whom He Himself
will guide.

XXII.

ON THE SPIRIT OF FAITH.

To understand what the spirit of faith really is, we,
must know that when a soul has given itself entirely
to God, God first of all inspires that soul with the
greatest confidence in Him, the greatest faith in His
words and promises, and the most utter resignation
to His guidance; but afterwards God may please to
try this confidence in every sort of way, by acting in a manner apparently contrary to all He has
said and promised, and by seeming to forsake those
who have forsaken all for His sake; by throwing
them into a state of such obscurity, of such desolation, of such a strange upheaval of all things, that
they no longer know how they stand, and are almost
inclined to believe that God intends their ruin.   In
spite of all this, these souls persevere in the service
of God: they relax nothing; they sacrifice one after
the other their dearest interests; they hope against
hope in the depths of their hearts, as Saint Paul says,
that is to say, they hope against all natural reasons
for hoping; and by acting in this manner they glorify
God exceedingly and amass an inestimable treasure
of merit.

All sacred history, of the Old as well as of the
New Testament, is full of examples of this conduct
of God; with this difference, that in the old law the

object of the Divine promises was temporal and figu-
rative, whereas in the new law the Divine promises
have a spiritual object, and are all directed towards
the salvation and perfection of souls. I will only
quote one instance, and it shall be that of the patri-
arch Joseph. God showed him in a dream, when he
was quite young, all his future greatness, and the
homage which his father and brothers would render
to him. But in what way did he attain to this greatness? In a way the very opposite apparently; in
a way which seemed only designed to compass his
ruin. His brothers, who were envious of him, made
up their minds to kill him; they threw him into a
dry cistern, intending to leave him there, to perish
with hunger; then they took him out from there, and
sold him to the Ishmaelites. Being sold as a slave
in Egypt, he was first thought well of and trusted by
his master; then calumniated by his wicked mistress
and cast into prison. There he was forgotten and
neglected by the man whose deliverance he had pre-
dicted. At last God sent to Pharaoh two dreams,
ot which Joseph gave the explanation, and all at once
he was promoted to the first dignity in Egypt. His
brothers trembled before him, and fell down before
him without recognising him; he provided food for
them and for his father; he became their saviour, and
gave them protection and a home in Egypt. See
by what a series of misfortunes Joseph attained the
summit of honour: for long years he only escaped
from one danger to fall into a still greater one; and
when he believed himself to be hopelessly forgotten
in the depths of a dungeon, God drew him from thence

and raised him to a position of the highest dignity. What was it that supported Joseph during this chain of adversities ? It was the spirit of faith : he never lost his confidence in God ; he always believed that God would accomplish what He had promised.

So it is in the law of grace with those souls whom God calls to a high state of perfection. He generally begins by unveiling His designs for them; He loads them at first with gifts and favours ; and when they think that they are far advanced in His good graces, little by little He withdraws from them : He takes away His gifts ; He casts them from one abyss into another ; and when He has brought them to a state apparently of utter loss, to an absolute sacrifice of themselves, He raises them up again, and, with the new life which He communicates to them, He gives them an assurance and a foretaste of eternal beatitude. This state of probation, which is a series of crosses, of bodily sufferings, of mental agonies, of desolations, humiliations, calumnies, and persecutions, lasts sometimes for fifteen or twenty years, sometimes longer, according to the designs of God, and the greater or less generosity and faithfulness of the soul.

Now what is it that supports these souls in a state so wearisome and so painful ? It is the spirit of faith ; it is their confidence in God : they have resigned themselves to Him ; they will never take themselves away again ; they will not withdraw from His guidance, whatever it may cost them. Even if they are to be lost, they will be lost rather than fail the least in the world in what they owe to God. They see nothing, they feel nothing, they take pleasure in nothing. If they pray, it seems to them that their prayers are rejected ; if they communicate, they fancy they are committing a sacrilege ; they no longer feel any confidence in their director ; they think he is leading them astray ; and notwithstanding all this, they continue to pray, to receive Holy Communion, and to obey. They have no comfort from within, no clear testimony of their conscience to reassure them ; they fancy themselves covered with sins ; it is as if the sword of Divine justice were suspended over their heads ; and it seems to them as if every moment it must fall upon them, and precipitate them into hell. From without, they have no consolation, no support from any man ; on the contrary, they are censured, they are condemned, they are loaded with calumnies and persecutions. And, in the midst of all this, strengthened by the spirit of faith, they remain firm and cannot be shaken ; they live, but with a life the principle of which is unknown to them ; they preserve an unchanging peace, but they are scarcely conscious of it, except sometimes for a short interval, and they do not reflect upon it, because God does not allow them to seek any consolation or pay any attention to what is passing within them. They live thus, suspended, as it were, between heaven and earth, having nothing upon earth which attracts them, and receiving no consolation from heaven. But, perfectly resigned to the good pleasure of God, they wait in peace until it is His will to decide on their fate.

What a miracle of faith, of confidence, and of resignation ! It is unknown, except by you, O my God ! For the soul in which this faith dwells, and which lives by this faith, knows nothing of it; and it is essential that she should be ignorant of it, otherwise her resignation would not be perfect. This is a state which, without doubt, gives more glory to God than any other; so that a soul of this kind glorifies Him infinitely more than all other souls who are holy with an ordinary holiness. Therefore, the devil, who is the great enemy of God's glory, has omitted nothing to cry down this state; he is its most fierce and terrible persecutor. He excites against it men who are either ignorant, or in bad faith, or of a proud spirit, and puffed up with their false knowledge: these men represent this state in the most frightful colours; they confound it with quietism, and they give it the odious names of hypocrisy, criminal indifference with regard to salvation, refined licentiousness, and so on; or they treat it as madness and the extravagance of a disordered brain. This is the way they describe it to good and pious souls, to draw them away from it, and to draw them away also from prayer, which is the gate of it; they try to inspire them with horror and aversion for persons who are in this state, for spiritual books which treat of it, and for directors who could guide them in it. God even permits sometimes that those who are in authority in His Church should be mistaken and misled in this matter, and that upon false reports, and without sufficient examination, they should condemn, unknowingly, the very holiest persons and the most marvellous works of God. God permits this, to put His favourites to the last trial of all, to confound the vain efforts of His enemies, and to draw from it His greater glory.

After what happened to our Lord Jesus Christ on the part of the high priests of the synagogue, there is nothing of this kind which ought to surprise us ; and after what happened to the synagogue for having condemned Jesus Christ, there is nothing too terrible for those to expect who wilfully condemn Him afresh in the person of His most faithful servants.

Therefore, in the midst of all the tempests which the devil may stir up against us, let us hold fast to the spirit of faith, and let us increase in it through the very means which are used to destroy it. He whom we serve is the All-Powerful, the Only True, the Ever-Faithful. Heaven and earth may pass away before He will suffer those to run any risk who have abandoned themselves to Him. He will try our love, for that is just : what is a love worth that has not been tried ? And He will carry these trials to an extreme extent, because He is God, and there is no love too great for Him.

A thousand times happy is the soul whom God tries thus, and to whom He gives the opportunity of showing Him the greatest love which He can expect from a creature. Is it not just that there should be a kind of love for God which will go farther in suffering for Him even than the excesses of the most violent human passion ? And the greatest favour He can grant to a soul here below is to inspire her with the efficacious desire of loving Him in this way. This love, stronger than death, more powerful than hell, is itself its own motive and its own recompense ; it is fed with its own flame. God kindled it ; God keeps it alive ; God will crown it after the victim of it is consumed.

XXIII.

ON THE LOVE OF OUR NEIGHBOUR.

"*A NEW commandment I give unto you, that you love one another, as I have loved you,*" said our Lord and Saviour Jesus Christ.

The precept of love for our neighbour belonging to the natural law, and being as old as the world itself, in what sense does Jesus Christ call it a *new* commandment?

He means that He Himself has made it new in a most decided manner, because, not content with ordering us to love our neighbour as ourselves, He wishes that we should love our neighbour as He has loved us; because by His death on the cross He gave us the greatest example of love for our neighbour which it was possible even for a God-man to give; and because He wishes that by this sign His true disciples shall be recognised.

In taking upon Himself our human nature, Jesus Christ became our Brother and the Head of the whole human race; He has raised us all, through Him, to the dignity of the Divine adoption, in such a manner that, in a supernatural sense, all Christians compose only one family, of which God is the Father and Jesus Christ the First-born Son. We share His rights to the heavenly inheritance; we all participate in the same graces, in the same sacraments; we are fed at the same table; we live by the same Bread; we are all, in fact, united to each other in Jesus Christ and in His Church in a most special manner. Thus, besides the relationship which we have with all mankind, there is between all the children of the Church a particular bond of union, founded upon their union with Jesus Christ, and cemented by His blood. Therefore it was with good reason that He called the commandment *new* which He gave to His disciples to love each other as He had loved them.

Now, how did Jesus Christ love us? To such a degree as to make Himself the Victim of the Divine justice for our sins; to give His life and His soul to purchase back for us eternal life; and this even when we were His enemies by original sin, and although He foresaw that we should almost all abuse His graces, grievously offend Him, and even take advantage of His goodness and long-suffering to sin against Him with more audacity. The conscience of every one of us must reproach us with these kind of things, more or less; and, in spite of all, Jesus Christ loved us, He loves us still, and to our last breath He will continue to love us, and will always be ready to apply to us the merits of His Precious Blood, and to reconcile us to His Father through His mediation.

Now, can we understand a little what is the extent of those words: *"Love one another, as I have loved you"*?

Have we a just idea of our obligations in this respect? I ought to love my brothers, as Jesus Christ has loved me; I ought to share with them, not only my temporal goods, but also all my spiritual gifts; I ought to pray for them as I pray for myself;

I ought to have the same zeal for their salvation as
I have for my own, and I ought to labour for it with
all my strength, by my prayers and good works, by
my words and by my example. I ought to be ready
to sacrifice everything, even myself, for the salvation of a soul. I ought to pardon everything, forget
everything, suffer everything, from my brothers, just
as Jesus Christ has suffered so much from me, and
has pardoned me everything. In short, I ought to
love them with the same love as Jesus Christ has
shown to me.

"Oh, my God! What charity would reign among
Christians if this precept was observed! and, as a
necessary consequence, what sanctity! For it would
not be possible for Christians to love one another
in this manner without all of them tending, each in
his own state, to the highest perfection; without their
all trying to induce one another to the practice of
perfection, and without their giving one another the
example of it.

All disorders, all scandals, all enmities—in fact,
all sins, would be banished from Christianity. This
beautiful spirit of charity did reign formerly amongst
the first believers; and even the heathen, when they
saw it, could not refrain from admiration. "*See*,"
they said, "*how these Christians love one another!*"

But alas! in these days, far from aspiring to this
beautiful charity, the greater part of Christians have
not even for their neighbour that natural love which
every man ought to have for another man; and the
great precepts of the natural law of love are violated
more frequently perhaps amongst us, and in a more

atrocious manner, than amongst savages and idolaters. Now, what is the cause of this? It is because we have ceased to be Christians, except in name; because we have given up the exterior profession and the essential duties of Christianity, and because, at heart, we are even more wicked than the pagans. This is not an exaggeration, and it stands to reason that it must be so. For a bad Christian must carry his corruption and malice further than a pagan, because he sins against light, he acts against supernatural graces, and he is far more guilty in thus abusing the light of reason and religion.

Let us mourn over these frightful disorders, we, whom God has specially called to the love of Himself, and of our neighbour for His sake. Let us recognise that self-love, which is the source of all sin, is the enemy of this love of God and our neighbour; that, as long as there remains in us any vestige of self-love, we can never love our brothers, as Jesus Christ has commanded us to love them. Self-love concentrates us on ourselves, and makes us exclusive; it makes us look upon our neighbour as a stranger, not only with regard to temporal things, but with regard to spiritual things also, in such a manner that the spirit of appropriation, of personal interest, of jealousy and envy, insinuates itself even into our devotion, and we end by thinking that the spiritual good of our neighbour may diminish our own. More than this, this same self-love is the cause of a thousand sins against charity. It makes us touchy, ready to take offence, ill-tempered, suspicious, severe, exacting as to what we think are our rights, easily offended: it keeps alive in our hearts a certain malignity, a secret joy at the little mortifications which happen to our neighbour, through our coldness, our distant behaviour, our indifference, and the injustice of our judgments; it nourishes our readiness to criticise, the unjust partiality of our words and actions, our dislike to certain persons, our ill-feelings, our bitterness against them, and a thousand other imperfections most prejudicial to charity.

I hold it as an impossible thing that any one who is not interior can attain to the perfect accomplishment of this precept of love for our neighbour, because, to do it perfectly, we must die in such a manner to our own spirit and our own will, that we may be guided entirely by the spirit of Jesus Christ and be animated by His charity. Otherwise, the occasions of wounding this charity, at all events slightly, present themselves incessantly; self-love, however little may remain of it, still has power to influence the heart; it still leads away and corrupts our judgment, rules over our affections, and does all this perhaps in a manner that is imperceptible to us. Now, in those persons who are not really interior, although they are supposed to be pious and holy, there is always a depth of self-love, which they know nothing about, which makes them blind and unjust with regard to their neighbour. And I must even add, that in many cases the duties of charity are so delicate and refined, that without a supernatural light it is impossible to distinguish them clearly or appreciate them justly; that these duties are so difficult to fulfil, that we have need, to do so properly, of a virtue

far above the common; and finally, that they sometimes require sacrifices, which can only be made by
those who are accustomed to die entirely to themselves.

Yes, the love of our neighbour, in a true sense,
is much more painful to nature than the love of God,
although it is also true that these two loves cannot be
separated. Thus our neighbour is the cause of almost
all the faults with which devout people have to reproach
themselves, and how many of these kind of faults do
they commit without perceiving them, without having
any idea of having done so, and which they would
have a difficulty in acknowledging.

Happy then are those souls who have embraced
the interior life, and who have given themselves
entirely to God, to accomplish perfectly, under the
guidance of His grace, these two precepts of love to
God and to our neighbour! They are not exposed
to be deceived, as so many are, in this matter of
charity, where self-love can so easily delude us, and
where the most skilful have often a difficulty in deciding as to what is right. They have nothing to
do but to listen for the voice of God, speaking in the
depths of their hearts, and in purity of intention and
uprightness of soul to beg of Him to guide them in
all their ways. God will never fail them if they are
resolved once for all to sacrifice their dearest interests
to the interests of charity : He will teach them how
far they ought to go, and where they ought to stop.
He will unveil for them the secret recesses of their
hearts, and will show them whatever therein that can
wound even the faintest shadow of charity. He will

never allow them, without instantly reproving them for it, to speak or act, or even to give way to a gesture or a smile, that is of deliberate ill-nature and unkindness ; He will put a stop to all their interior judgments of others, all their suspicions, all their imaginations ; He will kill all their natural inclinations and aversions, all their fancies, wounded feelings, and sensitiveness ; He will stifle all their resentment, and bitterness, and malicious joy.

And at the same time that He is destroying all their defects that are contrary to charity, He will establish in their hearts those great principles of love for their neighbour which Jesus Christ taught, and of which He gave the example. The God-Man will reveal Himself to them, and will animate them with His own feelings, with His generosity, His zeal for souls, His sweetness, His gentleness, His tenderness, and His mercy. He Himself will love their neighbours, through them, because being the absolute Master of their hearts, He will regulate and produce the very movements and affections of those hearts.

But to attain to this it is clearly to be seen that we must continually renounce ourselves, and keep ourselves always in a state of dependence upon God, always united to Him by prayer, always attentive and faithful to His inspirations. The exact observance of the two great precepts of the law of the Gospel is undoubtedly worth all the trouble we may have to take in subjecting ourselves for that end to those teachings of the interior life which may be hard and painful to human nature.

XXIV.

ON THE WORLD.

WHAT is the world ?   And what ought the world to be to a Christian ?   These are two most interesting questions for any one who wishes to belong entirely to God, and to assure his own salvation.

What is the world ?   It is the enemy of Jesus Christ, and it is the enemy of His Gospel.   It consists of that immense number of people who are attached to sensible objects, and who place in them their sole happiness ; who have a horror of poverty, suffering, and humiliation, and who look upon such things as real evils from which they must flee, and against which they must protect themselves at any cost ; who, on the contrary, have the greatest regard for riches, pleasures, and honours ; who consider these things as real and solid good ; who desire them and pursue them with extreme eagerness, without caring what means they use to obtain them ; who fight with one another over the goods of this life ; who envy one another, and try to take from each other what they have not themselves ; who only value another person, or despise him, in proportion as he possesses or does not possess these perishable goods ; in one word, who found upon the acquisition and enjoyment of temporal things all their principles, all their code of morality, and the entire plan of their conduct.

The spirit of the world is then evidently opposed to the spirit of Jesus Christ, and of His Gospel. Jesus Christ and the world condemn one another, and reprove one another. Jesus Christ, in His prayer for His elect, declares positively that He does not pray for the world; He announces to His Apostles, and through them to all Christians, that the world will hate and persecute them, as it hated and persecuted Him. And He commands them to wage a continual war against the world.

In the first ages of the Church, when nearly all Christians were saints, and the rest of men were plunged in idolatry, it was easy to distinguish the world, and to know with whom to associate, and whom to avoid. The world, openly in arms then against Jesus Christ, was distinguished by marks which could not be mistaken. But since whole nations have embraced the Gospel of Christ, and since discipline has been relaxed, there has gradually been formed in the very midst of Christians a world in which reign all the vices of idolatry—a world which is eager for honours, for pleasures, and for riches—a world whose maxims are in direct opposition to the maxims of Jesus Christ.

Now as this *world* still makes an exterior profession of Christianity, it becomes much more difficult to distinguish; and to associate with it has become much more dangerous, because it disguises its evil teaching with more cleverness, because it spreads it with more carefulness, and makes use of all its craftiness to reconcile its own evil maxims with the doctrines of Christianity. And with this end in view it weakens and softens as much as possible the holy severity of the Gospel ; and on the other hand conceals as carefully as possible the venom of its own false morality. From this comes a danger of seduction, all the greater that it is not easily perceived, and so we are not sufficiently on our guard against it ; from this comes also a certain spirit of accommodation and acquiescence, by which we try to reconcile the real Christian severity with the maxims of the world upon such matters as the desire of riches or the inordinate enjoyment of pleasures—a reconciliation which is impossible, a state of things which can only end in flattering human nature, in spoiling Christian sanctity, and in forming false consciences. It is almost incredible to what an extent this disorder can go, even in the case of persons who pride themselves upon their piety and devotion ; and it is a disorder which is in one sense more difficult to correct than that which results from conduct openly worldly and criminal, because such persons never will acknowledge themselves in the wrong, and succeed in deceiving themselves in these matters.

If we desire to live here below without sharing in the corruption of the world, there is only one thing to do, and that is to break with the world absolutely and entirely in our own hearts, and to enter into the feeling of Saint Paul when he said, " *The world is crucified to me, and I to the world.*"

Oh, what wonderful words ! And how deep is the meaning they contain ! Formerly the cross was the most infamous of all punishments—it was the punishment of slaves. When then the apostle says that the world is crucified to him, it is as if he said, I have for the world the same contempt, the same aversion, the same horror as I should have for a vile slave crucified for his crimes. I cannot bear the sight of it : it is for me an object of malediction, with which I can have no connection, no association, no relationship.

And there is nothing extreme, nothing but what is perfectly just and 'right, in this expression of Saint Paul, which ought to be that of all Christians; and the reason of this is evident. The world crucified Jesus Christ, after having calumniated Him, insulted Him, outraged Him ; and the world is crucifying Him now every day. Is it not just then that the world in its turn should be crucified to the disciple of Christ ? Is it not just that the disciple should have a horror of the chief enemy of his Master, his Saviour, and his God ? Therefore the renunciation of the world is one of the most solemn promises of the sacrament of baptism, and an essential condition, without which the Church would not admit us amongst her children. Do we ever think of this promise ? Do we ever think of the obligations it imposes upon us ? Do we ever examine ourselves as to how far this renunciation extends ?

The Christian's renunciation of the world ought to go as far as the worldly renunciation of Jesus Christ ! This rule is clear, and we cannot be deceived in it. There is nothing more to do but to make the application of it, and to do so to its fullest extent. The world has its own gospel. We have only to take that in one hand, and the Gospel of Jesus Christ in the other ; we have only to compare their teaching and their example with regard to the same things; we have only to oppose Jesus Christ on the cross, in suffering, in opprobrium and nakedness, to the world, surrounded and intoxicated with honours, riches, and pleasures, and say to ourselves, To which do I belong? To which do I wish to belong? Here are two irreconcilable enemies who will make war against each other for ever : on which side will I fight? It is impossible for me to remain neuter, or to take part with both of them. If I choose Jesus Christ and His cross, the world will hate me; if I attach myself to the world and its vanities, Jesus Christ will reject and condemn me. Is it a question of hesitating? Am I a Christian if I do hesitate for a moment? But if I do range myself once for all under the standard of the cross, is it not evident that the world must become from that instant an enemy with whom I can never again make peace or truce? Once more we may say, How far our obligations extend, and how holy Christians would be, if they were thoroughly penetrated with the greatness of their engagements !

It is not sufficient that the world should be crucified to us ; we must also consent to be ourselves crucified to the world ; that is to say, we must allow the world to crucify us, as it crucified Jesus Christ ; to make war against us, as it made war against Jesus Christ ; to pursue us, to calumniate us, to outrage us with the same fury ; to take away from us at last our goods, our honour, and even our life. And not only must we consent to all these sacrifices rather than renounce our holiness as Christians, but we must make so doing a subject of joy and triumph. The disciple must glory in being treated like his Master. "*If they have persecuted Me,*" said our Lord Jesus Christ to His apostles, "*they will also persecute you.*" It is an infallible rule. The world would not be what it is, or Christians cannot be what they ought to be, if they escape the persecution of the world.

We often seek to know something about the state of our souls; we would like to know if we are pleasing to God, if Jesus Christ recognises us for His own. I will give you a rule by which you can easily be enlightened, and by which your uneasiness can be set at rest. See if the world esteems you, holds you in great consideration, speaks well of you, seeks your society. If it is so, you do not belong to Jesus Christ. But, on the contrary, if the world censures you, laughs at you, speaks ill of you, avoids you, despises you, hates you, oh, what great cause for consolation you have! Oh, well may you then believe that you do belong indeed to Jesus Christ!

Let us then think seriously, before God, what the world is with regard to us, and what we are with regard to the world. Let us sound our interior dispositions, let us study the depths of our own hearts: we shall most surely find there much that will humble and confound us; we shall discover that the maxims of the world have left deep impressions on our minds, and that in many difficult and delicate matters our judgment is far too ready to follow the judgment of the world; we shall find that we do desire the esteem of the world, and that we do fear its contempt; that we do form attachments too easily, and break from them with too much pain;

that we are subject often and often to a kind of human respect, to a way of accommodating ourselves, to a *giving in*, as it were, to the world, which is a great hindrance to our perfection, and which keeps us in a state of constraint and dissimulation. We shall find, in short, that we are not such faithful and determined friends of Jesus Christ and enemies of the world as we thought we were.

But let us not be discouraged : to triumph entirely over the world, to brave it, to despise it, and to be pleased that in its turn it should despise and fight against us, is not the work of a moment. Let us exercise ourselves in the little occasions which present themselves to us : if God loves us, He will take care that these occasions are not wanting to us; and let us prepare ourselves by these little victories for greater conflicts. Let us remember, in all our necessities, those words of Jesus Christ : "*Have confidence, I have overcome the world.*"

Let us beg of Him to help us to overcome it also, or rather to overcome it Himself through us, and to destroy in our hearts the kingdom of the world, that He may establish there His own kingdom.

XXV.

ON THE DIGNITY OF MAN.

THE dignity of man is comprehended in this saying, "*Everything that is not God is unworthy of man.*" It is only necessary for this saying to be well understood,

and it would draw sinners from their vices, and raise
the good to the highest summit of perfection. I
believe that to convert souls and carry them on to
the most sublime virtue there is no need of a multitude
of considerations : one alone is sufficient, provided it
be well meditated upon, that the soul is penetrated by
it, that it is allowed to influence the conduct, and that
it is followed out in practice to its utmost extent.
Such is the consideration which I am about to propose.
Let us first convince ourselves of the truth of it, and
then let us make up our minds to practise it with the
greatest fidelity.

Everything that is not God is unworthy of man—
unworthy of occupying his mind, unworthy of occupying his heart, unworthy of being the motive or the
principal objects of his actions. Can we have any
doubts on the subject if we reflect a little upon what
we are, upon the intention God had in creating and
redeeming us, and upon what other creatures, whether
they are our superiors, our equals, or our inferiors,
are really with regard to us ? Can we have any
doubts about it if we consider that our mind was
created to know God, and our heart to love Him :
that our destiny is to possess Him eternally, and that
the present life is only given to us that we may
merit this great happiness ? Can we have any
doubts about it if we cast our eyes on the goods of
this world, and compare them with the nature of our
souls, with the grandeur of the ideas of the soul, and
the immensity of its desires ? The goods of this
world are either corporal, and so can have no proportion with a substance which is purely spiritual,

or they are based solely on the opinion of men, and so are false and visionary. Besides, they are in their very nature inadequate, fragile, fleeting, and perishable. Can we doubt this if we consult our own hearts, and observe that as long as our hearts are fixed upon created objects they are happy only in hope and in idea, never in reality : that they are always craving, always uneasy, always tormented by fear and desire ? On the contrary, from the moment that we give our hearts entirely to God they begin to be in peace and repose, and we feel that no man and no event can take away this peace from us unless through our own fault ?

If all these reasons agree in proving to us the truth of that saying, there is nothing more to do but to make it the rule of our lives, and follow it out to its extreme limits. For to believe it true, and yet make no use of it as regards our conduct, is to behave as fools and madmen, and to pronounce our own condemnation.

Everything that is not God is unworthy of me. I ought then to say to myself, I must not then esteem anything unduly or fix my affections on anything which passes away with time ; that is to say, on no created thing whatsoever, and without exception. This is the first consideration which will regulate my mind and my heart in the use of all the things of this life. All these things pass away, they fly away like shadows ; nothing is worthy of my love but that which is eternal.

God wishes me to make use of the things of time for a time ; but He does not wish me to make any account of them ; He does not wish me to place my happiness in them : He simply employs them as a means of proving my love and my fidelity, and He will punish or reward me according to the use I make of them.

What must I then think of all those things upon which men pride themselves, and which they desire so passionately ?   What must be my judgment as to the advantages of birth or rank which I have in this world, as to the consideration which I enjoy, or the honours which are rendered to me ?   Are these things worthy of me ?   Do these things deserve the least attention, the least regard on my part ? Have I any reason, for such things as these, to prefer myself to any other person, whoever he may be ?

What should be my judgment as to any advantages of mind or body which I may possess ?   What are in reality all these miseries of which some people are vain ?   What does it really matter to me if I have a little more or less of intellect, or talent, or friends, or knowledge, or beauty ?   Am I any better for these things in the eyes of God ?   Should they make me think more highly of myself ?   Or, if I do not possess these advantages, should it be a subject of complaint or affliction to me ?   Oh, how infinitely beneath me are all these purely natural advantages, and how I lower myself if I make of them a subject of self-congratulation !

And as to the gifts of fortune, which procure for me the pleasures and comforts of life, are they worthy of me ?   Everything of this kind which exceeds what is necessary, is it worthy of my desires or my eagerness ?

Riches, after all, have only for their object the body, and the well-being of the body : is it not to lower myself to the condition of the animals when I make of my body a god, an idol; and give all my care to a mass of flesh which only serves as a prison for my soul ?

And even health, and life itself, when looked at in the light of eternity, are they possessions worthy of me ? And should I distress myself so much to preserve them, and fear so much to lose them ? If this life is not given entirely to God, if it is not devoted entirely to His service, is it an advantage ? Is it not rather an evil, and a great evil, since long years will only heap up sorrows and sins ?

But we may think, is not honour at least, is not the care of our reputation, is not the esteem of men, an advantage which we may safely desire ? May we not fear what will make us lose this esteem, and seek what will gain it for us ? I agree that we must live in such a manner as to give no cause for scandal ; but that must be because God sees us, not because men see us. If our conscience reproaches us with nothing, why should we be alarmed, or grieved, or tormented by the false judgment and the vain conversation of men ?

Are their judgments and opinions the rule of what is true ? Is it in this way that God will judge us ? And if I have God and my own conscience on my side, what more can I desire ?

But, you may say, I pass for what I am not; I

cannot show myself anywhere ; every one is speaking against me, and spreading reports which cover me with shame, and contempt, and ridicule. Yes, humanly speaking, this is an evil undoubtedly, and even one of the greatest evils of this life. But is it an evil when we look at it from a religious point of view ? Is it an evil from God's point of view when we make to Him the sacrifice of our reputation ? Is it not rather a good, and a very great good, if our virtue and our piety draw down upon us the censure, the contempt, and the ridicule of the world ? And even if these things should go farther, if we should incur persecution, or even death, and the most terrible punishments, has not Jesus Christ Himself, the eternal Truth, pronounced that those who suffer such things are "*blessed;*" and we know that He chose for Himself this kind of blessedness.

Then, since God alone is worthy of me, that which God loves and esteems is also that which alone deserves my esteem and my love. Now, what is it that God esteems ? It is precisely that which the world despises ; and, in like manner, everything that is great, and high, and honourable in the eyes of the world is an "*abomination*" in the eyes of God : these are the very words of the Gospel.

The reason of this difference is that God looks upon things as they regard Himself, and His own glory, and His eternal designs for us, whereas men look upon things as they regard themselves and this present life.

Which of these two rules must I follow in my judgments ? What is it that God loves ? It is precisely that which the world hates. God loves poverty, crosses, humiliations, sufferings, everything that detaches us from the things of this life, and fixes our thoughts and affections upon future and eternal things.

The world, on the contrary, loves everything that attaches it more strongly to the things of time, and makes it lose sight of the things of eternity and the desire of heaven. Which of these two is the best judge of the greatness and dignity of man ? Which is the best judge of his happiness, and the means of obtaining it ?

What then must we do if we wish to be saints ? One thing, and one only : we must continually apply to our conduct and our actions this consideration : Everything that is not God, everything that is not infinite, eternal, immense, as He is, is not worthy of me. I am made for God alone. I ought only to love, and esteem, and seek after that which will bring me nearer to God, which will give me, even in this life, the enjoyment of Him by faith, and which will assure me of the eternal possession of Him one day in Heaven. I ought to despise, and hate, and avoid all which may separate me from Him, everything which drives Him from my soul, or exposes me to the danger of losing Him for ever. And where shall I find the just and unfailing discernment of these things ? I shall find it in the Gospel; in the teaching and example of Jesus Christ. God was made man ; He lived and conversed with man, to teach us what is our true dignity, our true greatness. It is only in the light of the Gospel that man is truly

great, because there alone he is seen in intimate relationship with God. Everywhere else, even in the
writings of the most sublime philosophers, he is
small, because there it is not seen that God alone
is his object, his centre, his first beginning and his
last end.

O my God! penetrate my soul with this sublime
truth, which makes of me a being so noble, so elevated,
in Your eyes : penetrate my soul with this idea of my
own dignity. Suffer me not to stoop, or to seek my
satisfaction in anything less than You! Be henceforth the sole object of my thoughts and affections ;
may I refer everything to You alone ; may the lessons
and the example of Jesus Christ be the only rules of
my conduct ; and may I trample under foot all creatures, my own pride, and my own self-love ; thus by
dying to everything and to myself also, to raise myself even to You, my beginning and my last end,
the sole and only source of my eternal happiness !
Amen.

XXVI.

ON THE HUMAN HEART.

"The heart is perverse above all things, and unsearchable : who can
know it?"—JEREMIAS.

BY these words, "the human heart," we mean
that depth of malignity, of perversity, and of self-
love, which is in every one of us, and the venom of
which extends over all our actions, even the best
of them : for there is scarcely any action we do

that is not spoilt by self-love and deprived of all its goodness.

This perverse and corrupt element in our nature is a consequence of original sin, which has led astray the primitive uprightness of our hearts, and has concentrated upon .our own selves that affection which ought to be given to God alone. If we observe ourselves carefully, we shall find that we love everything in proportion as it affects ourselves, that we judge of everything according to our own view of it, and solely with regard to our own interests : instead of which, we ought to love everything, and even ourselves, only in God and for God's sake ; and we should judge of everything according to the judgment of God, and solely with a view to His interests. And the source of all our vices——those of the mind and those of the heart, is that we will reverse this right order of things : this is the root of all our sins, and the sole cause of our eternal ruin.

If we study quite young children even, we shall perceive in them the first seeds of this disorder, and the germs of all the evil passions of our nature. These germs develop from day to day, and have already made serious progress before reason and religion can do anything to check them. And the saddest thing about the whole matter is that the first effect of this disorder is to blind us as to our own state : we can see the faults of others plainly enough, but we cannot and will not see our own ; we are angry with those who try to make us see ourselves as we really are, and we will never allow that they are right ; and the principal cause of our trouble

L

when we do fall into a fault is a secret pride
which makes us vexed and irritated at being obliged
to acknowledge our fall even to ourselves.   We
do all we possibly can to hide what we really are
from ourselves and from others.   We do not always
succeed with others, who easily find us out; but, unfortunately, we succeed only too well with ourselves:
and the knowledge of our own hearts, which is
the most necessary of all knowledge, is also the most
rare, and that which we take the least trouble to
obtain.   We live and die without really knowing
ourselves, without doing anything to acquire that
knowledge, and almost always after having laboured
all our lives to disguise ourselves in our own eyes.
What a terrible mistake, when we have to appear
at last before the God of truth, there at last to see
ourselves as we really are!   Then it will be too
late; there will be no help and no hope then; we
shall know ourselves but for our own misery and our
eternal despair !

It is necessary, therefore, to try in this life to
attain to a right knowledge of ourselves, and to
judge ourselves with a just judgment; and above all,
we must try to be firmly persuaded not only of the
importance, but of the absolute necessity of this self-
knowledge, and also of its extreme difficulty.   But
how shall we set about this, when from our earliest
childhood we are so profoundly in the dark on this
subject, and when increasing age only increases the
darkness and obscurity ?   We must have recourse to
Him Who alone knows us perfectly, Who has fathomed
the most secret recesses of our hearts, Who has

counted and followed all our footsteps. We must implore the light of His grace, and by the help of that light we must incessantly study all our actions and the secret motives of those actions ; all our inclinations, our affections, our passions ; above all, those which seem the most refined and the most spiritual. We must be inexorable in condemning ourselves whenever we see we are guilty, and never try to excuse ourselves either in the sight of others or in our own sight.

If we are in this good disposition of uprightness and sincerity, if we acknowledge humbly before God our own blindness with regard to ourselves, most assuredly He will enlighten us ; and if we will only make good use of these first rays of His Divine light, we shall see more and more clearly, day by day, into our own hearts ; we shall discover by degrees all our defects, even those that were most imperceptible ; even the cunning deceits of self-love will not be able to escape from our vision ; and, aided by the Divine assistance, we shall pursue this enemy relentlessly until we succeed in banishing him for ever from our hearts.

Now God, Who is infinitely wise, only gives us this knowledge of ourselves gradually and by degrees ; He does not show us our misery all at once— such a sight would drive us to despair, and we should not have strength to bear it—but He shows us first of all our most glaring faults, and as we go on correcting these, He discovers to us our more subtle and secret faults, till at last He lays bare to us all the innermost recesses of our hearts. And this goes

on our whole life long; and too happy shall we be
if before our death we attain to a perfect knowledge
of ourselves and an entire cure of all our evils!
This grace is only granted to those souls who are
most holy, most faithful, and most generous in never
forgiving themselves anything.

The most important point is, therefore, always to
walk under the guidance of the Divine light; to be
quite sure that, if we wander away from that light,
we shall lose ourselves; to mistrust our own intellect, our own judgment, our own opinions, and to be
guided in everything by the Spirit of God, to wait
for His decision, and to hold our own in suspense
until He decides for us and directs us. How rare
is such a practice as this, and what great fidelity
in mortifying ourselves it requires! But also, by it,
what errors we avoid, what falls we escape, what
progress we make in perfection!

What errors we avoid! It is quite certain that
whenever we judge of the things of God by our
own judgment, we are at fault; that we deceive ourselves in everything respecting the nature of holiness
and the means of attaining it; that we are as incapable of judging of our own actions, our own motives,
our own dispositions, as we are of the actions and
dispositions of our neighbour; that in him as in ourselves we condemn where we ought to approve, and
approve where we ought to condemn, on slight
grounds and without any knowledge of the true
state of the case. And as our judgments on such
matters are the principles of our conduct, into what
errors do not we fall when we take the promptings

of our own spirit for our guide! We construct our own ideal of sanctity; we are quite delighted with it, and adhere to it most obstinately; we will listen to no one else's ideas; we judge ourselves and we judge others by this rule, and we thus make terrible mistakes of which every one but ourselves is conscious!

What falls we escape! All our faults come from leaving the Spirit of God to follow our own spirit. We are not sufficiently careful about this in the beginning; we do not mistrust ourselves enough; we do not always consult God with the deepest humility; we lean upon our own spirit until insensibly it takes the place of the Spirit of God; we do not perceive this; at last we deceive ourselves completely, and fall into all sorts of delusions; we think we are following the Divine light, and we are only following our own imagination, our own passions; this blindness goes on increasing day by day; the wisest advice cannot bring us back; we are no longer in a state even to listen to it: and—I am not afraid to say it—with the best and most upright intentions in the world, we find ourselves incessantly in danger of committing the greatest faults unless we are really interior, and unless we are always on the watch against the artifices of self-love.

There is only one way of making a real advance in the way of perfection, and that is, never to guide ourselves, but always to take God for our Guide, to renounce ourselves in all things, to die in all things, to our own judgment and to our own will. Whatever progress we may have made in this way, the moment we attempt to guide ourselves we go back. The farther we advance, the more absolutely necessary is the Divine guidance for us; and if the greatest saint on earth were to think for a single instant that he could guide himself, in that instant he would be in the greatest danger of being lost for ever.

Since then it is quite impossible for us to know our own heart—since self-love can always lead us astray and blind us—since pride, which is the greatest of all sins, is all the more to be feared the farther we are advanced in the ways of God, let us never rely on ourselves; let us always keep ourselves in God's sight and under the guidance of His Hand, and let us beg of Him to enlighten us always and without ceasing.

The true knowledge of ourselves consists in believing that, however far advanced in perfection we may be, we are always of ourselves incapable in this supernatural life of one good thought, of one right judgment, or of one just action; and that, on the con- . trary, we are capable of falling into the greatest sins, and even of being hopelessly lost, if we turn away from God and His guidance ever so little. Whoever knows himself in this manner, and acts accordingly, will never go astray. But to know ourselves like this, and to act on our knowledge, we must be really interior, given to recollection, to prayer, and the constant thought of the presence of God.

XXVII.

ON TEMPTATIONS.

"Because you were pleasing to God, it was needful that you should be tried by temptation."—*The Angel Raphael to Tobias.*

THOSE who have given themselves up to the spiritual life have no difficulty in persuading themselves that they are pleasing to God, when He makes them feel the sweetness of His presence, and when He overwhelms them with His caresses, when they enjoy a peace which nothing seems to trouble, and when they experience nothing painful either from the attacks of the devil or from the malice of man. But when God withdraws His consolations, when He allows the devil to tempt them and men to put their virtue to the proof, then, if they are told that all this is a certain sign that they are pleasing to God, it would not be so easy to persuade them of it; on the contrary, they then think that God has forsaken them, that they please Him no' longer as they once did, and they seek uneasily to discover what there can have been in their conduct to induce God to treat them with so much severity.

Nevertheless, here is an angel revealing to Tobias that it was just because he *was* pleasing to God that it was necessary for him to be tried by temptation. Mark the connection : God, and the devil, and men all try you. What is the necessary cause of this treatment ? It is because you are pleasing to

God.   Temptations are therefore the reward of your previous fidelity ; and God allows them on purpose to make you still more agreeable in His eyes, and consequently more holy and perfect.   Every page of the Old and the New Testament contains proofs and examples of this truth.   And it is undoubtedly the most powerful motive for consolation which the servants of God can have in all their trials.

Thus, when they begin to give themselves to God, the first thing they must most certainly expect is this : that if they serve Him with their whole heart, if they are faithful to His graces, if they neglect nothing to make themselves pleasing in His sight, He will try them with every sort of affliction ; He will allow the devil to tempt them, He will send them humiliations and persecutions, and they must prepare themselves for all this by an entire resignation to the will of God.

But if, after several years passed in the service of God, their interior peace is uncrossed by any kind of trouble, if the devil and men leave them in tranquillity, then it is that they ought to mistrust their virtue, and believe that they are not really as pleasing to God as they thought they were.

It is, therefore, very necessary that temptation should try the true servants of God   What do we mean by the word *try ?*   We mean, first of all, that temptation makes clear and obvious the truth and genuineness of their virtue.   For what is a virtue worth that has never been exercised ?   It is a feeble virtue, a doubtful virtue of which we can make no account, and which we cannot rely upon.   Is it at all

difficult to walk when God is helping us on ? Or to
pray when we are inundated with spiritual consolations ? Or to overcome ourselves when the attractions of grace are so triumphant that they leave
scarcely any room for the smallest resistance on the
part of nature ? Is it a painful thing to rest peacefully in the bosom of God, sheltered from all winds
and tempests ; to be feared by the devil, who keeps
himself at a distance ; and respected by men who
pay homage to piety in our person ? Certainly
holiness would be neither difficult, nor rare, nor
terrible to corrupt nature, if it could be acquired
without any effort, without any combats, without any
contradictions ; and it would have been most unreasonable of Saint Paul to compare Christians to the
athletes who, after long and painful training, came
to struggle in the arena, and who gained the victory
at the cost of so much sweat and often of so much
blood. A virtue that has never been tried does not
deserve the name of virtue.

Next, what does *to try* mean ? It means to
purify. Just as metals are tried and purified from
all alloy by placing them in the crucible, so is virtue
purified in the crucible of temptation. And from
what is it purified ? From the alloy of that spirit of
self-interest which debases it, from the self-love which
corrupts it, from the pride which poisons it. It is
impossible for virtue to be what it should be—that
is to say, disinterested, unappropriating, expecting no
reward, free from all vain complacency—unless it has
passed through the crucible of many temptations.
The effect of every temptation against purity, for

example, or against faith, or against hope, is to strengthen these virtues in our soul and carry them to the highest degree. The effect of anxieties, of weariness in doing good, of disgust at everything, of evident repugnance to duty, of extreme desolation, so that all sensible grace is withdrawn from us, and God seems to have forsaken us—the effect of all this is to purify our love, to increase our courage, our fidelity, and our perseverance. The effect of calumnies, vexations, and persecutions is to raise us above all human respect, and at the same time to take away from us a certain good opinion of ourselves which the praise of men nourishes in us without our perceiving it. Finally, the general effect of all temptations is to detach us from the things of this world, to humble us in our own eyes, to inspire us with more trust in God, and to draw us into closer union with Him.

Temptations are entirely, therefore, in the designs of God, the recompense, the proof, and the consummation of virtue. How, after that, can we fear them? If humility does not allow us to desire them, because that would be to presume on our own strength, the zeal for our perfection also does not allow us to dread them, still less to be unhappy when they do come, and to think that all is lost. But you may say, "I am so afraid of sinning, I am so afraid of forfeiting grace, I am so afraid of being lost, and I see myself exposed by temptation to the danger of all this." You may as well say that you are afraid of fighting, of gaining the victory, and of being crowned; for the apostle says that the crown of glory is only destined for those who have fought

according to the rules. Do you not see that this
very fear of sinning, which makes you so weak and
cowardly, comes from your only considering your
own strength, and not thinking enough of the help of
God, which can render you invincible? I grant you,
that if you only look at your own weakness the least
temptation may be strong enough to overcome you.
Therefore you ought never to look at yourself, except
to acknowledge and distrust your own weakness; you
ought to throw yourself into the arms of God, that
He may be your support and your protection. Can
you be afraid of sinning when the arm of the All-
powerful sustains you? What can the strength of
all men and all devils do against Him? Can they
tear you from His arms without your consent? Is
not His help assured to you in all those temptations
which He permits, which you have not sought of
yourself, in which you mistrust your own strength,
and to which you have only exposed yourself at His
command?

Listen to the words of Saint Paul—it is to you he
speaks : "*God is faithful,*" he says ; "*He will not suffer
you to be tempted above that you are able to bear; but
will, with the temptation, also make a way to escape, that
you may be able to bear it.*" (1 Cor. x. 13.)

Weigh well these words, for they will fill you
with consolation and confidence in the midst of the
hardest trial. "*God is faithful:*" He owes it to
Himself, He owes it to His own promises, He owes
it to His love for you, to succour you in any danger
that threatens your soul. His glory is interested in
helping you, because sin is an offence against Him-

self.   He knows that you can do nothing without Him, and that you will most certainly fall if He abandons you.   If He failed you in these critical moments He would not be Himself.

"*He will not suffer you to be tempted above that you are able to bear.*"   The faithfulness of God towards us does not consist in delivering us from all temptation—for that would be to deprive Himself of His own glory, and to deprive us of the merit attached to the victory—but His faithfulness consists in never allowing the temptation to go beyond our strength for resisting.   God knows perfectly, and infinitely better than we do, what our strength really is, for we derive our strength solely from Him and His grace.   He moderates the action of the tempter, for He always remains the supreme Master of that action ; and He will never suffer the tempter to have more strength to attack than we have to resist.

This is not all : He will increase the power of His assistance in proportion to the strength of the temptation, so that we may be able to bear it and to come forth as conquerors.   Thus He gives us more strength to resist than He allows the devil to have to attack us.   The greatness of the help increases in proportion to the violence of the temptation.

We fight, under the very eyes of God, and for Him, with the arms which He supplies to us, and it is of faith that it is never for want of His Divine assistance, but always through our own fault, if we do not gain the victory.   He wishes to punish us either for our past infidelities, or for our presumption, or for our want of confidence in Him.   But supposing we give no occasion for our defeat, we are certain of victory through the help of God.

"But," you may say, "I do not feel this help." What does it matter, whether you feel it or not, provided you really have it ? God is only exercising your faith. Is it anything to be astonished at, that while the devil is stirring up tempests in your imagination, rousing all your passions, obscuring your understanding, shaking your will, and filling you with trouble, is it astonishing that you should not feel a help that is purely spiritual, and that is acting only in the very depths of your soul ?

"But I think I have consented : I am sure of it." Never judge that of yourself : God does not wish it ; you will deceive yourself, and you will by this give the devil power over you, and he will drive you to despair. Rely in this entirely on the decision of your spiritual father, and humbly submit your own judgment to his. "What !" you will say, "in such a matter as this, upon what passes in my innermost soul, upon what has to do with my conscience and the salvation of my soul ? " Yes : your spiritual father has a light from God, and sure rules to judge whether you have consented or not, and you have neither these rules nor this light to guide yourself. God wishes you to be guided by faith and obedience, to die to your own judgment ; He does not allow you to see clearly what is passing in the interior of your soul, above all in those terrible moments of trouble and darkness.

XXVIII.

ON WHAT OUR CONDUCT SHOULD BE WITH REGARD TO TEMPTATIONS.

AFTER having spoken of the usefulness and even the necessity of temptations, we must now say something about the manner in which we ought to act when the temptations come. This matter, which is quite practical, is not one of the least essential in the spiritual life. Whole treatises have been written upon it : I will confine myself to the most important points.

Temptations differ according to the different states of the persons they attack ; and this is something to which we must pay great attention, that we may discern them well. The temptations of the generality of Christians lead them to evil under the appearance of some sensible good. These temptations are quite easy to recognise ; and as they have nothing to do with persons who have given themselves entirely to God, for whom I am specially writing, I shall say nothing about them, except that the only means of sheltering ourselves from these sort of temptations is to resolve most firmly to be attentive and faithful to Divine grace even in the smallest matters, and to avoid not only mortal sin and all occasions which might lead us into it, but also venial sin and the slightest appearance of sin.

Whoever has generously decided on this course, and

who faithfully pursues it, will no longer be exposed
to this sort of temptations, which have no other root
than the indecision of our will, as long as it is fluc-
tuating between virtue and vice.

When we have given ourselves entirely and once
for all to God, He generally allows us to enjoy for
some time a certain peace and tranquillity of soul ;
He does not allow the devil to trouble us, wishing to
give us time to get up our strength and to put ourselves in a state to resist his attacks.   But, as virtue
has need of being tried, that thereby it may become
confirmed, the temptations will come when God sees
fit, or when the soul herself gives occasion for them
by leaning too much on herself, or reflecting too much
on herself.

The object of these temptations is, 1st, to withdraw
us from a certain good through the fear of committing evil.   For instance, the devil will try to keep a
soul away from Holy Communion through the fear
of communicating unworthily, or under pretence that
the soul derives no profit from it.   This fear is only
a vague fear with which he troubles the imagination,
and the only way is to despise it and take no notice
of it.   This pretence only comes because we wish to
judge of ourselves of the profit we derive from our
communions, which is what we ought never to do.

2nd. The object of these temptations is, to turn
us away from doing good under pretence of loss of
time and idleness.   This happens above all with regard to prayer, when we have no longer good thoughts
and affections, and when we are assailed with dis-
tractions.   Then we immediately think we are doing

nothing, and we are tempted to give up our way of prayer and return to ordinary meditation. This is a delusion which we must fight against strenuously. Prayer is the death of self-love, and it is never more effective for producing this death than when it is dry, distracted, and without any consolation or sensible devotion.

3rd. The third object of these temptations is, to propose to us another way of doing good than that which God wills for us. For instance, God draws us to Himself by a love of retirement, of solitude, by a desire of enjoying His Presence in peace and silence. And under pretence of zeal for souls, or charity, or edification to our neighbour, we allow ourselves to be drawn into all sorts of exterior good works, and association with the outside world, and we even wish to undertake the conversion of souls to God. This is a temptation which is very frequent; and we must resist it by waiting until God Himself furnishes us with the occasion of serving our neighbour, and shows us plainly that it is His Will: we should never take the initiative of ourselves.

4th. The devil will try to tempt us in the matter of obedience, either by giving us a bad impression of our director, or suggesting to us that he is deceived in our regard, or that he goes beyond his authority. On this matter I have only one thing to say, and it is this: when we once have sufficient proof (and we always have it in the beginning) that our director is a good and upright man, that he is learned and enlightened, and that he is guided by the Spirit of God, then we must obey him in all things as we

would obey God Himself; we must never allow ourselves to judge him; and we must listen to nothing
which might weaken our good opinion of him. Of
course I except those cases where there is palpable
and notorious evidence of his having conducted himself badly; but such cases are very rare, and they
are always easy to be recognised.

The temptations of more advanced souls are quite
of another order, and they are rather trials than
temptations. God, Who wishes to humble them, to
purify them, and to annihilate self in them, allows the
devil to try them with violent temptations against
purity, or against faith, or hope, or their love of God
and their neighbour; He allows a kind of universal
upheaval or unchaining of the powers of evil; He
may even allow exterior and evident faults, to which
the soul believes she has consented, though in reality
she is very far from having done so.

It is, above all, in these kind of temptations that
the guidance of an experienced and skilful director
is absolutely necessary, and we have need of a perfect
obedience of judgment and will; for the soul then is
so troubled, the understanding is so obscured, that
the soul is incapable of judging rightly on what is
• passing within herself, and she must absolutely rely
on the judgment of another. What she must do
then—and this is most essential—is to hide nothing
from her director, but to tell him faithfully and
honestly, without fear or shame, and with great
simplicity, exactly what she experiences; to let him
form his own judgment, without trying to influence
him by hers, and without disputing with him; to

M

agree with his decision, without examination or reflection, and then to do without hesitation whatever he may command; in spite of any fear she may have, or any feeling that she has offended or is going to offend God.

These states of the soul are very strange, undoubtedly, and the conscience suffers in them a terrible perplexity. But God allows them, that the soul may die completely to herself, to her own will, to her own interest; and the only way to pass through them safely is in a spirit of blind obedience, of perfect fidelity, and of entire resignation to the will of God.

Besides what I have just said as to the manner in which we ought to behave during these different temptations, there are a few general rules to observe before, during, and after the temptations.

Before the temptation comes, we must neither fear it, nor even think of it, nor take any measure to anticipate it or to prevent it. I am speaking of the temptations of *trial*, in which the soul is entirely passive: we must simply keep ourselves, like little children, in the arms of God, placing in Him all our confidence, and expecting everything from His help. The best preparation is an inviolable fidelity to Divine grace and a generous courage in overcoming ourselves in all things; for the more we conquer nature the less hold temptation has upon us; the devil is only strong against us in proportion as we are weak through self-love.

During the immediate time of the temptation, we must let it pass over us like a stormy cloud, we must hold fast to God, and we must not give up any of our ordinary practices of devotion. Thus, even if we are assailed by the most horrible thoughts during the time of prayer, we must not leave off our prayer until the usual hour for doing so; still less must we give up Holy Communion on the pretext of the impure or blasphemous thoughts which trouble us at that sacred moment. It is very often just this very time which the devil chooses to torment us. Let us make a rule to ourselves never to yield to him, however hard he may press us.

"*Resist the devil,*" says Saint James, "*and he will flee from you.*" He can do nothing against a soul which is firm and immovable; he must retire, overwhelmed with confusion. If our director has prescribed any particular practice during the time of temptation, we must be very faithful to it, because God always blesses obedience.

When the moment of temptation is over, we must enjoy the calm which is restored to our soul without examining whether we have consented or not: this could only serve to trouble and discourage us, for it is certain that it is not by the manner in which the soul is affected during the temptation that she can judge whether she has resisted or yielded. She is then too much agitated to be able to discern what is free and what is not.

It is her general conduct after the temptation is over which alone can tell her of her victory or her defeat. If she is humble, docile, obedient, faithful in the observance of all her duties, ready to renounce her own will, God will never allow her to be overcome, and it is upon this rule that the confessor must decide and reassure the soul, if he sees that it is right to do so. Therefore it is necessary for the soul to give him a faithful account of all she has experienced, neither adding to or diminishing anything, telling as certain what she believes to be certain, and as doubtful what she thinks doubtful. Everything else rests with the director.

What she ought, above all things, to forbid herself, are reasonings and reflections upon the temptation and its circumstances. She ought never to think about it at all, except to speak of it to her director, and when that is once done, she ought never willingly to let her mind dwell upon it at all.

XXIX.

ON THE HUMAN "I." (*Ego.*)

GOD alone has the right properly to say *I*, and to look at everything as it regards Himself, to be Himself the rule, the measure, and the centre of all things ; because God alone exists of Himself, and everything else exists only by His will, and for Him, has no value whatever but the value He gives it, and, considered by itself, is nothing, is worth nothing, and deserves nothing. This is true in the order of nature, and it is still more true in the order of grace.

When we can well understand this fact, it is easy to understand also how unjust is the human *I*. This injustice consists in man having a great consideration for himself, esteeming himself, loving himself, and thinking himself worthy of esteem and love; in his constituting himself the centre of everything, and referring everything to himself; in making the love he has for himself and his own interests the secret motive of all his thoughts, words, and actions. He looks at everything from his own point of view; he seeks himself in everything; it seems to him as if the whole universe, and all creatures, and even God Himself, only existed on his account. He has no esteem or love for others, except in proportion to the esteem and friendship they show to him. And if he ever does show them any sort of kindness, or oblige them or serve them in any way, it is only for the sake of his own interest, or if not for his own interest directly, for his own vain-glory. This esteem and love of himself insinuate themselves everywhere, even into his service of God, and are the source of all the imperfections and faults into which he falls.

The human *I* is the root of pride, and consequently of all sin. It is the enemy of God, Whom it attacks in His absolute and universal sovereignty. It is also the enemy of men, whom it stirs up one against another, on account of the opposition of their respective interests. It is the worst enemy of every individual man, because it draws him away from his real and true good, leads him on to evil, and takes from him all peace and rest.

If we could once annihilate the human *I*, all crimes would disappear from the face of the earth, all men would live with each other like brothers, sharing their possessions without envy, helping each other in all their necessities, and each one of them looking upon his neighbour as a second self. If we could once annihilate the human *I*, all the thoughts of man, all his desires, all his actions would be referred to God only, without any mixture of self-interest; God would be loved, adored, and served for Himself alone, on account of His infinite perfections and on account of His benefits. He would be loved whether He consoled a man or afflicted him; whether He caressed him or tried him; whether He drew the man to Himself with sweetness, or seemed to reject and forsake him. If we could once annihilate the human *I*, the innocent man would pass his days in an unchanging peace, because both from within and from without there would be nothing to trouble him.

There are two kinds of the human *I*: the first one, which is gross, animal, earthly, and which has for its object only the things of here below; it is that of worldlings, who are always occupied in seeking after the honours, riches, and pleasures of this earth, or regretting the loss of them; it is that of pretended philosophers and wise men, who by a refined pride, and to make themselves singular, affect to be independent of common prejudices and opinions, and seek their own glory and honour by the very contempt they pretend to have for such things. All the vices which brutalise man and desolate the world are the offspring of this gross and earthly *I*, which causes the misery of the human race here and hereafter.

The other *I*, which is far more subtle and delicate, is the spiritual *I*, the *I* of persons who are given to piety. And who can say what harm this *I* does to devotion—how it lessens it, and narrows it; to how many delusions and complications it exposes devotion; how it renders piety ridiculous and contemptible in the eyes of the world, which is always ready to criticise spitefully and pitilessly the servants of God? Who can tell of how many miseries and weaknesses and falls it is the cause? How it makes devout people scrupulous, petty, uneasy, officious, uncertain, eccentric, jealous, critical, spiteful, ill-tempered, insupportable to themselves and to others? Who can tell how often it frustrates and stops the operations of Divine grace; how it favours the cunning and snares of the devil; how it makes us weak in temptations, cowardly in times of trial, reserved and ungenerous in our sacrifices; how many noble designs it brings to nought; how many good actions it infects with its dangerous poison; how many faults it disguises and makes appear as virtues?

The especial characteristic of the human *I*, whichever it may be, the sensual or the spiritual, is to plunge us into the most deplorable blindness. We do not see ourselves, we do not know ourselves, and we think all the time that we do see and know ourselves. Nothing can open our eyes, and we get angry with any one who tries to do this. We set it down to unkindness, or at least to quite mistaken kindness, if any one attempts to advise us or correct us. It is no use to be very gentle with us, and to tell us what is wrong with all the sweetness and circumspection possible—our wounded self-love is at at once in arms, is very much offended, rebels against

and never pardons the good advice which was inspired simply by zeal and charity.

In the same way, we think we are quite capable
of guiding and judging ourselves, we even wish to
direct those who have been appointed to govern us,
and to teach them how they ought to act towards us;
we do not think we are properly guided and directed,
except by those who will guide us and direct us in
our own way, and according to our own opinion.

The true director, he who requires the submission
of our judgment and our will, who preaches to us
bare faith and blind obedience, is soon abandoned as
one who tyrannises over consciences.   When we are
spoken to about fighting with our self-love, or overcoming our repugnances, or conquering our aversions;
when any one tries to open our eyes about certain
cherished faults; when any one tries to show us the
imperfection or positive badness of our motives;
when certain sacrifices are asked of us—all these
things speak a language which we will not listen to;
all this is an intolerable burden which is being forced
upon us : no one understands us; every one is mistaken about us; they exaggerate things; they go
beyond what the law requires, and even beyond the
counsels of perfection !

Nevertheless, it is most certainly true that all
holiness consists in the destruction of the human *I*.
It is true that Christian morality has no other end;
that the object of all the operations of Divine grace
is to humble us and to annihilate in us the love of
ourselves.   It is true that the love of God and the
love of ourselves are like the two weights of a

balance, and that one can only go down when the other goes up. Therefore, the only means of perfection, that great practice which embraces all others, is to fight against ourselves, to do violence to ourselves in everything and always; and, as we are neither sufficiently clear-sighted or disinterested or skilful in the choice of means to undertake and successfully conduct a warfare of such importance, in which our own heart is the field of battle, we have only one thing to do, and that is to give ourselves freely to God, to leave to Him the care of this warfare, and to second Him as far as is in our own power.

Let us say to ourselves : My greatest enemy, the enemy by which my two other enemies, the devil and the world, can do anything against me, is myself; it is that "old man," that offspring and consequence of Adam's sin; it is that love of self which was born with me, which was developed in me before ever I came to the use of reason, which has been strengthened by my passions, by the blindness of my understanding, and by the weakness of my will, by the abuse I have made of my liberty, by my sins and my bad habits. How shall I fight against, how shall I overcome this terrible enemy ? What shall I do; how shall I begin ? Alas! this enemy will raise himself up again through the very blows which I give him; he will applaud himself for my victories, and will attribute them to the effect of his own strength ! He will contemplate and admire himself in the virtues I may have acquired and in the defects I may have corrected; he will be intoxicated with the praises which others may give to my piety; and

he will pride himself even on the acts of humility
which I may have performed! He will appropriate
to himself your work, O my God! and will deprive
You of the glory which belongs to You alone! Once
more, then, what shall I do? How shall I conquer
this terrible enemy, who makes of his very defeat a
subject of triumph?

Ah, Lord and God of my soul! it is *You* Who
must undertake this war for me. I cannot do it
myself.

My self-love is my enemy only because it is
Yours; attack it, conquer it, crush it, pursue it to
its utter destruction. I give myself up to You, I
abandon myself to You entirely with this intention.
You are All-powerful, suffer me not to resist You;
punish me for the least infidelity; permit me not the
least thought of myself, the least complacency in the
good which it may please You to work in me, the
least attachment to Your gifts, the least spirit of
appropriating anything to myself! Leave me not,
O my God and my all! until the old Adam is
entirely destroyed in me, and until the new Adam,
who is our Lord Jesus Christ, reigns in his place
and makes me holy with His own holiness! Amen.

XXX.

ON THE ANNIHILATION OF SELF.

"I am before Thee as one that is not."—PSALMS.

WHEN we are spoken to of dying to ourselves, of annihilating ourselves, when we are told that that is the foundation of Christian morality, and that in it consists the adoration of God in spirit and in truth, we do not wish to receive this saying; it seems to us hard and even unjust, and we rebel against those who announce it to us on the part of God. Let us convince ourselves once for all that this saying has nothing but what is just and right in itself, and that the practice of it is infinitely sweeter than we think for. Afterwards let us humble ourselves if we have not the courage to put it in practice; and instead of condemning the words of wisdom, let us condemn ourselves.

What does God ask of us, when He commands us to annihilate ourselves and to renounce ourselves? He asks of us to do ourselves justice, to put ourselves in our proper place and to acknowledge ourselves for what we really are. Even if we had been born and had always lived in a state of innocence, even if we had never lost original grace, we should still be nothing else but utter nothingness from our very nature; we could not look upon ourselves otherwise without making a great mistake; and we should be unjust if we expected God or men to look upon us

in any other light.   What rights can a thing have
that is nothing ?   What can a thing require that
is nothing ?   If his very existence is a free gift,
certainly everything else he has is much more so
It is then a formal injustice on our part to refuse
to be treated, or to refuse to treat ourselves, as if
we were really nothing.   But we may say that this
avowal costs us nothing to make with regard to God,
and that it is just as far as He is concerned ; but
that it is not at all so with regard to other men, who
are nothing as well as we are, and therefore have no
right to oblige us to such an avowal and to all its
consequences.   Certainly, this avowal costs us nothing
as far as God is concerned, if we only make it with
our mouth , but if we mould our conduct upon it,
and allow God to exercise over us all the rights
which belong to Him ; if we freely consent that He
shall dispose of us as He pleases, of our mind, our
heart, and our whole being, it will cost us a great
deal, and we shall even find a difficulty in not saying
that it is injustice.   Therefore, God has pity on our
weakness ; He does not make use of His rights in
all their severity, and He never puts us to certain
annihilating trials without first having obtained our
free consent.

As to what concerns men, I agree that of themselves they have no authority over us, and that any
contempt or humiliation or outrage on their part is
an injustice.   But we have not any the more for
that the right to complain of this injustice, because
in reality it is not an injustice against us, who are
nothing, and to whom nothing is due ; but it is an

injustice against God, Whose commands they violate when they despise us, or humble us, or outrage us. It is therefore God who should resent the injury they do to Him by ill-treating us; it is not for us to resent it, for in all that happens to us we ought only to feel the injury that is done to God.

My neighbour despises me; he is wrong, because he is of no more importance than I am, and God has forbidden him to despise me. But is he wrong because I am really worthy of esteem, and because there is nothing in me that deserves contempt? No. If he takes away from me my goods, if he blackens my reputation, if he attempts my life, he is guilty, and very guilty, towards God; but is he so towards me? Am I justified in wishing him ill for it, or in seeking revenge? No. Because all that I possess, all that I am, is not properly mine, who have nothing of my own but nothingness, and from whom therefore nothing can be taken away.

If we were always to look upon things thus, only as they regard God's side of the questions, and not ours, we should not be so easily wounded, so sensitive, so given to complaining and getting angry. All our disturbances come from thinking ourselves to be something of importance and assuming rights which we do not possess, and because we will always look at things as they regard ourselves, and not simply as they regard the rights and interests of God, Whose injuries are the only ones which ought to concern it.

I confess that this is a very difficult practice, and that to attain to it we must be dead to ourselves. But indeed it is a just thing, and reason has nothing to oppose to it.   For God requires of us nothing but what is reasonable when He requires of us that we should behave to Him and to our neighbour as if we were nothing, had nothing, and expected nothing.

This would be quite just, as I have already said, even if we had preserved our first innocence.   But if we were born in original sin, if we have stained ourselves over and over again with actual sins, if we have contracted innumerable debts against Divine justice, if we have deserved, I know not how many times, eternal damnation—is it not a chastisement far too mild for us to be treated as if we were nothing, and is not a sinner infinitely beneath that which is nothing?   Whatever trial he may suffer from God, whatever ill-treatment he may have to bear from his neighbour, has he any right to complain?   Can he accuse God of severity, or men of injustice?, Ought he not to think himself too happy to be able to save himself from eternal torments by patiently bearing these small temporal trials?   If religion is not a delusion altogether, if what faith teaches us about sin and the punishments it incurs is really true, how can a sinner whom God wishes to pardon dare to think that he does not deserve whatever he may have to endure here below, even if his life were to last for millions of ages?   Yes, it is a sovereign injustice, it is a monstrous ingratitude, for any one who has offended God—and which of us has not offended Him?—not to accept with a good heart and most thankfully, with love and zeal for the interests of God, all that it may please the Divine Goodness to send him in the way of sufferings and

humiliations. And what shall we say if these sufferings, these passing humiliations, are not merely to be
instead of the punishments of hell, but if they are to
be the price of an eternal felicity, of the eternal possession of God—if we are to be raised high in glory in
proportion as we have been humbled and annihilated
in this world? Shall we still fear this annihilation?
And shall we think that we are being wronged when
we are required to annihilate ourselves because we
are really nothing, and because we are sinners, while
all the time we have the promise of a reward which
will never end?

I may add that this way of annihilation, against
which nature cries out so strongly, is not really so
painful as we imagine, and it is even sweet. For,
first of all, our Lord and Saviour Jesus Christ has
said so. "*Take My yoke upon you*," He says, "*for it
is easy and light.*" However heavy this yoke may be
in itself, God will lighten it to those who willingly
take it up, and who consent to bear it for the love
of Him. Love does not prevent us from suffering,
but it makes us love our sufferings and prefer them
to all pleasures.

The reward, even in this world, of annihilating
ourselves, is a peace of heart, a calm of our passions,
a cessation of all the agitations of our mind, of all
murmurs and interior revolts.

Let us examine the proof of this in detail. What
is the greatest evil of suffering? It is not the suffering itself, but it is our rebellion against it, it is the
state of interior revolt which so often accompanies it.
A soul that is perfectly annihilated will suffer all the

evils imaginable without losing the sweet repose of
its blessed state : this is a matter of experience.   It
costs a great deal to attain to this state of annihilation, we must make the greatest efforts over ourselves ;
but when we have once attained it we enjoy a peace
and repose proportionate to the victories we have
gained.   The habit of renouncing ourselves and of
dying to ourselves becomes every day more and more
easy, and we are astonished at last to find that what
seemed to us once intolerable, what so frightened our
imaginations, raised up our passions, and put our
whole nature in a state of rebellion, does not even
give us the least pain after a certain time.

In all contempt we may have to suffer, in all
calumnies and humiliations, the thing which really
hurts us and really makes them hard to bear is our
own pride; it is because we wish to be esteemed
and considered, and treated with a certain respect,
and that we do not at all like the idea of being
treated with ridicule and contempt by others.   This
is what really agitates us, and makes us indignant,
and renders our life bitter and insupportable.   Let us
set seriously to work to annihilate ourselves, let us
give no food to pride, let us put away from us all
the first movements of self-esteem and self-love, and
let us accept patiently and joyfully, in the depth of
our soul, all the little mortifications which are offered
to us.   Little by little we shall come not to care in
the very least about what is thought of us or said
of us, or how we are treated.   A person who is dead
feels nothing; for him there is no more honour or
reputation ; praise and blame to him are equal.

In the service of God, the cause of most of the trouble we experience is that we do not annihilate ourselves sufficiently in His Divine presence; it is because we have a sort of life which we try to preserve in all our dealings with Him; it is because we allow a secret pride to insinuate itself into our devotion. Hence it comes that we are not indifferent, as we ought to be, as to whether we are in dryness or in consolation; that we are very unhappy when God seems to withdraw from us, that we exhaust ourselves in desires and efforts to call Him back to us, and fall into the most wretched depression and desolation if His absence lasts a long time.

From this cause too proceeds all our false alarms about the state of our souls. We think God must be angry with us because He deprives us of the sweetness of sensible devotion. We think our Communions have been bad because we have made them without any great fervour; the same with our spiritual reading, our prayer, all our other practices of piety.

Let us serve God, once for all, in the spirit of annihilation; let us serve Him for Himself alone, not for ourselves; let us sacrifice our own interests for His glory and His good pleasure; then we shall always be quite contented with the way in which He treats us, being persuaded that we deserve nothing, and that He is too good, I do not say to accept, but to permit our services.

In all great temptations against purity, or against faith or hope, what is most painful to us is not exactly our fear of offending God, but our fear of

N

losing ourselves through offending Him. We are much more occupied with the thought of our own interest than of His glory. This is why our confessor has so much difficulty in reassuring us, and in making us obey him. We think he is deceiving us, that he is leading us astray, that he is ruining us, because he requires us to pass over and set aside our vain fears. Let us annihilate our own judgment; let us prefer blind obedience to all else; let us even consent, if it is necessary, to be lost through obedience: then we shall find that all our perplexities, all the anguish of our soul, all our interior torments, will cease. We shall find peace, and a most exquisite and perfect peace, in the total forgetfulness of ourselves. There is nothing in heaven, or on earth, or in hell, that can trouble the peace of a soul that is really annihilated.

XXXI.

ON GENEROSITY.

THERE are two kinds of generosity, one which is natural, the other which is supernatural: both come from God; and the first kind of generosity disposes us for the second. To enter upon the way of perfection, to walk in it and to persevere in it to the end, we have need of a great foundation of generosity, because this way is only one continued series of sacrifices, each one greater and more difficult than those that went before. Thus, all the souls whom

God destines to great sanctity have in themselves a certain nobility of thought and feeling which raises them above the things of this earth, and at the same time a certain tenderness of heart which makes them deeply . sensible of the sufferings of others, so that they gladly deprive themselves of what they have to succour those who are in need. Now, it is from the union of these two beautiful natural qualities, elevation of thought and feeling and tenderness of heart, that true generosity springs. A soul that is low and earthly, and wrapped up in the things of this world, a soul that is hard and insensible to the sufferings of others, can seldom be generous ; it may practise devotion in the spirit of self-interest and to ensure its salvation, but naturally it will always be mean and narrow, will give to God the very least it possibly can, and will never have the slightest conception of the great sacrifices which God asks of His saints. But although natural generosity disposes us for supernatual generosity, the two things are very different, whether we consider them by themselves or in their motives.

Natural generosity scarcely consists in anything more than giving to others a part of what we have ; instead of which supernatural generosity makes us give to God not only all that we have, but all that we are. It carries us on to sacrifice to Him our mind, our will, our liberty, our health, our life, our reputation—to consent, in fact, to the total destruction of our own individuality and of all that belongs to us, and in which our dearest interests are concerned.

Now it is easy, says Saint Gregory, to give up what we have, but it is exceedingly difficult to give up what we are, and to renounce ourselves; and without the most special grace from God, and without the greatest efforts of generosity on our part, we shall never do it. We think we have done everything when, in certain moments of fervour and sensible devotion, we have given ourselves to God with all our heart, and have protested to Him that we are ready to pass through any trial, to suffer everything, to sacrifice everything, for the love of Him. But this is only a sacrifice in intention and preparation; the real sacrifice is quite another thing.

When God wishes to lead us by the way of real sacrifice, He generally begins by taking away from us all sensible fervour; He permits all kinds of repugnances, of rebellion of nature, and a general upheaval of self-love. It is then that we feel an inexpressible opposition and aversion to all that God asks of us, a violent interior combat which reduces the soul to a sort of agony. We desire that the chalice of bitterness may pass from us; we beg of God that it may do so: in fact, nature rebels with all her strength against her destruction. But at the same time our will, sustained by Divine grace in a manner that is very powerful, although it is imperceptible to us, our will remains unshaken in its submission; it receives the blows and feels all the weight of them, but it bears them with courage, and is not cast down.

Sometimes, at the moment when the blow first falls, the soul is in peace, strong and contented; but immediately afterwards trouble seizes her, the imagination begins to work, self-love awakes; and all these interior agitations weary the soul, leave her no rest, and only cease after a longer or shorter period, as long as it may please God to make the trial and the battle continue. This trial will come back again and again, until the soul is perfectly dead to the particular object which was the cause of the agitation. Then God passes on to another trial, and so on from sacrifice to sacrifice until the end.

But why does God permit these repugnances and these results, either before or after the sacrifice? For several reasons worthy of His infinite wisdom. First, to teach the soul to know herself, to understand how bad she is, how opposed to all that is good, how incapable of the least effort of generosity, and in this way to keep her in a profound humility; for she would be tempted to take credit to herself, and to attribute her sacrifice to her own strength, if God did not make her feel all the difficulty of it. Secondly, she learns by this to know better the value of grace, and how necessary it is for her to trust only in God, since she can find no strength, no support in herself. Thirdly, the more resistance she feels in herself, the more obstacles she has to overcome, the greater also will be her merit; the longer the combat lasts, the more complete will be the victory; the more nature is destroyed, the more God will be glorified and the devil put to confusion, and the more experience and skill will the soul acquire in the secrets of the interior life.

As all our generosity comes from God, He hides the knowledge of it from us for fear we should deprive Him of the glory which belongs to Him alone.

From the little I have just said it is easy to judge

how great is the difference between natural generosity
and supernatural generosity, and that the supernatural is exercised upon objects much more interesting to us, and also is incomparably more difficult and
painful for us, than the other. They do not differ
less in their motives. There is always a good deal
of self-love, and even a great deal, in the exercise
of natural generosity. It is often mixed with self-
interest, with vanity, and pride; we think ourselves
superior to those whom we oblige; we take credit to
ourselves for a nobility of feeling which raises us
above the common herd of mankind; we are delighted
with the praises bestowed upon us; we praise ourselves, and enjoy complacently a certain interior satisfaction.

Not one of these motives can sully the exercise of
supernatural generosity. Self-love can find no nourishment there, for it is against self-love and at its
expense that this kind of generosity is exercised.
Our own interest has no place there, for this generosity leads us to sacrifice it entirely to God's interest.
Our victories cost us so dear, and are so painful to
us, that we are not exposed to the danger of being
vain of them. Our interior and exterior humiliations
protect us from pride and from the praise of men.
Everything here is for God, and only for God; and
this it is which gives to this generosity a character
so sublime and Divine, that we see at once it can be
nothing else but the work of Divine grace.

When it pleases God to require great sacrifices of
a soul, He will give her a proportionate generosity,
He will enlarge her heart, He will elevate her senti-

ments; He will give her the highest possible idea of what His rights are, and will make her see that all she can do for Him is nothing, and less than nothing; that it is pure goodness on His part to be willing to accept of the little she can offer Him; that all the glory which the voluntary annihilation of all His creatures could procure to Him, would add nothing to His greatness and His felicity; and finally, that He does us an inestimable honour when He deigns to accept our offerings and our sacrifices.

When a soul is once penetrated with these ideas, she sees clearly that up to this time she has done nothing for God; she conceives an immense desire of devoting herself entirely to Him; and because all she could do and suffer for His infinite Majesty would not be worthy of Him, she begs of Him to glorify Himself through her in any manner which may please Him, and she gives herself up entirely to Him for this purpose. From that moment her heart opens, and, as much as a little creature is capable of such a thing, she becomes fit for the greatness of the designs of God. The yoke of the commandments, and even of the counsels, which seems so heavy and so burdensome to ordinary Christians, becomes to her light and sweet; she is astonished that God asks so little of her; she would like to do a thousand times more for the love of Him. This is what David experienced when he said, "*I will run the way of Thy commandments, when Thou hast set my heart at liberty.*" Before that he walked with difficulty and effort, he found the way too hard and too narrow, because his heart was narrow and ungenerous. Now that God, by taking possession of his heart, has communicated to it something of His own immensity, he walks no longer; he runs, he flies—no difficulty, no obstacle, can stop him.

It is only too true that in the service of God everything depends upon the disposition of our hearts, and that what appears a great deal to a soul that is mean and concentrated on itself is nothing at all to a generous soul who has come out of herself to lose herself in God. Let us then continually ask of God for this generosity. Let us beg of Him never to allow us to measure what we owe to Him by our own narrow and finite ideas, but to raise us up to His own ideas of Himself, and to teach us to serve Him as God ought to be served. To serve God as God! Oh! what a magnificent thought! But the execution of it is infinitely beyond us. There is only one way of accomplishing this service, and that is to offer ourselves to God, that He may dispose of us absolutely; that He may strip us of our own spirit and clothe us with His; that He may give us a heart according to His own heart. Let us ask this incessantly, and to deserve an answer, upon which depends the greater glory of God, and our own perfection, let us observe our inviolable fidelity to every movement of Divine grace. The less we are conducted according to our own views, the more we are conducted according to the designs of God; for there is no more proportion between the ideas of God, as to what constitutes holiness, and ours, than there is between His Divine nature and our nature; and as long as we are only generous in our own way we are not so in His way.

XXXII.

ON OBEDIENCE.

OF all the virtues, that of which the practice costs the most to man is obedience. To give up our own will, to sacrifice our own judgment, to depend upon another not only as to our way of acting, but even in our way of thinking and judging—and this not with regard to indifferent things, or things of no great consequence, but with regard to things pertaining to our salvation and sanctity—this is something much more difficult than privations, or fasts, or austerities. Obedience attacks a man in that which is nearest to him, in his liberty, in his right to dispose of himself as he likes. It attacks his self-love where it seems to be most reasonable and to have a good foundation. What is more just, apparently, than to judge of things according to our own reason, to guide ourselves according to our own light, and only to consult others as far as we think proper? What seems more revolting to our good sense, at first sight, than to give to another all authority over us in what regards our conduct, to do nothing without his consent, and to execute blindly whatever he advises or commands, without the least resistance even in the depths of our own souls? This sacrifice is, without contradiction, the greatest we can possibly make. It is a universal sacrifice, because it embraces every moment of our lives; and it is the most interesting of all, because it concerns our future life and our eternal happiness.

Now, this is the sacrifice which God specially requires from every soul which aspires to perfection. Yes, He requires it as a condition without which there can be for that soul neither holiness nor true virtue. Whatever she may do if she follows her own will, if she directs herself, if she considers herself the mistress of her own actions, she will never please God, because self-love and her own spirit spoil all her good works. God declared to the Jews, by the mouth of His prophet, that their fasts were not pleasing to Him because they did them of their own will. "Does God desire sacrifices and victims?" said Samuel to Saul. "What He desires, is it not rather that you should obey His voice? for obedience is better than sacrifices, and to hearken than to offer the fat of rams." These words are of great importance, for they show us that it is obedience before all things which can give any value to what we do, since even the acts of religion have nothing in themselves which can please God unless they are done through obedience.

God therefore requires this virtue of us as the one which is most pleasing to Him, and which gives a particular merit to all the other virtues. To speak more clearly : by the other virtues man gives to God what he possesses, but he does not give himself; he keeps back that which God asks of him above everything else. But by obedience he gives himself, and he gives himself entirely, for what does a man refuse to God when he sacrifices to Him his liberty, and desires to depend only on Him for all things ?

But you may say, " If I desire to depend only on God, what need is there that I should obey a man ? Is it not sufficient if I listen to the voice of Divine grace, and follow its interior inspirations ? "

My reply is, in the first place, that Divine grace and Divine inspiration would lead you to submit yourself to a man because this is the order established by God, Who in spiritual things as in temporal governs us through the ministry of men clothed with His authority. I reply, in the second place, that nothing is more dangerous or more exposed to delusion than to constitute ourselves judges as to what are Divine inspirations; and that we shall most certainly go astray if we take for the will of God or the voice of God any strange imaginations which rise up from our heart or pass through our mind. Finally I reply, that in all this there is evidently an insupportable pride, a presumption which God will not fail to punish by abandoning to his own reprobate senses that self-willed person who would not submit himself to the authority which was established to guide him. " But why," you may still say, " should I submit myself to a man who after all may be deceived, and may lead me wrong ? " The man to whom you submit yourself holds the place of God : you need have no doubts about it ; God has appointed him to guide you in the way of salvation. If you place yourself under his guidance in all good faith, solely with the view of obeying God, you may confidently believe that God will enlighten him, and will give you, through his lips, all the instructions necessary for you. You may believe that God will never allow you to go astray so long as you walk in the way which He Himself has marked out for you, and that His very Providence is engaged in preserving you from error. I am always supposing, however, that your director, in all his conversation and his conduct, has never given you any reason to suspect his faith or his piety, or his good life or his capacity; because if the contrary is the case, then you must of course leave him. But when you are once thoroughly convinced that he is a good man and an enlightened man, then you must resign yourself entirely to his guidance, without the slightest fear of running any risks as to your salvation or your perfection. God would never permit such a man to be deceived in anything that was essential, and He would set right, through His infinite goodness, any little mistakes into which he might fall, so that they should hurt neither you nor him. This is what you must believe with a firm faith. Without this, you would be for ever at the mercy of a host of doubts, uneasinesses, and scruples; the foundations of your obedience would have nothing of firmness and solidity about them; and it would be impossible for you to bear all those temptations and trials, in which God wishes us always to sacrifice our own judgment to that of our director.

The way of obedience is then not only a sure way, but the only sure way—the only way where we know God will take care of us, the only way to which He promises His grace and blessing. This way puts the soul in perfect safety, for in everything she does she may reassure herself by saying, " I am not acting of myself, I am not following my own will, I am not governing myself by my own decisions : it is God Who is deciding for me, it is God Who is guiding me by means of him who is for me the interpreter of God's will. I am more certain of doing the will of God, by following obedience, than if God Himself were to speak to me ; for then I might be deceived, and take for the voice of God the suggestions of the devil or my own imagination ; whereas it is impossible for me to be deceived as long as I accept as the commands of God all that is prescribed for me by obedience. What a sweet peace, what an ineffable calm, this certainty produces in the soul !

This way, as I have already said, gives an infinite value to the smallest things we do, through the principle of obedience ; because even in the smallest things is found that which is greatest of all, and that is the sacrifice of our own will. Wherever God does not see our will, He sees His own ; and wherever He sees His own will *only*, can He possibly see anything that can please Him more ?

This way is the way of annihilation, the way of adoration in spirit and in truth, the way of perpetual sacrifice. For what remains to the soul that has no longer either judgment or will of her own ? What has she reserved to herself ? Nothing · all is sacrificed, all is immolated. God has everything that was once hers, because He has her liberty, and disposes of it as if it were His own.

The merit of obeying a mortal man for God's sake is so great that it surpasses that of obeying God in His own Person; for if I were to see God, and if He Himself were to communicate His will to me, I should not have the merit of faith, and it would cost me nothing then to submit my judgment to His judgment and my will to His will. The practice of obedience embraces perfectly the practice of all the other virtues. It renders us invincible to the attacks of the devil; it raises us above all temptations and trials; it draws down upon us the choicest graces of Heaven. God can refuse nothing to an obedient soul; He looks at that soul with an extreme complacency; He delights in loading her with His gifts and favours.

Obedience is therefore a short way to perfection. Let us attach ourselves to it above all else. Let us neglect nothing which it prescribes for us. Let us take care never to reason about it, nor to try to submit it to our own light: for it is no longer obedience when we seek to know the reason of the commandment. We must believe blindly, we must bring our understanding into captivity, we must force all the aversions of nature; and, as soon as ever a thing is commanded us, we must do it, whatever it may cost us. Thus our Lord and Master Jesus Christ was obedient even unto death, even to the death of the cross. Let us take Him for our model; our obedience will never go so far as His did. From His birth to His death, He never did His own will in anything. "*He pleased not Himself.*" Can such a thing be said of us, reckoning from the time when we really gave ourselves to God!

XXXIII.

ON HUMILITY.

"Learn of Me, for I am meek and humble of heart, and you shall find rest for your souls."

MEEKNESS is the fruit of Christian humility; and Jesus Christ joins these two virtues together here, because one depends upon the other. Every man who is really humble of heart is meek; and whoever fails in meekness is wanting also in humility, which is the principle of meekness.

It is a strange thing that our Lord Jesus Christ does not tell us to learn by His example to be meek and humble of heart, but to learn that He is humble of heart. And why is this? Is it then a virtue which His example cannot teach us? Yes: we cannot be humble in the same manner that Jesus Christ was humble. If humility consists in abasing ourselves lower than we are, it is Jesus Christ alone Who could be truly humble. He Who, being of the nature of God, was made man, and took upon Himself everything that is vile and contemptible in the sight of men, He alone was truly humble, because He united Himself to a nature infinitely inferior to His own; He was humble, because in this nature which He assumed to Himself He submitted to all the humiliations which are due to a proud sinner who deserves to be the outcast of God and man. He was humble of heart, because His humility was a humility of choice, a sincere humility, accompanied by all those interior sentiments which befit the state of a voluntary victim for sin. It is therefore impossible for us to be humble in the same way that Jesus Christ was. As we are nothing from the very beginning, how can we make ourselves any less, or place ourselves below what we are by nature? Sinners by our own free will, deserving of the curse of God and of the punishments of hell, worthy only of contempt and horror, and thus infinitely below nothing, to what a state could we be further reduced which might pass for a state of humility? When we place ourselves on the level of nothing, we are only doing ourselves simple justice, even if we had never been guilty of any sin. And when we consent to be treated by God and all creatures as a sinner deserves to be treated, still we only do ourselves simple justice, even if we had only committed one mortal sin. How then shall we humble ourselves, how shall we lower ourselves, we who have been guilty of a host of mortal sins? Let us confess, once for all, that we are so low that it is impossible for us to descend lower. Let us confess that, in the natural order and the supernatural order, in this life and in the life to come, there is no confusion, no contempt, no ignominy, which is not less than we deserve. And even when we have acknowledged all this in the sincerity of our hearts, when we have submitted to all the humiliations which a guilty creature deserves, when we have fully recognised that we do only deserve these humiliations, we are still obliged to confess that to bear all this is *not* humility on our part, but simply the acceptation of a most just chastisement.

If this is true, if nothing is more evident in the very principles of faith, where are we, and what is our pride, when we cannot suffer either from God or men the slightest shadow of contempt or the least apparent neglect? The very idea of contempt disgusts us, troubles us, and makes us angry; we cannot persuade ourselves that when we are despised it is just what we deserve, and that it is impossible for us to be despised too much. We avoid with the greatest care everything that could make us lose the false esteem of men; we sacrifice our duties, our Divine inspirations, the most vivid and certain teachings of our conscience, through a fear of ridicule or of a false and contemptible opinion which others may have of us. It seems to us the most painful effort of virtue to appear in the eyes of the world as we really are in the eyes of God, and we are not capable of this effort; and in a thousand occasions we break our promises, and are false to our good resolutions.

Again I say, what pride! How unjust! How senseless! How abominable in the sight of God! And even if we were ashamed of this pride, if we humbled ourselves when we reflected on it! But no; we take credit to ourselves for it; we think we have very noble and elevated sentiments; we treat as mean and foolish and extravagant the esteem which the saints have had of humiliations, and the holy eagerness with which they have embraced them.

If we were really humble with the humility which is fitting for us, we should make no account, either

o

in ourselves or in others, of good birth, or of intellect, or of beauty, or of riches, or of any other natural gifts; we should never make of any of these things an occasion for thinking more highly of ourselves or for despising others who do not possess them. For all these advantages do not really belong to us, to us who are only nothingness: God has given them to us out of pure liberality, and His intention never was that we should be vain of them. More than this, these advantages are of no use in themselves for our salvation. And if we make a bad use of them, they are only for us so many occasions of sin. We have then no reason to think well of ourselves on account of them; on the contrary, we have every reason to humble ourselves. If we were humble with the humility which is fitting for us, we should think ourselves unworthy of the esteem of men, and we should refer to God alone all their praises, without reserving anything for ourselves, considering that as a theft from His Divine glory. Neither should we fear their contempt, knowing that we deserve it, inasmuch as we are great sinners. We should even be very glad to be despised, hoping by it to be able to satisfy the Divine justice. Undoubtedly we must not do anything which really deserves blame, but we must not take too many precautions to escape the judgments of men; and when our good actions draw upon us calumnies, and ridicule, and contempt on their part, we ought to rejoice for ourselves, and to pity them.

If we were humble with the humility which befits us, we should serve God thinking less of our own

interest than of His, convinced that we deserve
nothing, and that it is an excess of goodness on
His part to allow of our serving Him at all. We
should receive all His graces with gratitude; and
far from appropriating them to ourselves, or priding
ourselves on them, they would only serve to humble
us still more by the thought of our own unworthi-
ness, and we should refer them all to God with
the same purity as they came from Him to us. We
should not be at all surprised or distressed if He
seems to repel us, or if He seems to pay no attention to what we are doing for Him; we should not
expect Him to set any value on our fidelity, our
constancy, or our generosity; we should never be
jealous of the favours He may show to others, but
we should think, like the poor woman of Canaan,
that the children's bread is not for dogs, and that we
are too happy if we may pick up the crumbs which
fall from their table. If God turns His face from us,
or if He looks at us severely and seems to be angry
with us, if He makes us experience some of the effects
of His justice, we should humbly submit ourselves
to Him, saying with the prophet, "I will bear the
weight of the anger of the Lord, because I have
sinned against Him." It is quite right that, as I am
a sinner, I should satisfy the Divine justice; I ought
not to wish to dispute the right of God to punish me.

Thus the humble soul sees nothing that she does
not deserve in the hardest treatment that she may
have to bear, either from God or men. All she asks
for is for strength to bear it, and that God may
derive glory from it. As for herself, she consents

with all her heart to be destroyed utterly, and she
does not consider what happens to her as a trial, but
rather as a just chastisement, too slight in comparison
with what her sins deserve. Acquiescing with all
that God makes her suffer, she finds her peace, her
strength, and her happiness in humility; she is delighted that God should be satisfied, and that at the
expense of all that she has He should receive what is
due to His Divine justice.

But how shall we attain to this humility? By
resigning ourselves entirely to God and leaving all
our interests in His hands. We may give ourselves.
And when this gift is made absolutely and entirely,
and without thought of return, God will accomplish
His designs upon us, and will give us all that is
necessary for us to co-operate with Him. He will
give us above all things that perfect humility which
is so deep, so generous, so peaceful, so unchanging,
which on the one hand makes us, as sinners, less
than nothing, and on the other hand, raises us above
the world, above the devil, above ourselves, and
makes us great with the greatness of God, strong
with the strength of God, holy with the holiness
of God. This humility is an infused humility; it
grows in us in proportion to our temptations, our
sufferings, and our humiliations. We have it, but we
do not know that we have it, because if we thought
ourselves humble we should think we were lower
than we deserve to be; whereas such a thought
could never enter the mind of a saint, who on the contrary is always quite certain that God and men treat
him infinitely better than he deserves to be treated.

XXXIV.

ON THE PROVIDENCE OF GOD FOR HIS CHILDREN.

Saint Paul says that "*all things work together for good to them that love God.*" And as this maxim is used very often, when we are treating of the spiritual life it is important that we should quite understand the meaning of it, that we should discern the reason of it and examine its consequences.

First of all, the Apostle says, "*all things.*" He excepts nothing. All the events of Providence, whether fortunate or unfortunate, everything that has to do with health, or wealth, or reputation; every condition of life, all the different interior states through which we may have to pass—desolations, dryness, disgust, weariness, temptations, all this is to be for the advantage of those who love God; and more than this, even our faults, even our sins. We must be resolved never to offend God wilfully; but if unfortunately we do offend Him, our very offences, our very crimes may be made use of for our advantage, if we really love God. We have only to remember David, we have only to remember Saint Peter, whose sins only served to make them more holy afterwards, that is to say, more humble, more grateful to God, more full of love.

"*All things work together for good.*" It is not a temporal good, not an earthly good. The Gospel

warns us of that often enough.   We are no longer
under the dominion of the law, which promised
temporal rewards to those who observed it; but we
are under the rule of grace, which only announces
to those who wish to walk in the way of perfection
crosses and persecutions, and only promises to them·
spiritual rewards.   This is not difficult to understand : all things work together for the *spiritual* good
of those that love God.   Nevertheless, we must
understand this good not according to our own ideas,
which are often mistaken, but according to the designs
of God.   If there is one subject more than another
upon which we are liable to be deceived, it is upon
all that concerns our spiritual interests.   We form
the most false ideas about it, and often consider that
as hurtful to our soul which is in reality most useful,
and also that as advantageous which is in reality
full of harm.   Our self-love leads us on this matter
into the strangest delusions.   We must therefore
believe—but with a belief that is born of faith, and
that does not rest on our own judgment—that our
true good and our true advantage is found in the
events of Divine Providence, and in all the different
interior states through which God makes us pass,
although often we cannot understand what God
means to do with us, and are quite ignorant as to
what the end of these things is to be.

But all these Divine arrangements are only a good
for those who love God, that is to say, for those
whose will is united and submissive to the will of
God—those who in His service consider before all
things the interests of God, the glory of God, and

the accomplishment of His good pleasure—who are ready to sacrifice to Him everything without exception, and who are persuaded that there is nothing better for a creature than to be lost in God and for God, because it is the only means of finding one's self again in Him : this is what I call loving God truly, and with one's whole heart. And this is what Jesus Christ meant when He said, " He that loves his soul shall lose it ; and he that loses his soul for My sake shall find it in eternal life." Whoever loves God in this manner is quite certain, and certain with an infallible certainty, that everything that God wills or permits with regard to him will be for his good, and even for his greatest good. He will not see it at the moment, because it is essential that he should not see it, and the sacrifices he has to make would not be accomplished if he did see it, but he will see it at the proper time. He will admire the wisdom and the infinite goodness of God in the wonderful way in which He leads the souls which belong to Him entirely ; and he will see with astonishment that the very things which he feared would be for his hopeless ruin are those which have made his salvation assured.

It is not difficult to understand upon what foundation Saint Paul based this maxim.

God alone has the right idea of what sanctity is ; He alone knows, and He alone has at His disposal, the means which can lead us to it. He alone also knows what is in the secret depths of our souls, our sentiments, our natural character, and the obstacles which are to be found there against our sanctity ;

He alone knows what secret motives will move us, and how to bring us to the end which He intends for our sanctification without in any way constraining our free-will. He knows what effect such and such an event, such and such a temptation, such and such a trial, will produce upon us; and on His part all is prepared that it may have good success. God has loved us from all eternity; He loved us first before we could love Him, and there is nothing in us that is good, either in the order of nature or grace, which He has not given to us. He loves us with a love that is infinitely wise, infinitely enlightened; He loves us not so much with regard to this present life, which is only passing away, only a time of trial, but with regard to the future life, which is our destination and our final end. If then it is true that everything that happens here to the servants of God is over-ruled and arranged by infinite Love and Wisdom for their eternal happiness, it can only be through their own fault if the designs of God are not fulfilled; and if one single event happens which does not conduce to their spiritual advantage, it is most certainly through their want of love and trust, and their failing in conformity to the will of God. For, as long as they love God with a real, effective, and practical love, it is impossible for anything in the world to keep them back; on the contrary, everything will help to their advancement in perfection, and will contribute to it.

The consequences of this maxim of the Apostle extend to everything, and embrace every moment of life. The first is, that if we wish to make sure of our salvation, as far as it is possible to do so, we must give ourselves up, we must abandon ourselves to God without reserve and for ever; we must not wish to dispose of ourselves in anything; we must foresee nothing, arrange nothing, determine nothing, except in the most entire dependence upon God's good pleasure; we must not make one step or one single movement to take ourselves out of the actual situation where we are placed by the order of God; we must not even desire to come out of it; but we must allow ourselves, so to speak, to be drawn by the thread of Divine Providence, and submit to every event as it happens: and as to what regards our innermost soul, we must remain quiet, and without having any fears about the state in which God chooses us to be, without wishing for the change or the end of this state, however painful it may be to human nature.

The second conclusion to be drawn is, that when we have contributed nothing to bring about a certain event, either exterior or interior, we may be quite sure that this event or this disposition of soul is the will of God for us, and consequently that it is the very best thing for us at the present moment. Thus we ought to be very careful not to have a contrary opinion, nor to think that such and such a thing is unfortunate for us, or that it will do harm to our spiritual progress, or that God has forsaken us and will take no more care of us. We are very apt to judge in this manner when we find no more pleasure in our spiritual exercises, when we feel no longer that sweet peace and tranquillity of soul which we once enjoyed, when we are attacked by violent temptations, when God takes away from us all exterior support, even when He separates us from a person in whom we had placed all our confidence. Then we think all is lost, because we see ourselves alone and without a guide. But we are quite mistaken. God never acts so efficaciously as when He acts by Himself, and when He takes away all external and sensible help; and His grace is never more real and strong that when we have no sensible proof of it. And our cause for assurance is never greater than when we think we have lost all assurance.   But the chief thing is to know how to put our trust in God alone, in utter abandonment, in bare faith, without any reasonings or reflections, confiding ourselves and our interests entirely into the hands of God.   It is then that, hoping against hope, we must say to ourselves, "Yes, I believe most firmly that all this will be for my good, and that if I abandon myself entirely to God I shall not be confounded."

The third conclusion to be drawn is, that when we have once given ourselves to God we must expect all kinds of sacrifices, and above all the sacrifice of our own will and our own judgment; we must expect to meet with many things in God's dealings with us which will strangely try our reason, and will oblige us not to listen to its voice at all. We must expect all sorts of things that are most displeasing to our senses and most mortifying, all sorts of sufferings and humiliations, all sorts of interior and exterior disturbances which we could never foresee, which pass all our conceptions, and of which neither spiritual books nor the experience of others could ever give us the least idea. Finally, we must expect that God will carry fire and sword into the very depths of our hearts, that He will root out and burn up our self-love entirely, and that He will leave us nothing of our own. This is undoubtedly very terrible to human nature; but the love of God, if it is what it ought to be, and if we allow it to do with us as He pleases, will dispose us for all these sacrifices, and will not allow us to omit one. How could the maxim of Saint Paul be true, if among all the things which God requires of a soul, there was one single one that was not for her spiritual and eternal advantage, and which therefore she thought she might refuse to God? No: the Apostle says, "*all things;*" and that great and noble soul who, following the example of Jesus Christ, wished that he might even be accursed—without however any fault on his own part—for the sake of the salvation of the Jews, his brothers, never thought that such a wish, so glorious to God, and so in conformity with the sentiments of Jesus Christ, could do otherwise than turn to his own advantage. However great our sacrifices may be, they can never come up to those of our Divine Master; and if His immolation of Himself, which was perfect, has procured for His Sacred Humanity a glory and happiness above all that we can express or imagine; we may believe with a firm faith that our immolation, imperfect as it may be, will procure for us a glory and happiness in proportion to the extent and the generosity of the sacrifice.

XXXV.

ON THE PRICE OF A SOUL.

If, on the one hand, religion humbles a man by teaching him that he comes from nothing, that he was conceived in sin, that he is inclined to evil and incapable of any supernatural good, on the other hand it raises him up, and inspires him with great thoughts about himself, by teaching him what his nature is really capable of through the grace of God, what is the greatness of his destiny, and what it cost God to purchase his salvation.

The human soul, by its very nature, is endowed with the faculty of knowing God and the capacity for loving Him. The intelligence of the soul, transporting itself above all that is created and finite, has power to raise itself even to the contemplation of that Being Who alone is uncreated and infinite, Who is the source of all good and all perfection ; it is able to form of Him an idea that is clear, and accurate, and indelible. The will of the soul is made to love this sovereign Good which the understanding presents to it. The desires of the soul, which no created object can ever satisfy, and which reach far beyond the limits of this life, tend necessarily towards a Good that is supreme, eternal, and infinite, and which alone can content the soul and make her happy.

If the soul will analyse the desire which she has of happiness, and the idea of happiness which presents itself to her, she will find that the object of this idea and of this desire is only and can only be God. This is the impression which she bears in the depths of her nature, this is what reason will teach her if she will only reflect a little, and this is what neither prejudice nor passion can ever entirely efface. Everything that is not God, everything that does not relate to God, is unworthy of occupying the mind or the heart of man, has no proportion with the immensity of his ideas and desires, and can never fully satisfy them. The very heathen philosophers comprehended this truth up to a certain point; and this was what rendered man so great in their eyes. Happy would they have been if in their conduct they had followed the light of their reason and the secret instinct of their hearts!

Not only is man destined to know and to love God in this life, but in another life he is to possess God eternally. It is not enough for him to be immortal; he is one day to be united to the Source of immortality, and to be happy with the very happiness of God. Of what use, indeed, would immortality be to him, if he were to be for ever consumed with a desire for God without ever possessing Him? Such a desire, if it were never satisfied, would only be a torment.

This is, then, the final end of man—the eternal enjoyment of God! He will see God; he will contemplate God as He is in Himself; and this sight and this contemplation will overwhelm him with an ineffable joy. Reason puts us in the way of learning this great truth, but Divine revelation alone can

give us distinct instructions upon it. And as it is
a wonderful gift, which certainly is not due to our
nature, we should never have known of it unless
God Himself had expressly revealed it; therefore
there is nothing like it in the writings of the wise
men of antiquity. But this eternal possession of God
is not promised to man absolutely and without con-
ditions; he must merit it by the good use which he
makes of his free-will during this short life; and God,
on His part, gives him and offers him everything that
is necessary for making a good use of his free-will.
And in what does this good use consist? In loving
and serving God according to the knowledge with
which reason and religion supply him; in practising
a certain number of precepts which in themselves
have nothing but what is just and right, and which
reason cannot help approving of, towards which an
upright heart is drawn of itself, and in the observa-
tion of which man finds, even in this world, peace and
happiness.

How great is man when we consider him from
this point of view! How noble are his ideas, how
elevated his sentiments, how pure his actions, how
worthy he is of the esteem of God and of his fellow-
men, when he thinks and speaks and acts always
with a view to this sublime destiny, when he never
loses sight of it, and when he never allows himself
anything that could draw him away from it! What
more just and excellent use can he make of his
reason and his liberty?

But how small is he, how mean, how foolish, how
unjust and cruel to himself, if, confining his ideas

and affections to this life, which is passing away, to this life, of which not one single moment is in his own power, he lowers himself to the enjoyment of things which were not made for him, to things which will always leave him empty and craving for more! and if, to procure himself this enjoyment, he tramples under foot the law of God, and exposes himself to the danger of losing for ever the eternal happiness which is awaiting him!

Is there any folly to compare with such folly as this? Can the degradation of our being be carried farther? Can a man be a greater enemy to himself? "*Be astonished, O Heavens,*" God Himself exclaims at the sight of such a strange perversity; "*Gates of Heaven, give yourselves up to desolation! My people*"—that is to say, those men that I formed in My own image, whom I destined to be the citizens of My kingdom, to share My glory and felicity — "*My people have committed two evils: they have forsaken Me, the Fountain of living water*" (of true happiness), "*and they have hewed themselves out broken cisterns that can hold no water.*" These two evils, which one could hardly believe possible on the part of a reasonable being, are nevertheless two very common evils, very prevalent, and, we might almost say, universal. In every country, in the very midst of enlightenment and religion, nearly all men forget God, despise God, offend God, look upon Him almost as a mortal enemy; and why? Because He created them for Himself, because He has destined them to enjoy His new happiness, because He wishes to associate them with His own eternal felicity, and because, for this reason,

He forbids them to fix their affections on fleeting and perishable pleasures, which are unworthy of them and incapable of ever satisfying them. Almost all men fix their eyes upon this earth, which is only the place of their exile, and will not look towards Heaven, which is their true country. They only desire immortality that so they may always possess the goods of this world; and they console themselves for the frightful prospect of death by the hope of returning to the nothingness from which they came.

But that which puts the crown on the real greatness of man, and on the sad disorder of his abasement of himself, is the thought of what the salvation of his soul has cost God. The Word of God, the eternal Son of God, Who was God like His Father, and equal in all things to His Father, united Himself to our human nature, took upon Himself our passible and mortal flesh, conversed with men, condescended to instruct them by His teaching and example, and finally, as a voluntary victim, sacrificed Himself for them to the Divine justice, to expiate their sins, to reconcile them to God, to restore to them the grace of their first innocence from which they had fallen, and to grant them all the assistance and all the means necessary for their salvation. That which our Lord and Saviour Jesus Christ did and suffered for all men, He did and suffered for each one in particular; and He would not have thought it too much to do if it had only been a question of saving one single soul. The salvation of a soul is then the price of the blood of God, the price of the death of God, the price of the greatest sacrifice which God

clothed in our human nature could possibly make!
This is incomprehensible; I know it is; and if this
mystery were not supported by all the weight of the
proofs of a divine revelation, human reason could
never bring itself to believe it.

But if this mystery is of a truth, and a certainty,
and a moral evidence which no reasonable mind can
deny, what does it prove? It proves that the dignity
of a soul is beyond understanding; for God to abase
Himself, for God to annihilate Himself, for God to
sacrifice Himself, only to save that soul, and make it
happy for ever! Can we be afraid of deceiving ourselves, when we esteem that which God esteemed so
much? And if, that we may save ourselves, God
requires of us the same sacrifice to which Jesus Christ
willingly submitted Himself, can we say that He
requires too much?

Again, what does this mystery prove? It proves
that a Christian who knows and understands it, and
who, to satisfy a miserable earthly passion, consents
to the eternal loss of his own soul, renders useless
the sufferings, the death, and the sacrifice of God;
and this is not saying enough: he turns them to his
eternal damnation, and makes for himself a hell a
thousand times deeper than that from which Jesus
Christ died to deliver him.

And what shall we say of those who, because this
mystery is so incomprehensible, treat it as a myth
and an absurdity? They do not wish that God
should have thought them worth so much: it was
not worth the trouble, they say, that God made Man
should die for them on a cross. The human soul is

P

too small a thing for its happiness to cost God so much. To hear them speak, it seems as if they were taking the part of God, and regarding His glory; they seem to think that it is an unbearable pride on the part of men to imagine that their souls could have such a high value. As if a mystery so Divine, so above human reason, so incredible, could ever have been an invention of human imagination or the fruit of human pride! Let us leave these impious ones, who vainly try to justify their impiety.

As for us, who believe humbly and firmly all that God has revealed to us, let us learn, by the contemplation of God upon a cross, what is the value of our souls; let us not lose our soul, let us not prostitute it to creatures, and to make sure of our eternal salvation, which cost so much to the Son of God, let us beg of Jesus Christ Himself to take charge of it, to lead us in the right way and guide us always. Such an inestimable treasure runs too great a risk in our own hands. Let us trust it to God and our Saviour; let us make Him the Master of our liberty, which we may so easily abuse, and the abuse of which may bring about such terrible consequences. Once abandoned to the safe and infallible guidance of His grace, we have no more to fear. He loves us too much, He takes too much interest in our salvation, ever to lose the price of His Blood and His sufferings.

XXXVI.

ON PURITY OF INTENTION.

OUR Lord Jesus Christ said : "*If thine eye be single*" (that is, *simple and pure*), "*thy whole body shall be full of light.*"

The intention is the eye of the soul, because it is the motive which makes the soul act, the end which the soul proposes to herself, and the torch which enlightens and guides her. If this eye of the soul is single, that is to say, if the intention is simple and pure, if it only looks to God, if it is not double, if it does not seek its own interests, then our whole body —that is to say, all our actions—will be holy and will be enlightened by the true light, which is God.

The simplicity of the intention also includes its uprightness and its purity. The intention is upright when we do not seek to deceive ourselves, when we act in good faith, when we do all we possibly can to learn and to follow the truth. This uprightness of intention is very rare amongst men. Errors, prejudices, passions, vices, and even smaller defects and failings do it great harm, and create a false conscience often upon very important matters. As long as we are not upon our guard, and always upon our guard against self-love—the most dangerous of all deceivers —we have always reason to mistrust the uprightness of our intentions, and we are not free from reproach in this respect.

The intention is pure when it is not mixed, when

God alone is the object of it, and when it is not infected by any motives of self-love. This purity of intention has its degrees, and is only perfect in the most holy souls ; indeed, it is precisely in this purity of intention that holiness really consists. As long as we love God with some thought of our own advantage remaining—as long as we do not love Him for Himself alone—as long as we seek our own interest in His service—as long as we seek ourselves ever so little—as long as we strive after perfection for our own sakes and for the spiritual good which it will bring to us—in a word, as long as the human *I* enters into our intention, so long will that intention be, I do not say positively criminal and bad, but mixed up with imperfection and impurity ; it will not have that beautiful simplicity which is so pleasing to God.[1]

Simplicity of intention absolutely excludes all multiplicity ; it does not rest upon several objects, but upon one alone, which is God ; and even in God it only considers His own glory, His good pleasure, and the accomplishment of His will. The simple intention is all for God ; the soul has no thought of herself there, she counts for nothing there : it is not that her true interests are really neglected—God forbid !— but she pays no attention to them, she forgets them, she is even ready to sacrifice them if God required such a sacrifice of her, and she consents with her whole heart to serve Him for Himself alone without any hope of return. When we reach such a point as this, our intention is perfectly simple and pure, it

---

[1] See p. 236, 2nd. This applies not to a permanent state of the soul but to transient feelings and actions.

communicates to even our smallest actions a value which is inestimable; God accepts them, God adopts them, looks upon them as His own, because they are done only with the view of pleasing Him; and we may imagine, when the time for rewards is come, will He not reward them liberally!

I boldly affirm that the least thing done with this purity of intention is of far greater value in the eyes of God than the greatest actions, those that are most painful and most mortifying to human nature, if they contain the least mixture of self-interest. It is because God does not look at the matter of our actions, but at the principle and the motive from which they spring; and because it is not what *we do* that glorifies Him, but the disposition of our hearts while we are doing it. We find a difficulty in understanding this because we cannot agree to put ourselves entirely on one side, and because our wretched self-love will glide in everywhere, and will corrupt and poison everything. But from its very nature the thing is and must be so; and if we will only consider ourselves we shall see that in the services rendered to us by others we follow the same rule as God does, and that we value these services less for what they are in themselves than on account of the affection which prompts them, and that it is this disposition of love and goodwill on the part of our neighbour which makes his services of real value in our eyes. The great difference between God and ourselves is that we cannot always be quite certain about this disposition of the heart, but God always can, because He always sees and reads our hearts.

But the truth remains; we wish, as He does, to be loved and served for our own sakes; this is what gives us pleasure, this is what makes the smallest action dear and precious to us; indeed, we think far more of the affection and goodwill to oblige us, even if no actual benefit follows, than we think of benefits that are not accompanied by the will to oblige us.

Now, we do not deserve to be loved and served for our own sakes; it is an injustice, it is a theft from God, when we desire to be loved in this way. But God does deserve it, and He alone has the right to claim such a love as this; He would have a right to it for many reasons even if, through His infinite goodness, He had not promised to reward our love and service.

But what must we do to attain to this purity of intention? One thing only: not guide ourselves, not dispose of ourselves in anything, but leave ourselves in the hands of God, and beg of Him to take charge of us not only as to exterior things but still more as to all that concerns our souls; that He would take possession of our mind and our heart; that He would inspire us with thoughts and affections and motives worthy of Him; that He would purify us from this leaven of self-love which is corrupting the innermost depths of our souls; and that, by means which He alone knows, and can alone make use of, He would at last raise us to this sublime purity. These means are hard to human nature, and they must be so, as their object is to destroy it. We must then expect to pass through many severe trials; but God will give to a generous soul the strength to bear them. She will feel that these trials are purifying her, that they are detaching her from herself, and uniting her to God more entirely; and this feeling will make them not only light and easy, but agreeable and desirable; so that, notwithstanding the extreme repugnance of nature, which cannot consent to its own destruction, she will accept them and embrace them with all her heart, and would not for anything in the world be delivered from them or see them at an end until the moment comes when God wills to deliver her.

All that we on our part have to do is, as soon as we perceive in our intentions anything that is human, or natural, or imperfect, to cast it away from us and disown it, following the light which God gives us. This light will change, according to the different states of soul into which we enter. At first it will only show us our most serious imperfections and faults; let us confine ourselves then to amending these, and let us take great care not to wish to be raised suddenly to a purity of disinterestedness of which we are not capable. Let us suffer God to act. Let us only have the intention that He may purify us; let us act with Him, making the sacrifices as He presents them to us; let us not try to go too fast, through the fervour of our imagination; and let us be quite sure that God will purify us at last by ways we could never have expected nor foreseen.

But is it not necessary, in every action we perform, to have an express and marked intention, and to say to ourselves "I do such and such a thing with such an intention"? This is what is called the

direction of our intention. I reply that, when we
have given ourselves once for all to God, this is not
necessary, or even advisable. The general intention
of always pleasing God, and always doing His will,
is quite sufficient; and we always have this intention
when once we have really and truly given ourselves
to Him. As long as this gift of ourselves to Him
lasts, the intention lasts also; there is no necessity
to renew it or to reflect upon it, or, so to speak, to
render an account of it to ourselves. If we ever
perceive that we are seeking ourselves in anything,
we have simply to give back to God what we were
taking away from Him after having once given it,
and then go on our way in the path of abandonment
and resignation.

This general intention, which it is a good practice
to renew every morning, includes perfectly all particular intentions, and in itself has more perfection
than all the others put together. And if it is more
perfect, it is also more advantageous to the soul, and
gains for her more good than any other. Thus
there is no need for us to propose to ourselves to
satisfy for our sins by such and such a good work,
or by acquiring such and such a virtue, or by obtaining such and such a grace.

The general intention of doing the will of God
comprehends all this, and has the advantage of taking
off our thoughts from ourselves, which the others
have not. We need not then be surprised when we
hear Saint Catherine of Genoa say that she could no
longer think about gaining indulgences. Was it
because she set no value on these treasures of the

Church? It would be a crime if we were to think so. Was it because she had not the general intention of gaining them? Certainly she had that. Was it that she did not gain them for want of thinking expressly about them? God Himself was occupying her thoughts with something much better, and could He refuse the pardon of her sins, and the share in the merits of His saints, to a soul that lived only for His love, which was only governed by His Spirit, and which had no object but His glory?

Let us then have this pure intention, in the sense I have explained it, this simple look of the soul towards God, this zeal for His glory and His interests only. Let us think and act and suffer only for Him; and all our sins will be remitted, we shall acquire all virtues, we shall obtain all graces, and we shall in a manner oblige God to provide, because He is God, for all our needs, and to take care of our interests which we have neglected and forgotten and sacrificed for the sake of His.

This is the most holy and the most excellent method of all.

XXXVII.

MARTHA AND MARY.

NOTHING is more worthy of attention than what the Gospel teaches us about the two sisters, Martha and Mary. It is certain that Martha is a type of the active life, that is to say, of the life in which, by our own efforts, by our own labour, we try to show God

how much we love Him; and that Mary is the model
of the contemplative life, in which we try to keep our
souls in peace and repose, that God may act in them,
and in which we do not act except through the influence of God, and under His guidance.

These two sisters received Jesus Christ into their
house. Both of them loved Him, both of them wished
to show their love for Him; but they did so in a
very different way. Martha only thought of exercising her charity and hospitality towards our Saviour
by preparing a repast for Him. Her pious care was
worthy of all praise, but she put into it too much
activity, too much eagerness, too much anxiety; she
agitated herself, she disquieted herself. She cooked
many different dishes when one would have been
sufficient. Mary, on her side, did not agitate herself, she did not make great preparations for serving
our Lord well, but she sat at His sacred feet that
she might be fed by His words. The occupation of
Martha was all exterior, all action; that of Mary was
all interior, all silence and repose. The one wished
to give to our Saviour, the other wished to receive
from Him; Martha presented Him with all she had
with a generous heart, Mary gave herself.

Martha, believing that she was doing a great deal
more for Jesus Christ than her sister, and that her
sister ought to leave the feet of the Saviour to come
to her assistance, complains of Mary to Him, and begs
of Him to tell Mary to help her. She thought that
Mary was idle, and that her silence and repose could
not possibly be pleasing to Jesus Christ. But what
is His reply to her? "*Martha, Martha, thou art*

careful and troubled about many things : but one thing is needful ; and Mary hath chosen the better part, which shall not be taken away from her."

Let us meditate upon this reply of our blessed Lord. The instruction it contains is admirably suited to moderate and restrain too great activity and to reduce multiplicity, which are two great defects of even sincere devotion. It was quite right that the hostesses of Jesus Christ should prepare something for Him to eat, but a frugal repast only was necessary. One single dish would have been sufficient for the wants of nature, and Martha thought she should be failing in hospitality and respect for her Divine guest if she did not prepare a great number of dishes. This was the defect of multiplicity.

This frugal repast should have been prepared quietly, without losing interior peace of soul; and Martha excited herself, agitated herself, troubled herself. This was the defect of activity.

Martha preferred her own occupation to that of her sister. Jesus Christ reproved her for this, and told her that the choice of Mary was better. He taught her also, and us through her, that all exterior works, all works of charity, however good they may be in themselves, are only for this present life, and will end when this life ends; instead of which the repose of perfect contemplation will never end, but after beginning on earth it will continue for ever in heaven.

On another occasion, when Jesus came to raise Lazarus from the dead, Martha as soon as she was told He was come, always active, always eager, ran to meet Him.   Mary stayed in the house; she waited quietly, she did not go out until her sister told her that the Master was calling for her.   Martha acted as her own inclination prompted her, at once; Mary waited to act until Jesus Christ Himself guided her actions.

Let us draw from all this some safe rules by which we may direct our judgment and our conduct in matters of devotion.

1st. All exterior good works, even when they have Jesus Christ Himself for their object, and when they have to do with such a necessary thing as bodily nourishment, are in themselves of far less value than prayer and the repose of contemplation.   Consequently we must, as a general rule, prefer prayer to exterior acts, and must give much more time to it. By prayer I mean here all those exercises of piety of which the soul is the immediate object.

2nd. When exterior works of charity, which have to do with our neighbour, are not of absolute necessity, we must not multiply them to such an extent that they take the place of our prayers and our spiritual exercises.   It is all very well to speak of zeal and charity: zeal must be regulated, and charity must begin at home.

3rd. Even when exterior works are positively necessary, and when they are the express will of God, we must try to acquit ourselves of them without losing the interior peace of our soul; in such a manner that even while we are acting our soul may still be united to God, and may never be deprived of that spirit of recollection which ought always to accompany it. And as this practice is extremely difficult, and is only fitted for advanced souls, all the masters of the spiritual life recommend to beginners to give the least time possible to active works, and to apply themselves much more to prayer. A time will come when prayer will become to them, as it were, natural, and then, if God thinks it well for them, they may employ themselves a great deal in exterior works without ever losing the peace of their soul.

4th. Even with regard to spiritual exercises, activity, which really springs from self-love, is always bad, and we cannot repress it too much, that it may be completely under subjection to grace. What did Mary do? She was seated; her body was perfectly motionless, quiet, and tranquil; she was perfectly silent. Jesus spoke to her, and she listened to Him with all the attention of her heart. It is never said that she spoke to Him, or that she interrupted Him; she kept herself in His Presence like a disciple in the presence of his master; she received His lessons, and allowed them to penetrate sweetly into the depths of her soul. This is the model of perfect prayer: when the soul seeks no longer to exhaust itself in reflections and sentiments, but when it listens to Him who teaches without any sound of words. When God gives us the grace to call us to this kind of prayer, we must never abandon it under any pretext whatsoever—not for any sort of distraction, or dryness, or desolation, or weariness, or temptation—but we must always persevere in it; we must overcome all the difficulties which meet us there, and be quite certain that we are doing a great deal when we are doing what God wishes us to do, even though we ourselves may think we are doing nothing, and only losing our time. We have need of great courage, and great dominion over ourselves, to walk constantly in the desert of a way of prayer that is bare and obscure and apparently empty of thoughts and affections : but it is precisely this prayer which will advance us most in dying to ourselves and living only for God.

5th. As activity engenders multiplicity, so repose leads to unity and simplicity, to that simplicity which Jesus Christ declares is so necessary. Activity multiplies all sorts of practices : it embraces all kinds of devotions. It passes incessantly from one act to another ; it is always agitating itself, tormenting itself, never thinking it has done enough. The simplicity of repose concentrates our souls on God, and fixes us to one thing alone—to listen to His voice when we are in prayer, and when we are not in prayer to do His will quietly in the moment that is passing, without disquieting ourselves about the past or the future ; in such a manner that the soul never really has but one object before her eyes, and that she is never entirely given up to exterior things, being less occupied with her own action than with the thought of God, Who is its motive and its end.

6th. The soul learns thus not to separate the occupation of Mary from that of Martha, and to arrange them both in such a manner that one does not interfere with the other. She neglects none of the duties of her state, even those of ordinary politeness; but above all these duties she places her inseparable union with God and her continual dependence on His grace. She renders to her neighbour all the services which depend upon her, but she does not do this of her own will; she waits until God presents her with the occasion. She speaks, she acts in peace under the direction of His grace, and she desires above all things to find herself alone with God.

7th. Finally, even in the best things of all, in those which immediately belong to the glory of God, the soul never takes the initiative of herself: she does not even make a fresh step towards God unless God Himself calls her. " She remains where she is," as Saint Francis de Sales says, " because her present state is that which God wishes, and she has no desire to leave it but at His command."

How beautiful devotion would be, how glorious to God, how useful to the soul, how edifying to our neighbour, how respected even by a corrupt world, if it was always based on these rules! But alas! we wish to govern ourselves, we seek ourselves in our devotion, and that is what makes it subject to so many faults and contradictions.

XXXVIII.

ON THESE WORDS OF PSALM LXXII:—

" Ut jumentum factus sum apud te : et ego semper tecum."

(I am as a beast before Thee   nevertheless I am always with Thee.)

REMARK the connection between these two things : *" To be as a beast before God,"* and yet *" to be always with God."* This is scarcely in conformity with the ideas which we form to ourselves of the infinite sanctity of God, and of what is necessary for our union with Him. What! to attain to this familiarity, this close union with God, I must be before him as a beast? Yes, it is so, and it is the Spirit of God Who has revealed it to us.

But what does it mean to be a beast, and a beast of burden, before God? The beast of burden that is intended for the use of man employs in the service of man all its strength, not according to its own judgment and will, but according to the judgment and the will of man. It is loaded with whatever man wishes, as he wishes, and when he wishes. It goes by the road man chooses, and at the pace he pleases ; it only stops to take food and rest when and how he pleases. In short, the beast of burden is quite at the disposal of its master, and can resist him in nothing.

So should our soul be with regard to God. If our soul desires to be always with Him, she must always depend upon Him in everything and for everything. She must of herself have neither action, nor judgment, nor choice, but in all things she must judge and choose and act only under the guidance of God. She must be content to be moved as God pleases to move her in all things, but especially in spiritual things.

What must we then do to attain to this total dependence upon God? We must annihilate ourselves and suffer Him to annihilate us continually.

We must annihilate ourselves as to what regards our mind and intellect, not allowing it to be attracted by any object for its own sake, not allowing it to be exclusively occupied with anything, or to judge of anything by its own light, but rather leaving it as far as lies in our own power perfectly void and empty, that God may fill this void with the thoughts that please Him. When we are in prayer, when we assist at Holy Mass, when we communicate, we must keep ourselves in the simple disposition to receive from God just what He pleases to give us, without being very much distressed if He gives us nothing, if we are dry and distracted, or even a prey to many temptations. When we are reading a pious book, we must simply give ourselves up to the impressions which God sends us, waiting to receive from Him the light to understand and the feeling to enjoy what we read.

In our conversations with our neighbour we must not prepare anything beforehand, we must not reflect upon things, we must not notice the faults of the persons with whom we speak, or at all events we must try not to dwell upon them ; we must say

Q

honestly and kindly what we think, without troubling ourselves whether we are pleasing people or being approved of by them; and when once the conversation is over we must think no more about it after the persons are gone away.

When we are alone we must try always to keep our mind free, without allowing it to dwell either on the past or the future, or on the affairs of others, occupying ourselves only with the present moment. We must carefully repress all curiosity of whatever kind, or upon whatever subject; we must only be mixed up with our own affairs, or with those of our neighbour, when charity requires it; and for all the rest, we must try to be in the world as if we were not there, and see what is passing without fixing our attention upon it.

We must annihilate ourselves in all that regards our heart, attaching ourselves to nothing except according to the will of God, appropriating nothing to ourselves, desiring nothing, and fearing nothing. It is comparatively easy to detach ourselves from temporal goods, from human sympathies and natural affections; this does not cost us much when we have once given ourselves to God, and when once we have tasted the sweetness of living only for Him. But it is not so easy, it costs us a great deal, to be really detached from spiritual goods, to be indifferent about Divine consolations, to receive them with simplicity, to lose them without regret, and not to desire their return.

We do not consent willingly and easily to lose our sensible peace, our conscious recollection, our enjoyment of the presence of God. And yet we must prepare ourselves for this loss, so that we may never be astonished and disconcerted when it happens to us.

Neither do we ever willingly consent to be the object of ridicule and contempt, of calumnies, of the false judgments of men, and never to say a word or to make a step to justify ourselves; but to suffer in silence and in peace, waiting till it pleases God to declare Himself on our side, and making to Him, if He requires it, the sacrifice of our reputation.

It is still harder to see ourselves forsaken by God, to receive no longer any drops of celestial dew, but to find ourselves dry and insensible, without enlightenment or fervour; to experience every kind of conflict and agitation and interior desolation; not to know whether we love God or whether God loves us; and so on and so on through all those depths of spiritual trials which God does not spare to those who love Him most. Nevertheless we must expect all this, if we wish to be closely and intimately united to God, and if we wish to be purified from all love of ourselves, even where it seems most justifiable and most spiritual. Many souls run extreme danger of stopping on the way; they draw back from God, as Jesus Christ says, when the time of trial comes: they are those houses without foundation of which the Gospel speaks, which cannot stand against winds and storms and inundations. But generous souls, who are prepared for everything, who do not rely upon themselves but upon God, who love Him for Himself alone, and who prefer His glory and His good pleasure to their own interests, such souls are purified in these trials as gold is purified in the crucible : they resist, as gold resists, the full activity of the fire ; the fire only burns away from them the rust and dross of self-love with which sin has infected them, and restores them to their original purity.

If we will suffer ourselves thus to be annihilated by degrees, if we will look upon ourselves as consecrated and devoted to God, that He may do as He pleases with us, then we shall be always with Him ; we shall be united to Him all the more closely when we think He is farthest from us.

When our Lord and Saviour Jesus Christ, dying on the cross in every imaginable torment, exterior and interior, a victim to the passions of men and the justice of God—when He cried out to His Father, "*My God, My God, why hast Thou forsaken Me ?*" had His Father really forsaken Him ?   No, indeed : on the contrary, His Father had never loved Him so much as at that moment, when Jesus Christ was giving Him the greatest proof of love.   But God made our Lord Jesus Christ experience the most terrible effects of the Divine dereliction, to complete the most perfect Sacrifice that ever was consummated. And it is the same, only not in the same degree, with those generous and loving souls whom God wishes to try.   The more He seems to forsake them, the nearer He is to them in reality, the more He supports them, the more He loves them.   But He waits for eternity to give them the full proofs of His love for them, after they shall have given Him in this life the proofs of their love for Him which He has a right to expect from them.

XXXIX.

ON THE THOUGHT OF DEATH.

THE thought of death is a most terrible object for those who are living in sin; they have no other resource than to put such a thought entirely away from them. What a sad resource! They are like a man who, on the edge of a frightful precipice, shuts his eyes that he may not see his danger.

The thought of death is still more terrible for those who only serve God out of a spirit of self-interest, who look at their salvation only as it regards themselves, and who think more of the justice of God than of His mercy. And, as a general rule, this thought is very distressing for any one who is not completely detached from the things of this world, and who does not constantly practise a dying to himself.

But the thought of death is sweet and consoling to those interior souls who have given themselves to God in good faith, and who, occupied solely in loving and serving Him, have placed their fate in His hands.

The first persons, that is, the sinners, look upon death as the end of all their pleasures and the beginning of a misery which will never end; and this thought drives them to despair.

The second, that is, the self-interested ones, look upon death with the eyes of self-love, and, allowing

themselves to be too much afraid of the judgments of
God, they only see in death the terrible moment
which must decide their eternity ; the uncertainty in
which they are as to the lot which awaits them fills
them with consternation, because, on the one hand,
they have not sufficient trust in God, and on the
other hand, faith and their own conscience will not
allow them to rely on their good works or on the
pardon of their sins.

But the third, those who have given themselves
entirely to God, expect everything from His infinite
goodness. As they fear to offend God far more than
they fear hell, they look upon death with joy, as the
moment which will unite their will for ever to that
which is good, which will deliver them from all their
temptations, and which will shelter them for ever
from sin. As the love ot God is their principal, and
indeed their only employment here, they see in the
passage from this life only a happy change which
will assure to them the possession of God and the
ineffable bliss of loving Him for all eternity. It is
not that they have a positive assurance of their
salvation, but they have a firm faith and trust in
God, and their conscience bears witness to their
constant fidelity to Him. The sight of their past
sins does not frighten them, because long since they
have hated them with a sincere hatred, and they have
cast all their sins into the bosom of the Divine mercy.
They think that it is Jesus Christ who will be their
judge, and they say to themselves: "Why should I
fear Him Who has given me so many graces, Who has
preserved me from sin, or raised me up again when

I had fallen into it, Who inspired me with the desire of giving myself entirely to Him, Whom I love more than I love myself, and Whom I wish to love until my last breath ? "

What regret can these souls have for this life ? they have never been attached to anything in it. What fear can they have of the consequences of death, when after death they will belong more to God than they did during life, when they will be His irrevocably and for ever, and when they will never more have anything to fear from the inconstancy of their will ? As long as they were alive, they might perhaps have succumbed to temptation, and might have lost the grace of God : this was their only fear, and this fear will cease for ever at the moment of death, and they will be established in perfect safety.

In short, the manner in which we look upon death depends upon the disposition of our hearts. When the heart is purified from the poison of self-love, when the assiduous exercise of prayer and interior mortification has broken down all the barriers between the soul and God, when we have passed through trials which have led us by degrees to the greatest sacrifices, and when we have attained to a state of perfect union with God, it is impossible for us to fear death ; we no longer look at it as it regards ourselves, but only as it regards the will of God ; and in this holy will death loses all its terrors : it is only amiable and desirable for those whose will is absorbed in the will of God.

To understand what I have just said, and to feel

the truth of it, we must have attained to this happy state of conformity to the will of God.   But although we may not yet be able to understand it completely, we may rest assured that it is so, and we may believe the experience of so many holy souls, who have only found peace and sweetness and joy in the thought of death.

Another thing which is equally true is that the thought of death is one of those that least occupy interior souls.   The reason of this is that God, Who is the sovereign Master of their spirit, turns their thoughts to other objects more conducive to their spiritual advancement.   And as all that is so terrible about death comes in a great measure from the imagination, and from the natural dread man has of it, in proportion as the imagination dies and we are detached from our bodies and become spiritualised, we lose all the fear we once had of death, and accustom ourselves to look at it as God wishes we should look at it.   Now, God certainly does not wish a soul that has given itself to Him to be terrified at the thought of death.

Besides, it is not by reflections drawn from our reason, nor even by the motives which faith teaches us, that we succeed in looking upon death with calmness and assurance.   This assurance is a gift of God, and He only gives this grace to those who have placed their temporal and eternal interests in His hands, who are no longer anxious about themselves in any way, and who have but one sole object, which is the accomplishment of His Divine will.   When we are absolutely lost in God death has nothing that can hurt us.

It is quite right to exhort the generality of Christians to reflect upon death, to consider its uncertainty and its consequences, because this is one of the most efficacious means of inducing them to lead a good life. But this practice, so salutary for the rest of the faithful, is not necessary for interior souls, because they ought not to restrict themselves to any particular practice, but to abandon themselves entirely to the guidance of the Spirit of God. Now the Spirit of God does not lead them to dwell in detail upon the thought of death, but it leads them to die incessantly to themselves by a mystical death—to purify their senses, to renounce their own will, to lose themselves, to forget themselves, that they may live only in God and for God. This mystical death is their great object: they work at it on their part while God is also working at it on His part, and when they have at last attained to this blessed death, natural death becomes for them only a passage from this present life to eternal felicity.

It is not necessary then for an interior soul to take the thought of death as a subject for her meditations, or willingly to occupy herself with it It is neither necessary nor useful for her since the happy moment when she gave herself to God and when God took possession of her. All she need do is to suffer herself to be guided by Divine grace in this thought as in all others. If the thought of death comes prominently before her while she is in prayer or making a spiritual reading, she must notice whether God seems to wish to draw her to this thought, and to occupy her with it by an interior attraction not to be mistaken.   But if not, she need not go against her attraction, neither need she force herself to a thought which is not good for her present state. The love of God, generosity towards God, fidelity to His grace, a constant care to deny herself, and not to be anxious about herself or her own interests, these are the thoughts with which God inspires her; it is to these that He continually directs her meditation.   These thoughts, which all tend to the attainment of the mystical death, are far more useful for her than thoughts about her natural death, for they draw her powerfully to renounce herself, and to allow herself to be annihilated by the Divine operation.

In conclusion, an interior soul has nothing else to do, with regard to her natural death, but not to think about it, unless God draws her to do so, and to abandon herself absolutely to Him as to the time of her death, the manner of her death, and what is to happen to her after death.

XL.

ON THE THOUGHT OF ETERNITY.

WE are terrified at the thought of eternity, and in a certain sense we have great reason to be so, for this thought is indeed very terrible.   But if we knew how to be frightened at it usefully, if we could draw from it, as a guide for our lives, the just conclusions which ought to arise from this fear, soon we should grow familiar with the thought of eternity, and we

should end by taking pleasure in it and finding
consolation in it. For if this thought has its terrible
side, it has also a consoling side, and an extremely
consoling side. Since, then, this thought comes to
us quite naturally, since it is associated so closely
with our ideas of God and of religion that the two
cannot be separated, since it is impossible for us to
get rid of this idea, so that in spite of ourselves it
pursues us everywhere, it is of the greatest importance that we should look at it as we ought to do,
in order that it may only inspire us at first with a
salutary fear, and afterwards, far from troubling us,
it may only inspire us with courage and joy.

The thought of eternity terrifies, and ought to
terrify, those who are the slaves of their passions,
and who are resolved to gratify those passions
at any cost whatever. But since this troublesome
thought embitters all their pleasures, instead of turning a deaf ear to it, as they do, and avoiding with
care everything that can remind them of it, they
ought calmly to examine from whence this thought
springs; if it is not a serious and right thought,
equally demonstrated by reason and revelation. And
when they are once thoroughly convinced of the truth
of it, it will be easy for them to go on to the conclusion that as they were not created for time, but
for eternity, they are the most foolish and misguided
of men to sacrifice their eternal happiness to objects
that are passing away and that can never satisfy
them. And from this conclusion to a perfect conversion to God there is only one step to make. For
indeed, if eternity is real, what do they gain by blind-

ing themselves to it and turning away from the remembrance of it? A truth upon which we will not think, and upon which we do not wish to think, is it any the less a truth for that? And if it is of the very greatest importance to us, do we lessen its importance by obstinately refusing to consider it?

The thought of eternity terrifies, and ought to terrify those who, without being hardened sinners and determined seekers after pleasure, are nevertheless too much attached to the things of this life and to life itself. But let them reflect that if they are destined to enjoy eternal things one day, it is towards those things that they should direct the desire of their hearts, and that all immoderate attachment to the things of this present life is a mistake. Let them think how unreasonable it is to love passionately that which incessantly escapes them, and which they must one day lose without hope of recovery, and to be cold and indifferent towards that which will last for ever and will for ever make their happiness or misery. If they would thus consider eternity it would be no longer for them an alarming object, but they would say to themselves: "I was not made for the things of this earth; why then do I take such an intense interest in them? Another life, which will never end, is to follow this life: why then do I not do everything in my power to secure the enjoyment of that unending felicity which religion promises me in that other life?" Then there would be no more eagerness to acquire the perishable goods of this world: we should make use of them according to the designs of God, but we should have no attachment to them;

all the desires of our minds and hearts, all our affections, would be drawn towards eternity.

The thought of eternity also frightens those timid
and half-hearted Christian souls who serve God more
for their own interest than for His own sake, who
fear Him more than they love Him, who are always
uneasy about their salvation, and who wish to be
certain about it, a certainty which it is impossible that
they should ever have. "I may perhaps be lost after
all," they say to themselves ; "I may be eternally miserable ; I do not know whether I am in a state of grace or
not ; I do not know if I shall not die in mortal sin."
And these kind of thoughts freeze them, fill them
with consternation, and plunge them into depression
and despair. It is quite contrary to the intentions
of God that they should trouble themselves in this
manner, and the thought of eternity was never meant
to produce such an effect as this. Let them be persuaded that God loves them more than they love
themselves, that He desires their salvation more than
they can desire it, that the means of securing it are
in their own hands, that they have only to make a
good use of those means, and after that they may
leave the care of their eternal interests to God in the
utmost peace and tranquillity. They do not see that
this excessive fear comes from self-love, and from
their referring everything to themselves instead of to
God. As to their salvation, they only think of it as far
as their own interest is concerned ; it is not the love
of God, the glory of God, the will of God, which is
their end and their centre—it is their own happiness,
and that as it affects themselves. Let them at once

correct this disorder; let them raise themselves a little above the thought of themselves only, and without neglecting their own interests, let them subordinate them to a far greater interest, which is God's interest: soon love will take the place of fear, they will put all their trust in God; they will expect their salvation, not for their own merits, but from the goodness and mercy of God; they will serve Him in peace, and the thought of eternity will terrify them no longer.

But it is not enough that this thought should not bring us fear and discouragement; it ought to become sweet and consoling to us, in such a manner that the soul should love to remember it, that she should never even lose sight of it, and that she should make use of it to support her and to animate her courage in all the crosses and evils of this present life. And what must she do to attain this? She must be penetrated with this thought of Saint Paul: "Our light afflictions, which are only for a moment, will obtain for us an immense and eternal weight of glory."

"What is this present life?" we ought to say to ourselves. "A time of trial, in which I may merit an eternal happiness. God has created me for the eternal possession of Himself—that is to say, of the Source and the Centre of all good. What a destiny for a being drawn from nothing! How great, how far superior to all our thoughts and desires! How, after that, can I lower myself to the things of this earth? how can I attach myself to them? how can I condescend to look at them? I am born for that

which is eternal, and I suffer myself to be enslaved
by that which is passing away. I am born to possess God, and I give my heart to creatures !

" But God wishes to give me this eternal possession
of Himself by way of reward. And what does He
ask of me in return ? He asks that here below I
should occupy myself with the thought of the happiness of one day possessing Him ; that when I consider such a great benefit, such a sublime destiny,
I should adore Him and love Him and serve Him
with my whole heart. He asks that if ever I have
the misfortune to offend Him, I should return to Him
at once ; that I should listen in the inmost depths of
my soul for His voice, which will call me back to my
duty. He asks that, in the hope of this blessed
eternity, I should suffer willingly and for the love of
Him all the troubles of this present life, and that I
should despise its false pleasures, or only use them
with the greatest moderation, according to His will.
This is all He asks of me."

Now, can there be a sweeter thought or a more
consoling thought than that of eternity looked on
in this light ? Is there one more fitted to raise
the soul above herself, above the delusions of this
deceitful world, above all the temptations and difficulties she may meet with in the practice of virtue ?
Everything I may have to suffer in this life, privations, mortifications, crosses of every kind, even if it
were to last for a hundred years, or for a thousand
years—what is all that in comparison with eternity ?
My sufferings, if they were a thousand times greater,
are only light evils when weighed in the balance

against the immense weight of glory and felicity which is waiting for me.

Take courage, then, my soul! Everything that passes is nothing when it is once over. I ought not to count as true good or true evil anything but that which lasts for ever. The deprivation of this pleasure saves me from an eternity of misery; what would its enjoyment have cost me? The practice of this virtue which costs me so much will procure for me a good that is boundless and unending.

Is there one evil that such a thought as this cannot sweeten, one temptation that it cannot vanquish, one act of virtue that it cannot make easy? Why then should we have such a great fear of eternity, since it is the greatest motive for consolation we can have in this life; the most sublime and the most encouraging motive?

"*What effect will this have on eternity?*" a great saint used to say. "Will this contribute to my eternal happiness, or will it endanger it?" This is a rule of conduct that is very safe and very decisive, and that can be applied to every circumstance of life. Let us make up our minds to follow this rule, let us call it to our recollection every day, let us familiarise ourselves with it, and then we shall live in this world as though we were already dwellers in eternity, and we shall taste its delights in advance, through the peace of our conscience and the joy and satisfaction of acting in all things according to the teaching of reason and religion and the will of God.

XLI.

GOD ALONE.

" God *alone*" is a great word in the interior life.   The first step we make in the way of perfection is to devote ourselves to God alone.   And in proportion as we advance in it, we detach ourselves more and more from everything that is not God, and from ourselves above all.   We reach the summit of perfection when we find ourselves united to God alone, in a most close union, and with nothing to come between us.

It is impossible to conceive what this possession of God alone really is, when He is united in Himself, by His very substance, with the centre of the soul ; we must experience it to be able to know what it is, and even then we shall find the greatest difficulty in making others understand what we experience.   But the purity of soul which is necessary to merit this blessed possession, the trials through which she must pass beforehand, are no less incomprehensible ; and whatever we may read about it in spiritual books, or in the lives of the saints, we can never really form any idea of it until we have ourselves experienced it.

It is not ourselves, it is not our director, however spiritual and enlightened he may be, it is God alone Who can give us this blessed possession of Himself. This work is His own work above all others ; and it is a work incomparably greater than the creation and government of the universe.   The only thing the

R

soul can do, to co-operate with this work, is to suffer
God to do as He pleases without examining what He
is doing, to keep herself faithfully and peacefully in
the state in which God places her, to oppose no
voluntary resistance to His operation, and to allow
herself to be despoiled by degrees of all that is not
God alone and His good pleasure. As long as she
can act at all of herself the soul must correspond with
Divine grace with the greatest exactitude ; she must
forbid herself a look or a word, a taste or a fancy,
or even the most innocent and permitted thing ; as
soon as God calls her she must rise above every
human consideration, without troubling herself in any
way as to what is said about her or thought about
her, or anything vexatious and painful that may happen to her ; she must stand firm against her natural
inclinations, her natural aversions, every rebellion of
nature, every suggestion of the evil spirit.

When God takes entire possession of her, so that
she is no longer mistress of herself nor of the powers
of her soul, neither of her memory to recollect anything, nor of her understanding to make reflections,
nor of her will to produce affections, then her duty
is to allow herself to be ruled and governed absolutely by God, to suffer all the trials He chooses to
send her without thinking either of what use they
can be or what will be the end of them, without
desiring to be delivered from them, and at the same
time never to relax any of her exercises or practices.
God may seem to withdraw from her ; the heaven
may be like brass and iron to her ; she may no
longer receive one single drop of dew or of consola-

tion ; she may have no more assurance either from God or man ; everything may appear to declare itself against her ; she may think herself hopelessly lost ; and yet she will persevere always in devoting herself, in sacrificing herself to the good pleasure of God, never thinking about herself, never being anxious as to what will become of her, and being confident that, provided she remains inviolably united to God, she can only lose herself in Him to find herself in Him again and for ever.

This is what the soul has to do with regard to God.

As to what regards him whom God has given to her for a guide, she ought to see God only in him, and to open herself to him as she would do to God Himself ; never to hide anything from him, or deceive him in anything, place an entire faith in all he says, obey him as she would obey God Himself ; but at the same time she must only attach herself to him as a means which God will make use of as long as He pleases, and which He will take away from her when He thinks proper. Thus, she ought to keep to him as long as God leaves him to her, and never give him up of her own accord ; but when God takes him away from her, however much this loss may cost her, she must acquiesce in it, and believe firmly that God has no need of any one particular man to guide her, but that He will either send her another guide or supply the place Himself, and be Himself her Guide, instead of using any human means. It happens sometimes that God leaves a soul without any direction : the trial is terrible, but if the soul is generous and faithful, she will lose nothing by this, and will only be

all the better directed, being under the infallible direction of God Himself. A soul in this disposition, and
that keeps in it by a faithful correspondence with
Divine grace, will most certainly attain to the possession of God alone.

It is not, therefore, a question of intention, or
project, or plan; no method, no book, no director,
can lead us to God alone. I repeat it again : God
alone can draw us and unite us to Himself. He alone
knows what means are necessary ; He knows how to
take each individual soul, and by what way to lead it :
we have nothing to do but to give ourselves up to
Him, to allow Him to act in us, and to follow Him
step by step.

If I am asked what it is necessary to renounce
to attain to the possession of God alone, I reply in
general terms that we must renounce without exception everything that is not God alone. And I add
that God only can comprehend the extent of this
renunciation ; that man, with the ordinary light of
grace, cannot form the slightest idea of it ; that what
he reads about it in spiritual books he may have a
dim perception of, but cannot thoroughly understand ;
and that unless he has a particular inspiration he
will never know what it is to give himself fully and
entirely to God. It is then for God Himself to lead
us by degrees to a perfect death to ourselves ; it is
for Him to inspire us one by one with the sacrifices
He expects of us and to give us the courage to make
them.

Let us not be frightened, and let us not presume
on our own strength. If we listen to our imagi-

nation, it will throw us into discouragement, and will
make us look upon this utter despoilment of ourselves as a phantom idea and a thing impossible to
human nature; our mere reason even, if we consult it,
will possibly tell us the same : but if we consult faith
only, if we cast our eyes on the cross of Jesus Christ,
if we meditate attentively on the great mystery of His
passion, then we shall understand how far we ought
to carry the renunciation of ourselves, that we may
attain to a perfect union with God alone.   Let us
beg of our Divine Saviour to open our eyes, that we
may understand those wonderful words of His : "*All
is consummated,*" and "*Father, into Thy hands I commit My spirit.*"   Let us beg of Him to make us understand what He did when by a voluntary death He
commended His soul into the hands of Divine justice
to expiate our sins.   And when we think of that
great Sacrifice, imagination, reason and all created
intelligence must keep silence, and we shall confess
that there is no renunciation too great for a man to
make with all his heart to merit the possession of
God alone.

Let us not presume either upon our own strength,
and let us not think ourselves capable of a generosity
which is beyond a feeble creature.   To cure ourselves
of blind presumption, and to conceive as much as
possible the extreme horror with which the perfect
renunciation of self inspires human nature, let us
consider our Lord and Saviour in the Garden of Olives ;
let us listen to what He said to His Father : "*If it be
possible, let this cup pass from Me*"—this very cup
which He had so ardently desired to drink.   If God

made Man was willing, for our instruction, to experience this extreme repugnance for the sacrifice which He had accepted from the first instant of His life, what a powerful grace is necessary for us, I do not say to make a sacrifice like His, but a sacrifice which may have some faint resemblance to His! Let us humble ourselves, let us be confounded, let us tremble at the sight of our own weakness and cowardice, but at the same time let us say: "God is all-powerful; provided only that I do not resist Him, He will do with me and by me whatever shall please Him: He will render me capable of the greatest efforts of generosity; He will detach me from myself, and will teach me to lose myself that I may live again in Him."

God alone! What a word! How great it is! how many things it expresses! No more of creatures, no more of one's self, no more of the gifts of God: a total void, an utter loss of all that is not God, God alone, God in Himself, God in closest union with His creature, a union that can never be broken!

XLII.

ON CONTINUAL PRAYER.

JESUS CHRIST has told us that we ought "*always to pray, and not to faint*"—that is, not to grow weary of so doing. And St. Paul recommended the first Christians to "*pray without ceasing.*" What kind of prayer must we understand by this precept, or rather,

by this counsel ?   And how is it possible to accomplish it ?

It is quite evident, at first sight, that it cannot be
a question here of *vocal* prayer, which can only be
engaged in at certain times.   Neither can it be always
the regular exercise of fixed mental prayer.   It is
also impossible for us to occupy our mind continually
and without interruption with the thought of God or
the things of God.   . An uninterrupted attention to
the presence of God is beyond mere human strength,
and is incompatible with all the anxieties and occupations of this life.

How then, and by what kind of prayer, can we
fulfil the intentions of our Lord and Master ?   By
the prayer of the heart, which consists of an habitual and constant disposition of love to God, of
trust in Him, of resignation to His will in all the
events of our lives ; in a continual attention to the
voice of God, speaking to us in the depths of our
consciences and unceasingly suggesting to us thoughts
and desires of good and perfection.   This disposition
of heart is that in which all Christians ought to be ;
it was the disposition of all the saints, and it is in
it alone that the interior life consists.

God calls all the world to this disposition of heart,
for it is without contradiction to all Christians that
Jesus Christ addressed Himself when He said that we
must always pray ; and it is certain that all would
attain to this state if they would faithfully correspond
to the attractions of grace.   Let the love of God once
take entire and absolute possession of a heart, let it
become to that heart like a second nature, let that

heart suffer nothing that is contrary to it to enter, let it apply itself continually to increase this love of God by seeking to please Him in all things and refusing Him nothing that He asks, let it accept, as from His hand, everything that happens to it, let it have a firm determination never to commit any fault deliberately and knowingly, or if it should have the misfortune to fall into one, to be humbled for it and to rise up again at once—such a heart will be in the practice of continual prayer, and this prayer will subsist in the midst of all occupations, all conversations, even of all innocent amusements. The thing is not then so impracticable nor so difficult as we might imagine at first sight. In this state we are not always absolutely thinking of God, but we never willingly occupy ourselves with a useless thought, still less with a wicked thought. We are not incessantly making direct acts, we are not incessantly pronouncing vocal prayers, but our heart is always turned towards God, always listening for the voice of God, always ready to do His holy will.

We deceive ourselves if we think that there is no real prayer except that which is express, formal, and sensible, and of which we can give an account to ourselves. And it is because of this mistake that so many persons persuade themselves that they are doing nothing in prayer when there is nothing marked about it, nothing that their mind or heart can perceive or feel ; and this often induces them to give up their prayer. But they ought to reflect that God "*understands,*" as David says, "*the preparation of our hearts ;*" that He does not need either our words or our thoughts to know the most secret disposition of our souls; that our real prayer is found already in germ and substance, in the very root of our will, before it passes into words or thoughts; in short, that our most spiritual and direct acts precede all reflection, and are neither felt nor perceived unless we are keeping a most careful watch for them. Thus, when some one asked Saint Anthony what was the best method of praying, "It is," said he, "when, in praying, you do not think that you pray." And what renders this way of praying most excellent, is that self-love can find nothing in it to rest upon, and cannot sully the purity of it by its touch.

Continual prayer is therefore not difficult in itself, and nevertheless it is very rare, because there are very few hearts in the right dispositions to make it and courageous and faithful enough to persevere in it. We cannot begin to enter on this way of prayer until we have given ourselves entirely to God. Now, there are very few souls who give themselves to God without reserve; there is almost always in this gift something that is kept back, something that self-love secretly keeps hold of, as is very soon seen in the sequel.

But when this gift is really full and entire, God rewards it at once by the gift of Himself; He establishes Himself in the heart, and forms there that continual prayer which consists in peace, in recollection, in a constant attention to God in the interior of the soul, in the midst of all ordinary occupations. This recollection is at first sensible; we enjoy it, we feel we have it. But afterwards it becomes quite spiritual; we have it, but we feel it no longer. And if we regret the loss of this feeling, that was so sweet and so consoling, if we try to bring it back, we are yielding to the insinuations of self-love. If we think that we are no longer recollected, and that we are no longer practising continual prayer because we feel nothing, we are making a great mistake. If the thought comes to us of giving up our prayer because we are no longer doing anything in it, that is a temptation, and a very dangerous temptation. If we yield to it, if we relax our fidelity, if we seek in creatures and from creatures the consolation we can no longer find in God, we shall lose the gift of continual prayer, we shall fall back, and advance no more, and we shall expose ourselves to the danger of becoming much worse than we were before we gave ourselves to God.

What must we do, then, to keep ourselves in the practice of continual prayer? First, we must be well persuaded that our prayer becomes more excellent and more pleasing to God just in proportion as it becomes less sensible and less perceptible to us. Second, we must give up by degrees all that watching and reflecting upon what is going on in our own souls which we are in the habit of making. This watching is frequent in the beginning, because we are so surprised to see what God is doing in our souls, and self-love also seeks its satisfaction there. But when our power of feeling is taken away, we must no longer permit ourselves this watching of the operations of grace and these reflections upon what God is doing for us; it is a sign that God wishes to draw us out of ourselves, to make us enter into Him and

lose ourselves there. Third, we must resist strongly
all thoughts which may come to us that we are losing
our time, that our prayers, our communions, our
spiritual readings are quite fruitless, because we make
them without sensible devotion and without consolation to ourselves. It is the devil, it is our self-love,
it is our nature, always so eager for consolation, that
suggests these thoughts to us ; they will not torment
us long if we are generous enough to make to God
the sacrifice of our own interests, if we are determined
to seek only Him and to forget ourselves, and if we
are sensible enough not to pretend to be saints in our
own way and according to our own ideas—as if we
could know of ourselves what sanctity really is and
the ways that lead to it. Let us then be reasonable
enough to believe that sanctity can only be the work
of God Himself, let us suffer Him to act as He will,
and let us abandon ourselves to Him without allowing ourselves to form one single judgment upon His
operations. Fourth, finally, we must be more faithful than ever in never seeking any kind of consolation or support from creatures ; in never giving ourselves up to any dissipation, but willingly consenting
to be separated at the same time from the joys of
heaven and from those of earth, even the most innocent, if grace inspires us to deprive ourselves of them.
By observing faithfully what I have just said, we
shall pass without danger over the most difficult part
of the spiritual life, and we shall be ready for still
more purifying trials when God sees fit to send them
to us.

The effects of continual prayer, in the beginning,

and when there is sensible fervour, are to teach us
by experience what the interior of our souls and the
reign of God there really are—to inspire us with a
love for retirement and solitude—to disgust us with
the world, with its vain conversations and false
pleasures—to purify our senses, and to communicate
to them a certain innocence which raises them above
the earthly objects which would otherwise ensnare
them.

When this prayer is no longer sensible and perceptible, its effects are to detach us from spiritual consolations, and to make us capable of receiving them
with far greater purity when it pleases God to give
them to us ; to make us die by degrees to self and
self-love ; to concentrate our attention on the thought
of our own nothingness by teaching us that we cannot have any good thought or any good impulse of
ourselves ; to make us simple, by putting a stop to
all our considerations and reflections about ourselves ;
to annihilate gradually our own judgment, our own
spirit, and to dispose us to judge of everything by the
Spirit of God ; finally, to establish our soul in a certain disposition of disinterestedness with regard to
God and His service, in such a manner that we begin
to forget ourselves entirely, and to be content to be
nothing provided only that God may be all.   Then
God will draw the soul to make a real sacrifice of herself, and to offer herself willingly to receive all kinds
of crosses, both exterior and interior, so that she may
become a sweet-smelling holocaust in His sight.   God
may apparently stain that soul by temptations of all
kinds : she may think herself guilty, she may see no-

thing but sin in all her actions; it may seem to her that God rejects her prayer, that He forsakes her, that He is angry with her, and that she has nothing to expect in this life and in the other but the effects of His just vengeance. Sometimes all men may turn against her; and whilst in her secret soul she thinks herself hopelessly lost, outside she is calumniated, condemned, and persecuted. Notwithstanding all this, she keeps herself always resigned and abandoned to the will of God, always under the hand of His good pleasure: provided He can derive glory from her and her sufferings in any way whatever, she is content.

This trial lasts as long as is necessary until she is completely lost in God, and until she is dead to self-love in all its forms. And after this mystical death she rises again, and enters, even in this life, upon the enjoyment of a foretaste of the life of beatitude in heaven. This is where continual prayer will lead us, if it is well understood and well practised.

XLIII.

ON TRUST IN GOD.

OF all the virtues, the most necessary to man is trust in God, because without it he can do nothing, and with it he can do everything. This virtue is the just medium between two extremes which are equally to be avoided, and into which, nevertheless, fall the greater part of men. Some fall into presumption, and the others into cowardice. The first form to them-

selves a false idea of the goodness of God, and abuse
it either by offending Him or by relaxing their pursuit
of perfection.   " God," they say, " will never condemn
me for such a little thing ; He will give me time to do
penance ; He is not so exacting, He does not look into
everything so closely."   The second class have a too
lively fear of the justice of God, and of the severity of
His judgments ; they scarcely ever think of His mercy.
This fear freezes them, destroys their courage, and
often throws them into despair.   Self-love and errone-
ous ideas are the source of these two extremes.   We
must keep the right middle course, which consists in
so putting all our trust in God that we can never
presume on His goodness, and also at the same time
that we can never despair.   It is only the souls that
are truly devoted to God who know how to keep this
just medium, all others deviate from it more or less.
Men fall more easily into presumption, women into fear
and mistrust.

Trust in God is founded, on the one hand, on a
right knowledge of God, and on the other hand, on a
right knowledge of ourselves.   The knowledge of God
teaches us that He is infinitely good in Himself ; that
He loves the creatures He has made ; that He cannot
help loving them and wishing well to them ; and that
their loss, if they are lost, can never be His doing.
Religion teaches us that He loves us incomparably
more than it is possible to imagine or conceive ; He
loves us to such a degree that He gave up His own
Son, and delivered Him to death for us ; He presents
us with His grace ; He is always ready to receive the
sinner who returns to Him ; He will pardon the

sinner and forget all his faults, provided only that he sincerely repents ; and He never ceases to follow the sinner, in all his wanderings, in order to bring him back to Himself. If we will only enter a little into ourselves, and reflect on the course of our life, experience will teach us that in all God has behaved towards us with a mercy that is infinite ; that He has preserved some of us from sin, and has withdrawn us from the occasions of it ; that He has for a long time borne with the constant falls of others of us ; that He could have damned us after our first mortal sin, and that He did not do so ; that He has contrived all kinds of assistance to help us to return to Him ; and that it is to Him alone that we owe our escape from the power of sin or our perseverance in doing good. Let us bring back to our memory all the personal graces we have received from Him, and besides those we know of, let us be quite sure that there are many many others which we are either ignorant of or have forgotten. How many motives may we draw from all this to place all our trust in God !

And the motives drawn from the knowledge of ourselves are not less important. I can do nothing, absolutely nothing, of myself, in the spiritual life. Not only am I weak, but my strength is nothing at all. I can make a bad use of my free-will, I can ruin myself for ever, if I choose, but my free-will without God's grace cannot save me ; I cannot save myself. I need the help of an ever-present grace, and this help is only granted to an earnest prayer that is inspired by a perfect trust in God. If I fall it is impossible for me to rise again unless

God stretches out His hand to me; and He will stretch it out to me as soon as I call upon Him. I can never rely on my own promises, or my good impulses, or my good resolutions; experience has proved this to me a thousand times. As to the dangers and temptations which surround the path of virtue, it would be the greatest blindness and folly on my part to think I could protect myself against them by my own strength.

In short, the whole work of my salvation, from the beginning to the end, depends upon God alone. He has in His hands the infallible means of bringing it to pass; and in spite of all my weakness, and my misery, and my inclination to evil, He will most assuredly bring about my salvation if I never lose my confidence in Him, if I expect everything from His mercy, if I keep myself always united to Him. It is therefore quite true that the more humility we have—that is to say, the better we know ourselves—the more trust we have in God. Now, a trust that is based upon humility can never be presumptuous. And, on the other hand, a trust that has for its basis the infinite goodness of God, His great love for His creatures, and His great power, such a trust can never be timid and cowardly. For what can he fear who finds all his support in God? "Throw yourself into His arms," says Saint Augustine; "He will not take them away; He will not let you fall." And when once we are in the arms of God what enemy can harm us? what temptation can tear us from Him?

"But the justice of God is very terrible," you may

say, "and I ought always to fear it." That is quite true; but for whom is His justice terrible? Is it for those children of God who love Him and serve Him as a Father, who are determined to refuse Him nothing and to displease Him in nothing? No. If these children love God, God loves them still more; He sees that their faults are not faults of malice, but of imperfection and human weakness: at the first look of love and sorrow that they turn to Him He will forgive them; and even if He has to punish them He will punish them in this world, in the way that is most advantageous for their salvation.

Is it for the sinners who return to God sincerely that His justice is terrible? No. They experience the effects of His great mercy; and often they are treated with so much tenderness and love that even the just are jealous of them: we have only to think of Mary Magdalen and of the Prodigal Son.

The Divine justice is only terrible for those who will not have recourse to His mercy, either through presumption or through despair; for those who love sin and do not wish to give it up; for those whose will is not straightforward and upright, and who would like, if they could, to deceive God Himself. But it is quite clear that such sinners as these have not and cannot have any real trust in God; it is clear that they have no right to this trust; for real trust in God can only begin from the time that we begin sincerely to desire to renounce sin, and to be overcome with shame and sorrow at having offended God.

God wishes us to fear His justice, that for this

s

reason we may avoid sin, that we may forsake it as soon as possible, that we may expiate it by penance, that we may never think we have expiated it sufficiently, and that we may not lightly presume on the hope of pardon.   But at the same time He wishes us to trust in Him, to hope for all things from His mercy, to return to Him rather through love than fear, and never to allow ourselves to become the prey of a terror that is without foundation and injurious to God, and that can have no other effect than to discourage and dishearten us.

But how far are we to carry this trust in God ? As far as His power and His goodness ; as far as our own weakness and our own misery ; that is to say, our trust is to be boundless.   Thus, however difficult perfection may be, we must strive after it with humility and confidence, without being frightened at the difficulties and dangers in the way.   But, as, when we consider ourselves, we ought always to say, " I can do nothing," so when we consider God, Who will be our Guide and Support on the way, we ought to say, " I can do all things through Him, and by His grace I shall succeed."

But the world is very much to be feared.   *"Have confidence,"* said our Lord and Master, Jesus Christ ; *" I have overcome the world."*   He overcame it in His own Person ; He will overcome it again in ours.   Is the world more formidable for us than it was for so many martyrs and so many saints ?   Had these martyrs and saints any strength of themselves ?   Not any more than we have ; but they were strong with the strength of God, and we can be so, as they were.

But the snares of the devil are so crafty and so powerful. The devil can do nothing against a humble trust in God. Never presume on your own strength; expect everything from God, and all the powers of hell will never be able to hurt you.

But self-love corrupts everything, poisons everything; it is always to be feared, whatever progress we may have made. Always, then, distrust yourself; be always on your guard against your own judgment and your own will. Increase each day in the love of God, and each day you will weaken self-love. Sacrifice all your own interests to those of God; leave to Him the care of all that concerns you, and only occupy yourself with doing His will. Do not refer God to yourself, but refer yourself to God for everything that is of any consequence to you, in time and in eternity, and self-love will be lost in the love of God.

But we must pass through many trials and humiliations to die entirely to ourselves. Yes, and this goes much farther than you can possibly imagine or foresee. But the more generously you accept these trials and humiliations, the more God will support you. Your courage and strength will increase beyond measure; or rather, in proportion as you lose your own strength, you will acquire the strength of God, and with that you will become capable of everything, superior to everything. And your victory over the world, over the devil, and over yourself, will be the effect of your trust in God. "*Perfect love,*" Saint John says, "*casts out fear;*" all fear, except the fear of offending God or of refusing Him anything.

XLIV.

ON THE LOVE OF GOD.

IT is very strange that it should be necessary to excite and exhort man to the love of God, when we consider that God is his first beginning and his last end, and the only Source of his happiness; yet God has thought Himself obliged to make of it a precept. Is not the love we have for ourselves sufficient to engage us to love God, and do we require any other motive than that of our greatest and even our only interest?   " You command me to love You, O my God!" says Saint Augustine, "as if it would not be for me the greatest misfortune not to love You!" However this may be, God has made of it a commandment, and the first and greatest of all commandments, the one which contains all the others.

It is given in these words: *" Thou shalt love the Lord thy God with all thy mind, and with all thy heart, with all thy soul, and with all thy strength."*

Let us explain the words of this commandment, and let us see by what marks we can discover if we are keeping it or not.

We are to love with a reasonable love, with a love of preference, with a love as much above other loves as God is above all other things which can excite the love of man.   We are to love, not for a moment, or for a short time, or at intervals, but always and at every moment, from the first instant that our reason begins to know God until our last mortal sigh. This is to be the actual and habitual, the fixed and permanent disposition of our hearts. We are to love with a love proportionate to the state of innocence in which God created the first man, and to which He has restored us by the Sacrament of Baptism, with a love that is infused, and therefore supernatural, and we are to preserve always, as a most precious gift, the sanctifying grace which accompanies this love; and, if we have not yet attained this grace, we must do all we possibly can to obtain it; and if we have lost it through our own fault, we must omit nothing we can do to recover it later on. God offers His grace to every one, and with His grace the inestimable gift of His Divine love; and if a man has reached the age of reason, it is always his own fault if he does not receive sooner or later both these gracious gifts.

" *Thou shalt love the Lord thy God.*" The principal motives for the love of God are contained in these words. He is *God;* the Being that is infinitely perfect, the Being that is infinitely amiable—amiable in Himself, by Himself, and for Himself, the Source of all the amiability and perfection which there can ever be in created things. He merits therefore the purest, the most disinterested love, a love that is independent of all other loves. He is *our God.* We have with Him every sort of relationship that it is possible to have. He drew us out of nothing; He has made us what we are; He has given us every blessing we enjoy; and He preserves them to us, and preserves us also, every moment of our lives. He has done still more for us in the order of grace than in the order of nature; His Divine revelation has taught us the extent of His benefits; let us only meditate upon them, and we shall see what love and gratitude we owe Him. He has prepared for us still greater blessings in the order of glory; for He alone created us, He alone redeemed us, that He might make us happy for ever in the possession of Himself. The eternal love, which He has for each one of us, alone induced Him to create us, and to promise us and prepare us for such great benefits; and in return for all this He only asks us to love Him as our Creator, our Saviour, and our Rewarder. Is not this just? Can we refuse to fulfil this duty?

Again, He is "*the Lord,*" the sovereign Lord, the only Lord, the beginning of all things, the end of all things, the centre of all things. Nothing else is lovable, except by Him and through Him; we cannot refuse Him our homage without falling into the sin of rebellion, neither can we share it with any other object without the greatest injustice. His principal kingdom, and that of which He is most jealous, is in our hearts; it is by love that He wishes to reign over us; it is not sufficient for Him that we should fear Him; what He desires and commands above all things is that we should love Him. He requires this love of us under the penalty, if we refuse it to Him, of the greatest of all miseries, of an everlasting misery, of an inevitable misery, from which nothing can save us. Every motive of justice, and gratitude, and hope, and fear, unite together to subject us to this law of love.

Therefore we must love the Lord our God. And how? With our *whole mind*, which was only given to us that we might know Him. We are to have Him always present to our thoughts, in such a manner that we at once banish from our minds any thought that might offend Him, any thought that might distract us and fix our attention on any other object to the injury of the attachment we ought to have for Him alone. This law of love commands us to seek instruction, and to occupy ourselves with the things of God and with all belonging to His service, with the duties of our state of life ; in short, it commands us to lead a serious life, as is fitting for a creature made only for God.

We must love Him *with all our heart.* Our chief affection must be for God, and all our other affections must be referred to Him. And we must renounce them if we find that they are drawing us away from Him. God will have *all* our heart : He will not share it with any one ; because He made it for Himself alone, and we cannot love Him as He deserves to be loved if we love at the same time anything else that we do not love for His sake.

We are to love Him *with all our soul;* that is to say, we are always to be ready to sacrifice everything for Him—our wealth, our honour, and our life itself; and we are to consent to renounce everything, to suffer everything, to lose everything, rather than transgress the commandment of the love of God. Our love for Him must raise us above all the pleasures of sense, above all human respect, above all human fear, above all promises and all threats, above all the advantages which the world may offer us, and of which it can deprive us.   And we must always believe, and act as if we believed, that if we lose all for God's sake we gain all.

Finally, we must love Him *with all our strength ;* that is to say, we must put no bounds to our love, because the measure of the love of God is to love Him without measure.   We are to strive continually to increase our love ; all our intentions, all our actions must tend to this end, and we must make it the object of all our prayers and practices of piety.   Oh how noble this intention is ! how worthy of God and man ! To pray, to frequent the Sacraments, to exercise works of charity, to suffer all the pains and sorrows of this life, solely with the view of increasing in us this holy love ! That indeed is to love God with all our strength !

But by what marks can we know if we love God in this manner ?   For this is a matter that torments many good and faithful souls, who can scarcely be reassured about it.   And on this subject I will say to them—

1st. That this very fear of not loving God enough, our very uneasiness about it, our desire to love Him more, is a most unequivocal proof that our heart belongs to Him.   But I must add that often there is a good deal of self-love in this fear and uneasiness, when they are excessive ; and we must always be guided by the decisions of a wise confessor, and not trouble the peace of our soul by examining ourselves with too much anxiety.

2nd. That it is not by the feeling of a sensible love that we can judge of its reality, but by the effects it produces. Sensible affections and sensible joy in loving do not depend upon us; God gives them or withholds them as He pleases. These feelings are deceptive; they come sometimes from the imagination, or from a naturally loving and tender disposition, or from indiscreet efforts; it is dangerous to be too much attached to them; and the devil may send them to us sometimes to deceive us and lead us astray. In this extreme attachment to sensible devotion we love God less than we love ourselves. It is therefore by its effects that we must judge of the reality of our love : if we are courageous in undertaking all for God, and in suffering all for God; if our own consolation counts for nothing in the service of God ; if we seek ourselves in nothing; if we persevere in spite of temptations and disgust, and weariness and desolation—these are the true proofs of love.

3rd. In proportion as we advance in the spiritual life we reflect less upon our love to God and our disposition with regard to Him : we abandon ourselves to Him in this matter, as in all others; we love Him without thinking of it, scarcely knowing that we love Him; and it is then that we love Him with the greatest purity. We are no longer exposed to the danger of looking on ourselves with vain complacency : the soul flies straight to God without thinking of herself at all. Love is her life, and her life is in God. She is engulphed and lost in Him ; and if she were to become capable of reflecting and telling herself how much she loves Him, she would be no longer in that blessed state, and would be in danger of falling from it.

4th. It is not generally by reflections or frequent self-examinations that the love of God is acquired and preserved, but by a direct looking towards God, by a pure intention, by a constant renunciation of all self-interested views, and by a continual fidelity in following all the movements of Divine grace and never listening to the promptings of our own spirit.

Love has its source in God : it is He who places it in our hearts ; He alone can increase it there. He alone knows what its nature and perfection really are.   Let Him do what He will : He who has given us the beginning of His love will give us progress in it, if we keep ourselves constantly united to Him and suffer ourselves to be guided by His Spirit.   Our Lord and Saviour Jesus Christ said : "*I am come to bring fire upon the earth, and what will I but that it be enkindled ?*"   Let us give Him our hearts, that He may kindle in them this Divine fire ; once lighted it will never be extinguished of itself, its sacred flames will consume all that is earthly and impure in our souls, and at last it will consume the soul itself, with all that belongs to it, and will unite it to God Himself.   Amen.   So be it.

XLV.

ON REST IN GOD.

"Come unto Me, all you that labour and are burdened, and I will refresh you : and you shall find rest for your souls."

THIS invitation was addressed to every man on earth ; no other than Jesus Christ has ever given them such an invitation ; and they have all the greatest interest in experiencing the reality of this promise. We all suffer in this world more or less, either from anxiety of mind, or sorrow of heart, or pain of body. And nevertheless we all long for rest, we seek it eagerly, and we wear ourselves out all our lives in this search without ever attaining the object of our desires. Where is rest to be found ? Where shall we seek it ? This is a most interesting question if ever there was one.

Some men, and in fact the greater number, seek their rest in the enjoyment of the riches and pleasures and honours of this life.

What care do they not take to secure these things for themselves, to preserve them, to increase them, and to accumulate them ?

Do they really find rest in these things ? No. How should rest be found in these perishing things, which cannot even satisfy the passion that desired them ; in things which have no proportion with the wants of the human heart, which leave it always empty, always devoured by a still more ardent thirst ;

in things that are always being disputed and envied
and torn furiously by one person from another?
What rest and stability can be found in things that
are change itself? If the foundation upon which we
build our rest is always moving, is it not a necessary
consequence that we must experience the same agitation? Let every one consult himself: experience is
the most positive of proofs. What man ever tasted
rest in the midst of the greatest treasures, the most
lively pleasures, the most flattering honours? Rest
is not in these things: every one knows this; and
yet it is in these things that man persists in seeking
it. Men exhaust themselves in desires, in projects,
in enterprises, and they never succeed in finding one
single moment of rest; and if they would only consult their reason, it would tell them that in this way
they never can find rest. What blindness! What
folly!

Others establish their rest in themselves, and in
doing this they think they are much wiser than those
who seek it in exterior things. But are they really
wise? Is man made to be sufficient for himself?
Can he find in himself the principle of his rest?
His ideas change every day; his heart is in a perpetual state of unrest; he is constantly imagining new
systems of happiness, and he finds this happiness
nowhere. If he is alone, he is devoured with weariness; if he is in company, however select and agreeable it may be, it soon becomes tiresome to him; his
reflections exhaust and torment him; study and reading may amuse him and distract him for a time, but
they cannot fill up the void in his heart. This is

the kind of rest which human wisdom promises to its
followers, and for which it invites them to give up
everything else, to isolate themselves, to concentrate
their attention on themselves. A deceitful rest, which
is not exempt from the most violent agitations, and
which is at least as hard. for man to bear as the
tumult of his passions !

Where then is rest to be found, if we can find
it neither in the good things of this world nor in
ourselves ? It is to be found in God, and in
God alone. Jesus Christ came into the world to
teach us this truth, and it is the greatest lesson that
He has given us. But how few there are that profit
by it !

"*Thou hast made us for Thyself*," cries out Saint
Augustine, "*and our heart finds no rest until it reposes
in Thee.*"

This truth is the first principle of all morality ;
reason, religion and experience all unite in proving
it to us.

But to repose in God, what must we do ? We
must give ourselves entirely to Him, and we must
sacrifice to Him everything else If we only give
ourselves partly to Him, if we make some reservation,
if we keep back some attachment, it is quite clear that
our rest cannot be entire or perfect, because trouble
will glide in by the place in our heart that is not
united to God and resting only on Him. This is why
so few Christians enjoy a real peace—a peace that is
continual, full and unchanging. They do not fix their
rest in God alone, they do not trust everything to
Him, they do not abandon everything to Him. Never-

theless, there is no true and solid rest to be found but in this utter abandonment.

This rest is unchangeable, as God is ; it is elevated, as God is, above all created things ; it is most secret and intimate, because it is only God, the enjoyment of Whom pierces to the very depths of our hearts ; it is full, because God completely fills and satisfies the heart ; it leaves nothing to desire, and nothing to regret, because he who possesses God can neither desire or regret anything else. This rest calms the passions, tranquillises the imagination, composes the mind and fixes the inconstancy of the heart. This rest subsists in the midst of all changes of fortune, of every imaginable evil and misfortune, even in the midst of temptations and trials, because nothing in these things can reach the centre of the soul which is reposing in God. The martyrs upon the scaffold, a prey to the most horrible tortures, the confessors in poverty, in prison, in exile, in persecution, tasted this rest in the depths of their souls, and were happy. The saints have tasted it in solitude, in the exercise of a most austere penance, in hard and excessive labours, in calumnies, in humiliations, in infirmities and sicknesses. A crowd of Christians have tasted it in the painful duties of their state of life, in the crosses attached to it, in the common life and all the cares and anxieties it entails. It only depends upon ourselves to enjoy it as they did. If we really wish it, God will be to us what He has been to them. He only asks of us, as He asked of them, one single thing, which is that we should lean only upon Him, and seek our rest and happiness in Him alone.

The experience of this is certain, and has never failed. From the moment that we give our hearts to God, that we put our conscience in order, that we take measures to avoid all sin, venial as well as mortal, that we make a firm determination to be attentive and faithful to Divine grace, and to refuse nothing to God, that we put ourselves under the direction of an enlightened guide, and resolve to obey him in all things—from that moment we enter upon a rest and a peace which we have never before experienced, of which we could have formed no idea, and at which we are utterly astonished. This rest is at first very sweet and pleasant. We enjoy it, and we feel that we are enjoying it; it draws us and concentrates us within ourselves. When we have this rest nothing troubles us, nothing wearies us. Any position, however painful it would otherwise be, is agreeable to us; all other pleasures, whatever they may be, become tasteless and insipid to us; we avoid carefully everything that could withdraw us from this sweet enjoyment of the peace of God. No miser ever feared so much to lose his treasure as we fear everything that could take away from us our rest or change it in any way. This is that blessed sleep of the soul, in which she wakes for God alone and sleeps for everything else.

This may seem like a dream, or a fancy, or an illusion to those who have never experienced it. And it is not only worldlings who think thus; all those to whom rest is unknown, because they have not really given themselves to God, treat it as a delusion, or as the wandering of an overheated imagination. But let us rather believe the saints who speak of it from their own experience; let us believe Saint Paul, who speaks to us of the "peace that passes all understanding;" let us believe our Lord Jesus Christ, who calls this rest His peace, a Divine peace, which the world can neither give nor take away. A peace which we can never obtain by our own efforts, because it is the gift of God, and is His reward for the absolute and irrevocable gift of ourselves which we have made to Him.

I have said before that this peace has its trials, and often even very severe trials; but far from shaking it, these trials only strengthen it: this peace of God rises above all evils, and raises us with it. It renders a Christian so happy in the midst of all his sufferings that he would not change his state, however terrible it may seem to human nature, for the most exquisite pleasures which the world could offer him. Such is the life of a perfect Christian who goes to God by Jesus Christ, and who adores God, as Jesus Christ adored Him, in spirit and in truth; who sacrifices everything to God, and himself above all. Nothing can destroy the rest and peace of his soul, and death will only be for him a short passage from his rest in time to his eternal rest.

What a terrible misfortune it will be for those who will not try to experience the truth of the promises of Jesus Christ, and who torment themselves vainly in this world, to be tormented for ever in the next!

XLVI.

ON THE LIFE OF THE SOUL.

THE Holy Scripture tells us to "*seek after God,*" and our "*soul shall live.*" Here, in two words, is the principle of the whole duty of man and the source of his happiness. The life of the soul, its true and only life, consists in happiness; the soul would rather not exist at all than exist only to be miserable; and, as long as she does not enjoy, at least in hope, what she imagines to be happiness, she does not think she is living at all. But where is this happiness to be found, and what must we do to seek it? Holy Scripture teaches us that our happiness is to be found in God, and only in Him. Now, guided by this rule, which is infallible, let us judge of the so-called happiness of the greater part of mankind, and while we pity them sincerely, let us try to secure our own true happiness. But this is a matter which requires more explanation.

The body has its own life, and it derives that life from the soul. If the body were only formed, without being animated, it would be only a machine, which could not preserve itself, and which would soon fall into corruption and decay. It is therefore on account of its union with the soul that the body is living; and as long as this union lasts, its life lasts. It is also the soul which preserves the life of the body, by giving it food and sleep as it needs

T

them, and by curing it of the illnesses to which it is subject. And if the body had not in itself a principle of corruption, from which all the efforts of the soul cannot deliver it, the soul would obtain immortality for it by remaining always united with it.

That which the soul is to the body, God is to the soul, but with a very remarkable difference. The soul has in herself a principle of natural life, which consists in her power of knowing and loving, and in the exercise of this power. But the soul is not sufficient for herself, and if she were reduced to only knowing and loving herself, she could not attain to her end, therefore, all the curiosity of her understanding and all the desires of her will carry her out of herself, towards other objects which she believes to be worthy of her knowledge and her love, and able to satisfy her eagerness to know and to love. The soul then is only happy when she is fully satisfied on these two points of knowing and loving—that is to say, when, by means of her understanding and her will, she is in possession of an object which leaves her nothing more to desire on the score of knowledge and of love. She rests in this object, and if the possession of it is assured to her for ever, she is also for ever assured of perfect felicity. All this is quite evident, and it only needs a little reflection on our parts to be entirely convinced of it.

But what is this object, to which the soul must be united by knowledge and love, if she would be truly happy?

It is not any sensible object. These objects have no relationship with the soul, except on account of the body which she animates, and they can only obtain for her a knowledge and love dependent on the body. But the power which the soul has of knowing and loving belongs to her as a spiritual substance, and quite independently of her union with the body; therefore this power must have its own proper object, upon which it can act immediately and without any dependence on the body. Besides, sensible things are evidently beneath me, and less than me; they were made for me, and for my use, because I have a body. But the wants of my soul are something quite different to those of my body, and my soul can find nothing in these sensible objects which can possibly satisfy her knowledge or her love.

What then is the object to which my soul must attach herself, that she may live with a true life and enjoy rest and happiness. Is it my fellow-creatures? No: their souls are in the same state as mine; I cannot make their happiness, they cannot make mine. My relationship with them is only accidental, they were not created for me, I was not created for them; we both have the same common principle of existence, our souls have the same needs; they aspire to the same life; they must seek it and find it from the same source.

This source of the soul's true life is God, and it can be none other but Him.

To know God, and to love God, this is the fulness of life and happiness. But can I know Him, can I love Him as I ought, of myself? No. My reason is not sufficiently enlightened, my will is not sufficiently pure and upright. I must go to God Him-

self, and ask Him to teach me how to know and to
love Him.   And for that even I have need of a
supernatural light to illumine my mind, and of a
supernatural impulse of grace to excite my will.   It
is in this light and this impulse that Divine grace
consists ; and this grace is to my soul what nourishment is to my body.   This desire, this necessity of
knowing and loving God, is the hunger of the soul,
and a hunger which God alone can satisfy.   He offers
His grace to all, to sustain their souls and to give
them life ; but before He gives it He requires that
we should ask for it, and He will always give us the
grace of prayer by which we can obtain all others.

The soul is therefore dead when she is separated
from God, just as the body is when it is separated
from the soul.   The death of the soul does not consist
in not existing, but in no longer knowing and loving
God.   It consists in the soul having neither peace
nor happiness, in being in a constant state of agitation
and uneasiness.   It consists in her experiencing a
continual hunger to know and to love her one sovereign
Good, and in never being able to satisfy this hunger.
It is to distract themselves, and to cheat this hunger,
as it were, that men of the world give themselves up
to their passions, and throw themselves with a sort of
fury into every pleasure that presents itself ; they let
their minds wander from one thought to another, they
fix their heart on one affection after another, and all
the time their disgust, their weariness, their inconstancy, their continual change, prove that they can find
nowhere, and in nothing except in God, what can
satisfy or refresh them.   Their souls are always

wandering, always passing from one desire to another; always seeking; always flattering themselves that at last they have found what they want and can be at rest, only to be disappointed again and again in all their hopes and expectations. Thus life passes away, and death surprises the wretched soul and takes away from her for ever the objects of all her desires, and leaves her nothing else but Him Whom she has never wished to know and to love, Whom she never can love now, and Whom she will only know too late to her eternal misery. What a frightful void in that soul! What an inexpressible agony! What a devouring hunger! What remorse! What despair!

The soul, on the contrary, who faithfully seeks after God in this life, will find Him; she attaches herself to Him alone, she is inseparably united to Him. And in this union she finds her life—not yet a life of perfect happiness, but of a happiness that is beginning; she finds a rest that remains in spite of all troubles, temptations, and sufferings; she finds a sweet and secret peace in the midst of the tumult and warfare of the passions, and which exists unchanged in all the events and changes of this mortal life. Such is the life which God promises her here below—a life traversed by all sorts of crosses, which she looks upon as necessary trials of her love and fidelity. Far from fearing these crosses, she desires them, she embraces them, she carries them courageously, because they only serve to make her know and love God more. She would not think she was living if she had not always something to suffer, because without suffering she would think she knew and loved God no longer.

This disposition of spirit may seem incredible, but it is real. And it is quite certain that, the more we die to ourselves, by sufferings and humiliations, the more we live to God; the more we come out of ourselves, the more we are buried and lost in God.

But after this loss of self in God, which is only for this life, we shall find ourselves again, at last, in God for all eternity; and we shall find ourselves again the more there, in proportion as our loss of ourselves in Him has been deepest in this world. Then we shall acknowledge the truth of those words of Holy Scripture: "The Lord gives death, and restores to life again; He sends down to hell, and brings back again." He gives us death to ourselves, and restores to us life in Him. He makes us die to our senses, to our passions, to our own spirit, to our own will, that He may make us live to Him and in Him. Life of knowledge, life of love, life of glory and happiness! All this will be the inheritance of all the elect. But what an incomprehensible difference between the degrees of knowledge and love, and of glory and happiness! God can be infinitely known and infinitely loved; He can increase to infinity the power which His intelligent creatures have of knowing and loving Him, and He will increase this power to His elect in proportion as they have loved and known Him here by suffering and dying to themselves. The life of glory will correspond then to the life of grace.

O my God! O true Life of my soul! teach me to seek Thee. My choice is made; I have no wish to attach myself to anything but to Thee; I wish for nothing but to know Thee and to love Thee. But I

do not know how to come to Thee; I have no strength
of myself. I give myself entirely to Thee, that Thou
mayest enlighten my mind and guide my will. To
live to Thee, and in Thee, I must die to myself. I
know this great truth, but Thou alone canst make
me pass through that happy death which shall obtain
for me the true life. Once more I give myself to
Thee. Teach me to die, to renounce all, and to lose
myself, to find myself for ever in Thee! Amen.

XLVII.

ON THE PEACE OF THE SOUL.

" Great peace have they that love Thy law."—PSALM cxviii.

To have this *"great peace"* of which David speaks,
it is not sufficient for us to observe the law of God—
we must love and cherish it. To observe it, only
through the fear of being lost if we transgress it or
to observe it even because our salvation depends on
its observance, is to think less of God than of our
own interest; it is to obey the law as a slave or a
mercenary. With such a disposition, which is very
common amongst Christians, we cannot expect to
have that full and abundant peace which is only
promised to those who observe the law in a spirit of
love. This spirit of love, which belongs to *children,*
not slaves, teaches us to look upon God as our Father,
to consider His law as a yoke infinitely sweet, His
glory and the accomplishment of His holy will as the

first of our desires, and the happiness of pleasing Him as our greatest advantage. This disposition does not entirely do away with the fear of hell and the desire of paradise, but it raises us above all self-interest, and leads us to serve God for a more perfect motive, as is proposed to us in the Lord's Prayer.

As soon as a soul, by a generous effort of love and a faithful correspondence with the attraction of grace, has made a firm resolution of refusing nothing to God, and of giving herself to Him for ever, to be and to do as He pleases in time and in eternity, from that moment God fills that soul with an ineffable peace, a peace that she never tasted before, a peace which satisfies her every desire, and which inspires her with a profound contempt for all the things of this world. This peace is the effect of the presence of God in the heart, and as long as we preserve this precious peace so long we may be sure of keeping ourselves in the presence of God. This peace is our consolation, our strength, and our adviser; it is the principle of our advancement. The deeper it becomes, the closer, the more immovable, the more inaccessible to all that could trouble it, so much the more shall we increase in perfection; in such a manner, that the height of this peace and the height of perfection are one and the same thing.

The whole secret of this, therefore, consists in preserving and increasing this peace amidst all the changes of the spiritual life. And here are a few rules for doing so.

The first rule is to enjoy this peace as we enjoy good health—that is, without thinking about it. If anyone is continually feeling his pulse, to see if he is not very ill, he will soon end by becoming so. And in the same manner, we expose ourselves to the danger of losing our peace of soul if we pay too much attention to it and are always looking to see if we possess it. Sometimes also we confound real peace with the feeling of peace, and we think we have it no longer because we do not feel it. This is a great mistake. In the beginning of our spiritual life, this peace is generally accompanied by a most exquisite feeling, because then we are entering upon a state of which we have had no previous experience. But as time goes on, and we grow accustomed to this peace, the sweet and sensible feeling of it diminishes; 'and we may even at last lose it entirely, without the real peace of our soul suffering at all. On the contrary, that only becomes more solid and more perfect. Thus, a sick man, when he becomes convalescent, feels his strength and health returning to him. But when he is perfectly well again, he feels nothing at all. We must not then regret the feeling of peace, any more than the sick man regrets the feeling of returning health and strength when his convalescence is at an end.

The second rule is to do all our actions with the greatest simplicity, without thinking too much about them either while we are doing them or after they are done. All self-examination that is too anxious and troubled is contrary to peace. As long as our conscience reproaches us with nothing it is useless to interrogate it; we must only be very attentive when it does speak, and follow its suggestions. But

when our conscience is silent, what is the use of asking ourselves continually: "Have I done well? Have
I done ill? Did I have a good or a bad intention?"
And so on.   All this only serves to perplex the
mind and to torment the soul.

The third rule is that every thought and every
fear which is vague and general, and without any
positive object, does not come from God or from our
conscience, but from our imagination.   We fear we
have not said everything in confession, we fear we
have expressed ourselves badly, we fear we did not
have true contrition, we fear we have not the right
dispositions to go to Holy Communion, and so on,
with a thousand other vague fears with which we
fatigue and torment ourselves   All this does not
come from God.   Whenever God reproaches a soul
His reproaches have always a clear, precise, and
determinate object, and we cannot mistake it.   We
must therefore despise all this kind of vague fears,
and boldly pass them by.

The fourth rule is that God never troubles a soul
that wishes sincerely to go straight to Him.   He
may warn her, He may even severely reprove her,
but He will never trouble her; the soul will see her
faults, she will repent of them, she will repair them,
but all quite peacefully, quite calmly.   If she is
agitated and troubled, it is always the work either of
her own imagination or of the devil, and she must do
all she can to put this trouble away from her.

The fifth rule is that we must change absolutely
nothing in our general conduct while we are in
trouble.   Thus our communions, our prayer, our

spiritual reading, all our other pious exercises, must go on as usual. Then peace will most certainly return to us, and the devil will have gained nothing that he hoped to gain.

Finally, the great rule of all is to do everything by obedience, and never to allow ourselves anything against the known will of our director. When we are once thoroughly convinced that our director is guiding us, and is guided himself by the Spirit of God, there is no other course to take but to abide by his decisions as if they came to us from the mouth of God Himself. God never fails to give, and that for a sufficiently long time, proofs which may reassure the soul as to the wisdom and enlightenment of her guide. And after she has once had these proofs, it is to doubt God Himself if she still doubts and hesitates and fears.

Peace therefore is maintained by a great fidelity in listening to the voice of God, in obeying our director, and in never listening to self-love or our own imagination.

We must also never lose our peace of soul through the faults into which we fall. We must humble ourselves for them before God, we must repent of them, we must repair them, if possible, and then think no more about them. It is only from love of self when we go on troubling ourselves because we are always the same, and because we do not correct ourselves, and do not make any progress in virtue. We deceive ourselves if we think this trouble comes from humility. A soul that is truly humble is neither astonished or troubled at her falls.

XLVIII.

ON FUNDAMENTAL TRUTHS OF THE INTERIOR LIFE.

The First Truth.

God has only given free-will to man that he may consecrate it to Him; therefore the best use we can make of our free-will is to put it in the hands of God again, to renounce all wish to guide ourselves, and to allow God to dispose of us in all things, because in the designs of God everything that happens to us by the arrangement of His Providence must be for our eternal salvation.

Saint Paul says that "All things work together for good to them that love God." If I govern myself in anything whatever, in the first place it is very much to be feared that I shall govern myself badly; and in the second place I am then answerable for the consequences, and if they are bad I cannot be sure of being able to remedy them. If on the contrary I allow myself to be governed by God, I am no longer answerable for anything—God takes charge of everything; I am quite sure of being well guided, and that nothing can happen to me that will not be for my greater good, for God loves me infinitely more than I love myself.

God is infinitely wiser and more enlightened than I am, and if I make Him my absolute Master, it is impossible that anything can prevent the execution of His designs of goodness and mercy towards me. This first truth is self-evident.

SECOND TRUTH.

The second truth is not less certain by experience, and it is this : that the source of the true peace of man is in the gift he makes of himself to God, and that when this gift is full and entire, generous and irrevocable, the peace which he will enjoy in return will be uninterrupted, and will increase and be strengthened from one day to another even by events which apparently might change it or do it harm. The only happiness in life, the only happiness we can obtain for ourselves by the good use of our free-will, is peace of heart. And this peace is not for the wicked, as God tells us in Holy Scripture. The peace also of those devout persons who have not fully given themselves to God is very weak, very tottering, very much troubled either by the scruples of their conscience or their fear of the judgments of God, or the various accidents and events of life. When is it then that a deep, solid, and unchangeable peace takes root in a soul? From the moment that she gives herself entirely to God she enters into a rest and a peace that is none other than the peace of God Himself, upon Whom she leans. We share, of necessity, in the nature of the things to which we attach ourselves. If I unite myself to things that are continually in motion, I experience the same agitation myself; if I unite myself to God, Who alone

is unchangeable, I share in His immutability, and
nothing can shake me so long as I do not separate
myself from Him.

Third Truth.

We are not capable, of ourselves, either of great or
little things for God ; but we must rather desire little
things, leaving it to God, when He thinks fit, to make
us do great things.

Little opportunities of serving and loving Him
present themselves every day, almost every instant—
great ones rarely offer themselves to us. Little
things conduce no less to our sanctification than great
ones, and perhaps they even do so more, because they
keep us humble, and give self-love nothing to feed
upon. Fidelity in little things, a carefulness to please
God even in the smallest trifles, proves the reality
and the delicacy of our love. We may do little things
with such an exalted motive that they may be more
pleasing to God than the greatest things done in less
perfect dispositions. Let us cast an eye upon the
holy house of Nazareth, and the simple and wonderful
lives led there, and we shall be convinced of the truth
of this. Finally, one thing is certain by the teaching
of Holy Scripture, and that is that he who neglects
and despises little things will also neglect greater
ones. Let us then aspire to the perfect practice of
little things, and of all that can nourish in us a
child-like and simple spirit.

FOURTH TRUTH.

The love of God has in us only one enemy, which is the love of ourselves; the devil is only strong against us, and only has power over us, through this self-love. Human respect, which is so terribly strong in so many souls, is the child of self-love. All the obstacles we meet with, all the interior disturbances we experience, only come from self-love. And in proportion as self-love is weakened, and we give up our own judgment and bend our own will to the will of God, which is His own glory and His own good pleasure, so will our difficulties be overcome, our conflicts will cease, our troubles will vanish, and peace and calm will be established in our hearts. Self-love, which at first is open and coarse and plainly seen, becomes more delicate and more spiritual as we advance. And the more spiritual it is, and the deeper and more secret it is, so much the more difficult is it to uproot, and so much the more distress and agony of spirit does it cost us to deliver ourselves from it.

We only know self-love as far as the Divine light discovers it to us, and God only shows it to us by degrees, in proportion as He wishes to destroy it: thus, self-love is only known to us by the blows that God deals at it and that we deal at it conjointly with God, and gradually Divine love occupies the place from which self-love has been driven, until at last Divine love succeeds in driving it completely from the centre of the soul, and reigns there alone, without a rival. When once a soul belongs to Divine love, she is perfectly purified; she may still have to suffer, but she resists no more, and she enjoys the most profound peace in the midst of her sufferings.

Let us follow the different states of the spiritual life, and let us see in a general manner, without going into details, how God pursues self-love from place to place in each of these states.

The most gross kind of self-love lives in the senses, and in the attachment to the things of sense. God drives it out by purifying the senses with His own sweetness and with heavenly consolations, which inspire the soul with disgust and contempt for all earthly pleasures.

Then self-love attaches itself to these consolations, to this peace, to this sensible recollection, until God takes away that support, and withdraws little by little all sensible feeling, leaving to the soul, at the same time, its real peace and tranquillity.

At last, by various kinds of trials, He apparently disturbs this peace completely upon which self-love was relying. We begin to lose ground, and to find no longer any resource in ourselves.

Then to the trials which come from God are joined the temptations of the devil. The soul finds herself stained with thoughts against purity, against faith and hope and charity; then she begins no longer to rely on her own strength or her own virtue; she thinks herself stained with sin, and her director has much trouble in persuading her that she has not consented to the suggestions of the devil. The temptations are always increasing, and her resistance, I do not say really, but apparently, is always growing weaker, in such a manner that at last the soul imagines she has consented ; she sees herself covered with sins, and for this reason she imagines herself rejected by God and forsaken by Him : it is now that self-love is really desolate, and finds the greatest difficulty in serving God for Himself alone, without any consolation. This state lasts until the soul learns to seek herself in nothing. Then self-love leaves her at last and for ever.

And when the soul is thus dead to herself, God gives her a new life, which belongs more to heaven than to earth, in which she possesses God with the firmest confidence, I might almost say with the assurance of never losing Him. She feels that she is united closely with Him in the very depths of her being and in all her faculties—her body even, in a manner, shares in this blissful union. She loves, and she is loved again ; no more fears, no more troubles, no more temptations ; her sufferings, if she still has any, only serve as food for her love. She waits for death in the greatest peace, and dies in the purest act of love.

FIFTH TRUTH.

In the whole course of the sanctification of a soul, the action of God always goes on increasing, and the action of the soul herself is always growing less, until at last all her care is to repress her own activity in order to place no obstacle in the way of the Divine operation. The soul then becomes more and more passive, and God exercises His power over her more

U

and more, until the will of the creature is entirely transformed into the will of God.

The great point, therefore, when we have once given ourselves completely, is to allow ourselves to be despoiled of everything ; for God will take all that we give Him, and will scarcely leave to the soul her own being—I mean her moral being, and her love for herself—but God alone takes all, to bring that all to a state of perfection and excellence above anything that we can think or say.

Sixth Truth.

Let us explain by a comparison what passes with regard to the soul in the way of perfection. A son, influenced by his good natural disposition, protests to his father that he loves him with his whole heart, without any thought of self-interest. The father shows at first by his caresses and his favours how sensible he is of this love of his son. At last, to try if this love is really true and sincere, he withdraws his caresses, he rebukes and neglects his son, he seems to despise his services, he has no attention except for his other children, and seems to forget this one entirely ; he exacts everything from him with the utmost severity, and punishes him severely for the least faults. Not only does he give this son nothing, but he despoils him of everything, and leaves him, so to speak, in a state of entire nakedness ; he takes occasion to ask of him the greatest sacrifices, and at last goes so far that he allows this son to think that he will have no share in his inheritance. In spite of all this, the good son perseveres to the end in giving his father every proof of his love that he possibly can; he spares himself in nothing, he seeks himself in nothing; he looks to nothing but the good pleasure of his father. Forsaken, despoiled, and ill-treated, he still loves his father with a strength, a generosity, and a disinterestedness which rises above all trials.

Now, what will not this father do for a son who loves him so much? Will he not give him, during his life and after his death, everything that he possibly can give him without being unjust to his other children?

A love which counts the cost, which calculates, which looks at its own interest, in a word which will only go so far and no farther, is not a perfect love: to be truly worthy of God, a love must be without measure and without bounds; it must rise above human reason and prudence, and must go as far as folly, even the folly of the cross! It is so that our Lord and Saviour Jesus Christ loved His Father; it is so that He loves each one of us. We shall gain in eternity all that we have lost for God in time, and we shall lose in eternity all that we have refused to Him in time.

XLIX.

ON THE DIVINE LIGHT.

WE have only to read the Psalm cxviii. to see at each verse how necessary the Divine light is for us during the whole course of the interior life. "*Give me understanding*," says David, "*that I may know Thy commandments.*" And again he says, "*Give me understanding, and I shall live.*"

To be thoroughly convinced of this necessity, we must know first that human reason is strangely obscured and dimmed since original sin overshadowed it ; and secondly, that the most enlightened reason would not be sufficient of itself to guide us in the way of grace, a way of which God keeps the secret to Himself. As His intention is that we should always walk in the spirit of faith, He only enlightens us gradually as we go on step by step, and only just so much as is necessary for our present needs. He does not wish us to look before us, or even around us, but He always gives us enough light to convince us that it is impossible for us to go astray if we will only follow Him, even though we may seem to be in the midst of a thick darkness.

The first thing, then, which a soul ought to do, when she wishes to belong entirely to God, is to renounce her own spirit, and all the ideas she may have formed beforehand on the subject of virtue and sanctity, being persuaded that these ideas are either false or very imperfect; not to think she can guide herself, nor judge of things by her own light, nor constitute herself a judge of the way in which her director guides her. All these pretensions will end by filling her with pride and presumption, by withdrawing her from obedience, by leading her astray, and perhaps by ruining her eternally; instead of which it is quite impossible for a soul who has renounced her own judgment entirely, who listens to the voice of God within her, and to the teaching of her director from without, whom she willingly obeys in all that is not sin, it is impossible, I say, for such a soul to run any risk of falling into delusion. God, in Whom she places all her trust, is interested in never allowing anything of the kind, and such a thing has never happened.

After this she must humbly pray for the Divine light, begging of God to enlighten her from one moment to another; she must never undertake anything of importance without consulting God, and without asking the advice of him whom God has given her for a guide.

The light of God is generally very abundant in the beginning. We receive it in prayer, and in Holy Communion; we are surprised at being able to understand books which treat of the spiritual life, and to see clearly in things of which we understood nothing before. This light is a sure light, and bears with it an evidence which leaves us no room for doubt. We feel that it is an infused light, and that we owe it neither to our natural intelligence nor to our careful application, nor to our continual efforts. More than this, it is accompanied by a sweetness and fervour which feeds and elevates and ravishes the soul as well as enlightening her.   As this Divine light is never the fruit of our own reflections, we must receive it passively, without reasoning upon it, without striving to retain it, or to recall it when it is passing away.   At the moment it is given to us it has its effect; and when there is a necessity for making use of this effect God will bring back the memory of it to us, or He will give us the same grace again.   But He does not wish us to appropriate it to ourselves, as if it were an acquired science, nor does He wish us always to have it at our own disposal.   The Spirit of God cannot be constrained nor subject to the will of a creature.

We must therefore let it come and go as God pleases, and believe that it will never be wanting to us when we have real need of it.   We may sometimes write down the lights and graces we have received, to communicate them to our confessor, when they have to do with some particular object; but to write them down only to refresh our own memory, or even to assist ourselves when we think it necessary, this is what we must never do, for it would be showing a certain want of trust in God.   It might perhaps, however, be done, if a person were very far advanced in the spiritual life, and if he were writing, in obedience to his director, more for the instruction of others than for himself.

We must be very careful also in these beginnings, when we are, as it were, surrounded with Divine light, never to speak about such things to others, even if we think we are speaking for God, or to guide and instruct others. This is a temptation we must always resist. A very special vocation from God is necessary before we attempt to guide our neighbour, particularly when we are not called to it by our state of life. And more than this, the light which is suitable for us may not be suitable for others, because God may be leading them by a different way.

Finally, we shall most certainly exhaust ourselves if we are always communicating our graces to the exterior world. But this does not mean to say that we are never to try to bring people to God, by our conversation and example, when we see them in good dispositions, and when they give us an opportunity of influencing them for good.

The use of the Divine light, either for ourselves or for others, is an extremely delicate and difficult matter, and presupposes a real death to ourselves. This is why we must never be the first to decide for ourselves, nor must we always receive as a Divine inspiration whatever comes into our mind with the semblance of good. Saint Paul tells us that Satan can transform himself into an angel of light; he very often mixes himself up with the Divine operations, acting upon the imagination at the same time that God is acting in the understanding and the will. We are therefore very liable to be deceived in all those things that are called interior locutions, attractions and inspirations; and we must always submit all those sort of things to the judgment of our confessor, waiting for his decision before we make any use of them.

To act of our own will and by our own judgment

in anything of this kind, is to fall directly into the snares of the enemy.

To dispose ourselves to receive the Divine light, we must, as much as we possibly can, never listen to our imagination, never rest on our own understanding, and have an extreme distrust of our own reflections and reasonings. We can scarcely believe how very little God communicates Himself to those who wish to be always reflecting, always reasoning. The best use we can make of our own reason in the things of God is to command it to keep silence before Him, and to keep it always in a state of annihilation. It is to the "little ones," to those who are like children in their simplicity and purity, that God communicates Himself freely. He has no regard for mere acquired knowledge, profound wisdom, or the natural light of the intellect; He wishes us to trample all that under foot when we wish to come to Him; He wishes us to renounce all that we have learnt from other sources, and humbly to be taught by Him alone. Such a man was Saint Augustine, the greatest doctor of the Church. He consulted God in everything with the simplicity of a child.

Such are not those people who, with minds very inferior to his, set themselves up as judges of the ways of God and of His dealings with souls. They will not be persuaded, as the Gospel teaches them, that the first step we must take, if we wish to understand the things of God, is to humble ourselves, and to confess that of ourselves we can understand nothing—to pray to Him, and to have recourse to Him as the only source of all light.

If it is true, as the Prophet Isaias says, that the thoughts of God are as far removed from the thoughts of man as the heavens are from the earth, how can we presume to build upon our own light in spiritual things ? Why is our mind not continually over-whelmed with confusion before God ? Why do we not incessantly open the " door of our heart," as David says, to breathe in and draw to ourselves the Spirit of God ? What is the adoration of " God in spirit and in truth," if it is not this constant and practical confession that God alone is Light and Truth, and that we are nothing but darkness and lies ?

This is, it seems to me, the true homage of the mind, and is also an infallible means of never going astray.

Let us then say to God, " Give me understanding, that I may know Thy commandments. It is impos-sible for me to practise them if I do not understand them, and I cannot understand them if Thou dost not give me the intelligence to do so. How can I understand what it is to love Thee with all my mind, with all my heart, and with all my strength ? Who but Thou, O my God ! can penetrate the depths of this precept, and communicate the knowledge of it to Thy creature ? Who but Thou, also, can make me understand what it is to love my neighbour as myself ? Do I know, can I know, in what way Thou hast commanded me to love myself ? And if I do not know how I am to love myself, can I know what is the love I owe to my neighbour ? Nevertheless, the whole law is contained in these two precepts.

It is evident then, that unless I wilfully blind myself, I understand nothing of Thy law, and can understand nothing, if Thou Thyself dost not enlighten me !

But Thy law is the source of life, of the true life, of the eternal life; we cannot gain this life without practising Thy law; and the more perfectly we practise it the more shall we enjoy that true life, which is none other than the possession of Thyself. Give me then understanding, and I shall live.   Yes, O my God and my All ! grant me to understand the necessity of Thy love, and the extent of Thy love; grant me to understand how in the love of Thee is contained the love I ought to have for myself and the love I ought to have for my neighbour.   Give me this Divine light, that, assisted by Thy grace, I may practise Thy whole law ; then I shall practise it in all its fulness, and I shall attain to the fulness of the true life—the life eternal !   Amen.

L.

ON SPIRITUAL CHILDHOOD.

OUR Lord Jesus Christ said, *" Suffer the little children to come to Me : for of such is the kingdom of heaven."*

And He said again, when He placed a little child in the midst of His Apostles, *" Unless you become as a little child, you shall not enter into the kingdom of heaven."*

The meaning of these words of our Saviour is,

that if we wish to have the kingdom of God within us, we must become, in our supernatural dispositions, just like a little child is in its natural disposition. And in short, there is a spiritual childhood, and this state is the first step we must take to enter upon the spiritual life. It is impossible to form any idea of this state of holy childhood unless we know it by experience; it is a gift of God—we cannot acquire it by any labour or reflections of our own. God Himself must lead us into it; and when we have the happiness of being admitted therein, we experience in ourselves, in our mind as well as our heart, a most wonderful change.

To picture to ourselves this state as much as is possible, let us compare it with the state of natural childhood.

A child does not reason, and does not reflect; he has neither foresight, nor prudence, nor malice. It is just the same with real spiritual childhood. The first thing God does when He places us in this state is to suspend the operations of the mind. He suspends that crowd of reasonings and reflections which swarm incessantly around it, and replaces them by simple and direct operations of which the soul is scarcely conscious; in such a manner that she believes she is not thinking when she is always thinking, and thinking in a way far higher, and nearer to God's own way, Who has only one thought, and that thought infinitely simple.

The soul, thus reasoning no longer, reflecting no longer, occupies herself no more with the past or the future, but only with the present; she forms no more

projects of any kind, but she allows herself to be
directed in all things, from one moment to another,
within by the Spirit of God, and without by Divine
Providence. There is no longer any malice in her
actions or her words, because she does nothing
and says nothing designedly or with premeditations.
Despoiled of her own prudence, she is clothed with
the prudence of God, Who makes her always speak
and act as she ought to do, as long as she is faithful
in never consulting her own spirit. The state of
utter dependence upon Him, in which God keeps her
in this respect, is so great, that it does not leave the
soul a single instant in which she is able to act of
her own accord.

A child has no dissimulation, no concealment.
As soon as he is capable of deceit he is no longer a
child. In like manner, nothing can equal the openness and candour of the spiritual child. He does
not compose his exterior; his recollection has nothing
constrained about it; his actions, his conversation,
his manners, everything in him is simple and natural ;
when he says anything, he really thinks it; when he
offers anything, he wishes to give it ; when he promises anything, he will keep his promise. He does
not seek to appear different to what he really is, nor
to hide his faults ; he says what is good and what is
evil of himself with the same simplicity, and he has
no reserve whatever with those to whom he ought to
disclose the state of his soul.

A child shows his love with artless innocence :
everything in him expresses the feelings of his heart,
and he is all the more touching and persuasive

because there is nothing studied about him. It is the same with the spiritual child, when he wishes to show his love for God and his charity for his neighbour. He goes to God simply, without preparation; he says to God without set formulas or choice of words all that his loving heart suggests to him; he knows no other method of prayer than to keep himself in the presence of God, to look at God, to listen to Him, to possess Him, to tell Him all the feelings with which grace inspires him, sometimes in words, but more often without speaking at all. He loves his neighbour sincerely and cordially, bears him no kind of malice or envy, does not ridicule him, does not criticise him, does not despise him, and never deceives him; he does not flatter his neighbour, either; he has lost the art of using those vain compliments which do not come from the heart—he only makes use of the courtesy and kindness which the Gospel authorises, and raises it still higher by his charity and cordiality. He loves none the less when he is obliged to reprove, he condemns as kindly and justly as he praises and approves; he is always doing good to others without affectation, without ostentation, in the sight of God, and without expecting any gratitude or return.

A child is docile and obedient—he feels that he is not made to do his own will. And the first thing also which the spiritual child renounces is his own will, which he submits entirely to the will of God, and to all that holds the place of God to Him. He does not wish to govern himself in anything, but in all that relates to the guidance of his soul he abandons

himself without reserve to the Spirit of God, and to
the minister of God, to whom he has given his confidence ; and as for his exterior conduct, he willingly
yields obedience to all who have authority over him
In indifferent things he prefers to accommodate his will
to the will of others, rather than to bring others to
his way of thinking. Finally, he wishes for nothing
because it is his own will, but only because it is the
will of God; therefore, when he once wishes a thing,
he does not change.

A child does not know himself, he does not reflect
upon himself; he is quite incapable of studying himself or observing himself.   He leaves himself as he
is, and walks straight on, always looking before him.
The spiritual child also is no longer curious about
looking into his soul and seeing what is passing
there.   He takes what God gives him, and is quite
content to be from one moment to another just what
God wishes him to be.   He does not attempt to
judge of the goodness or perfection of his prayers,
his communions, or any of his other pious exercises,
by the passing feelings which he may experience in
them, but he leaves the judgment of all these things
to God ; and, provided only that the interior disposition of his soul does not change, he rises above all
the vicissitudes of the spiritual life.   He knows that
the spiritual life has its winters, its hurricanes, its
tempests, and its clouds—that is to say, its times of
dryness and disgust, its interior weariness and its
temptations.   He passes courageously through all
these trials, and waits in peace for the return of fine
weather.   He is not uneasy about his progress ; he

is not always turning round to see how far he has advanced on the road; but he goes on his way quietly, without even thinking if he is walking, and he advances far more because he is not looking to see how he advances. In this way, he is not troubled, he is not discouraged. If he falls, he humbles himself for it, but he gets up again directly, and runs with fresh ardour.

A child is weak, and feels his weakness; this is what makes him so dependent, so distrustful of himself, and so full of trust in those whom he knows take an interest in him. The spiritual child feels, in like manner, that he is weakness itself, that he cannot support himself or make a single step without stumbling. Therefore he never leans upon himself, he never relies upon his own strength, but he puts all his trust in God; he keeps himself always near to God, he stretches out his hand to God, that God may hold him and sustain him in all the difficult paths he may have to tread. He is infinitely far from ever attributing to himself any good he may do or any victory he may gain, but he gives the glory of all to God. He does not prefer himself to others, but is firmly convinced that if God were to leave him to himself he would fall into the greatest crimes, and that if others had the same graces that he has they would make a much better use of them than he does. For the same reason, as he feels himself to be so weak, he is not astonished at his falls; his self-love is not annoyed by them, but feeling his powerlessness to rise of himself, he calls upon God and implores His assistance. This feeling of his weakness is also the principle of his courage, because God is his strength ; and, assured of the protection of God, he sees nothing that can frighten him or shake him.   He undertakes nothing of himself, he exposes himself to nothing by his own will; but the moment God speaks he undertakes all, he exposes himself to all, and he is sure of succeeding, in spite of all the efforts of men and of hell.

Innocence, peace, and pure joy is the heritage of little children ; they are happy without thinking they are happy ; they have no care, no anxiety.   Their parents, their nurses, their governesses, think of everything for them.   They are in a continual state of enjoyment.   And this is only a weak and imperfect image of the state of the spiritual child of God.   His happiness, like the happiness of the other child, is neither perceived nor reflected upon ; but it is real— he enjoys it.   God fills his soul with it, God thinks of everything for him, God provides for everything. This happiness is maintained in the midst of the greatest storms of the spiritual life, and it cannot be affected by the events and changes of human life.   It is not that the state of spiritual childhood renders us insensible, but it raises us, by our perfect resignation to the will of God, above all feeling to the enjoyment of an unshaken peace.   No one can judge of this except by experience.   But the experience of it is such that the whole universe could never succeed in persuading a soul that is so blessed that she is deceived and deluded.

PRAYER.

O Lord of my Soul! can I think of the happiness which Your children enjoy even in this life without imploring of You with all my heart to call me also into the number of those children in whom You find delight—of those children who are Your true worshippers, who depend entirely upon You, and who accomplish Your adorable Will in all things?

Suffer me, O my Saviour! to come to You in like manner! Take me in Your sacred Arms, lay Your Hands upon me and bless me; take away from me for ever my own spirit and replace it by the instinct of Your Divine grace; take from me my own will, and leave me only the desire of doing Your Will. Give me that beautiful, that lovable, that sublime simplicity which is the first and the greatest of Your gifts. Adam was created in this simplicity. He lost it for himself and for me by his sin. I have deserved myself, by my innumerable faults, to be deprived of it for ever. But, my Lord and my God, O Supreme Good, and my Rest! You can give it to me again; You desire to do so, and if I put no obstacle in Your way, I hope that You will restore it to me. Then You shall receive from me that tribute of homage which is only perfect from the mouth of children! Amen.

x

LI.

ON THE JEALOUSY OF GOD.

In many places in Holy Scripture God calls Himself a jealous God ; and He even goes so far as to say that His name is *jealous*, to show us how essential that character is to Him, and that He cannot despoil Himself of it any more than of His very Being.

But of what is God jealous ?   Of one thing only, and that is, of the homage of our mind and our heart —not a barren homage which rests on simple speculation, but a true homage which influences all our feelings and all our actions.

Now, in what does this homage of the mind consist ?   It consists in acknowledging God to be everything, the beginning of everything and the end of everything, and that without Him all is nothing.   It consists especially in humbling our minds before Him, and in submitting to Him all the light our intellect may receive ; or rather in being convinced that He Himself is our true Light, both in the natural order and the supernatural ; that we cannot see well or judge well, except in so far as we see as He sees and judge as He judges : and this will bring our mind into a state of absolute dependence on Him, into a continual dying to our own spirit to consult His only, and into a constant fidelity in never acting in conformity to our own will, but only as He wills. This is the homage which He requires, and which

He has a right to require from our minds, and of this homage He is infinitely jealous. If we refuse it to Him we go against His most essential right, we arrogate to ourselves independence in a matter which concerns the finest quality of man, that is, his capacity for knowledge, his intelligence, and his reason; we pretend either that we do not hold this intelligence from God, or that we can make a very good use of it without regulating it by the Divine Intelligence—a most foolish pretension, injurious to God, and the source of all the wanderings of His creatures.

On the contrary, when we render to God this homage of the intellect, we acquit ourselves of our first duty towards the Supreme Intelligence, we place all our glory in depending utterly upon Him for all our knowledge, or for all our powers of judgment; and this homage is for us a principle of wisdom and good conduct, and an assurance of never going astray. All the errors of the human spirit, in matters of faith and morality, only proceed from not consulting the Source of Light Himself, "*the light that lightens every man that cometh into the world.*" We must therefore in everything, but especially in supernatural things, upon which our salvation and perfection depend, keep our mind annihilated, so to speak, under the Mind of God.

And the homage of the heart, in what does that consist? In establishing God as the centre of all our affections, in loving Him for Himself alone, with all our strength, in loving ourselves only for Him and in Him; in loving no other creature except in a very subordinate manner and even then referring all our love for creatures to Him. Is not this just, when we consider that God is infinitely lovable, that we hold from Him alone our power of loving, and that He cannot permit our affections to be concentrated on ourselves or on any creature whatsoever? Does not the most simple light of reason teach us that this homage of the heart is due to God alone; that it is due to Him in all its fulness, that it is due to Him at every moment of our existence, and that a heart which does not love God, and does not love Him above all things—loving everything else and itself also for God's sake only—must be a depraved heart, a monster in the moral world? If we reflect for a moment upon Who God is, and what we ourselves are, can we doubt that all our love belongs to Him, that He requires the homage of it, that He is essentially jealous of this homage, and that He cannot suffer the contrary disorder without reproving it and punishing it?

Besides, this homage, that is so just and so natural, is the principle of our fidelity. Let us bestow our love where we will, but we shall never be happy in this world until we fix it upon God alone. This is a matter of experience. Every love that is not a well-ordered love is the torment of the person who loves, even if he were possessed as well of all the good things of this earth. And on the contrary, every love that is well-regulated, and that has God for its first object, is for the heart a never-failing source of peace and joy which no evil in the world can trouble.

But to what degree is God jealous? He is jealous

infinitely and without measure. He to Whom all is
due, Who deserves all, Who exacts all, is necessarily
jealous of all, and can let nothing pass. O my God!
let me conceive, as much as I am capable of doing
so, how far Your jealousy extends, that I may never
be so unhappy as to wound it in anything. If it is
true that I ought to love You only for Your own
sake alone, and that I ought to refer all other love
to You—if it is true that all love that is not love of
You is self-love, then Your jealousy with regard to
this self-love must be infinite ; it must go so far as
not to be able to suffer the least vestige of self-love
to remain in a heart, and to pursue it to its utter
destruction. O my God, I firmly believe this ; faith
and reason both teach it to me.

But if this is so, how can I destroy this self-love
which is so deeply rooted in me, which began with
my very existence, which corrupts and stains all my
affections ? Alas! I do not know it in all its extent ; and even if I did thoroughly know it, how could
I fight against it ? This love is a part of myself;
it is in me and clings closely to me. What strength
can I find in myself against myself?

It is quite true that no man can fight against
self-love in his own strength ; but he can give himself up to God, he can suffer the just jealousy of
God to fight against his own self-love, he can second
this jealousy with his own earnest efforts ; and when it
is a question of dealing the last blow at the wretched
human *I*, he can consent to bear this blow and not
to shrink from the hand that is crucifying him.

He must pass through many conflicts and trials

before he comes to this ; but a faithful and generous soul which leaves itself in God's hands, and never wishes to draw back however God may treat it, will infallibly attain to this. The jealousy of God is too much interested in the matter to leave His work unfinished. This work began from the moment that God took possession of the soul and established His kingdom there. If this soul does not withdraw herself from the kingdom of God, she may be quite sure that God will not desist until He has finished His work in her according to His designs. Now this work of God consists in purifying her entirely from self-love, in not leaving a single fibre of it in her, and in utterly destroying the human *I*, in such a manner that the soul can lose nothing and desire nothing. Then God finds no more self-love, no more self-interest in that soul, and His jealousy is satisfied.

And it is so essential that this jealousy of God with regard to self-love should be fully satisfied, that if it is not satisfied in this world it will be in the other. It is of faith that self-love, which is the fruit of original sin, can have no place in Heaven, and that the sole love which can exist there is the pure love of God. If then a soul, however holy she may otherwise be, leaves this world with some remains of self-love clinging to her, the fire of purgatory must purify her from them ; and this fire, as we know, is the same as the fire of hell, and purgatory only differs from hell because *hope* finds a place there, and because it is not eternal.

. But why is God jealous in this way ? Because

He is God, infinitely holy, and the infinite lover of order ; and because His love, as He communicates it to the blessed in Heaven, cannot exist with self-love. If one of the blessed in Heaven could cast a single look of complacency on himself, if he could for one moment love his happiness for his own sake, if he could see in this happiness anything but the pure goodness and mercy of God, the glory of God, and the will of God, at that very moment he would fall from Heaven, and could never enter there again till he had expiated that act of self-love.

O my God! exercise upon me here, in this life, all Your most just and holy jealousy ! Annihilate my mind, purify my heart, and make them both render to You the homage which is due to You in all its fulness ! Amen.

LII.

ON PURE LOVE.

PURE love is the love of God, unmixed with the love of self. Thus, from whatever motive we may produce an act of love to God, whether on account of His infinite perfections or from a motive of hope or of gratitude, this act is pure as long as it is not stained with self-love. God alone knows if we love Him sincerely and purely. And He has thought fit to conceal this knowledge from us on purpose to keep us humble and in an entire trust in Him.

Self-love is therefore the great enemy of pure love ;

these two loves cannot exist together; one must necessarily exclude the other.

Now, what is self-love? It is that love of ourselves which begins and ends with ourselves, and which has not God for its final end. This self-love intrudes even into spiritual things, when we love virtue, and the gifts of God, and the holiness of God, and God Himself, only for our own sakes, or for the enjoyment we find in these things, or for the advantage we derive from them, in one word, when we set up our own selves as the centre and object of our affections. Now when this self-love carries us to desire grievously forbidden things and to seek after them, it becomes mortal sin. But it is only venial sin or mere imperfection when it attaches us to objects which are really good and holy in themselves, and when it still gives to God the love of preference which is due to Him, because in this case the disorder is not in the foundation and essence of our love, but in our manner of loving.

The love of God is always infinitely pure in its source, which is no other than God Himself. It is pure, although in different degrees, in the angels and the blessed souls in Heaven. It is a most certain truth, that self-love can never enter Heaven; our heart must be purified from it either in this life or in purgatory.

As the ordinary course of grace is to draw us to God by a certain sweetness and sensible fervour, our love for God in the beginning is almost always mixed with self-love; and God is not offended at this mixture then, because it is a necessary consequence of our misery. He even makes use of this self-love then to detach us from the things of earth, and to give us a taste for those of Heaven ; He makes use of it, in these beginnings, to induce us to make a quantity of sacrifices which otherwise we could not make. It is really the love of God which leads us on to detachment and sacrifices and the practice of prayer and mortification ; but if self-love did not also find something to feed upon, which seems very delicious, and quite superior to all the pleasures of earth, never should we embrace the interior life.

The love of beginners is not then entirely pure, and, as a general rule, it cannot be so and ought not to be so. But by degrees God purifies this love on His part, and He teaches the soul to purify it on her part. God takes away from time to time, and sometimes for a long period, all sensible consolation : we become dry and distracted in prayer and at Holy Communion, our enjoyment of spiritual things, our extreme fervour, our transports of love, become very rare, and last but a short time. The soul at first is very unhappy ; she thinks God has forsaken her ; she is tempted to give up everything. But if indeed she did give up everything, it would be a proof that she was only mercenary, and that she was only loving and seeking herself in her devotion. Instead of which, if she remains faithful through all these times of dryness, if she relaxes nothing, if she gives to God with the same generosity all He asks of her, then she begins really to love God for Himself alone, and not for the sake of His gifts. These are the first purifications of Divine love.

After longer or shorter alternations of consolation and dryness, if the soul is really noble and generous, God takes away sensible fervour from her altogether, and only allows her to taste His love most rarely, and for one moment, as it were. A love thus despoiled and naked becomes constantly purer and more simple. The soul feels no longer either that she loves or that she is loved; she perceives it no more, she reflects upon it no more. Nevertheless all the time she is loving infinitely better and more intensely than ever, but without the slightest thought of herself, self-love can find nothing more to attach itself to. The creature disappears and leaves to God the whole heart. In this state the soul produces rarely formal acts; she lives in the simple and continual exercise of one act of love. The proof that she loves is no longer in her feeling it, but in her utter forgetfulness of herself; she no longer enters into her interior to see what is passing there or to enjoy it, but she withdraws farther and farther away from herself to bury and lose herself in God.

But these even are not yet the greatest purification of love. This is done, 1st, by temptations, which seem to destroy in us all virtues, when in reality they are only strengthening and perfecting our virtue. Temptations against purity, temptations against faith, temptations against hope, temptations against charity to our neighbour, temptations to impiety and blasphemy, often an upheaval of all the passions. But all this passes on the borderland of the soul, the soul is not really affected by it; but she does not know that; she fancies she has consented, and however much she may be reassured and comforted, she lives in a constant fear of having sinned. Behold her, then, clothed and covered and penetrated with the conviction of her own misery : she sees nothing in herself but filth and corruption, she is very far now from loving or esteeming herself, she despises herself, she hates herself, she looks upon herself as a monster ! Can you not see now that self-love is not only not acting any longer in that soul, and staining her actions and motives, but it is even changed into a disposition totally opposite ? It is the love of God, and the purest love of Him, that has produced this effect, for the soul only hates herself in this manner because she fancies she has offended God, and because she believes herself to be the greatest of sinners. But oh ! how far she is now from consenting to sin ! She would prefer hell. Yet the misery she experiences persuades her that she is nothing but sin and abomination ; and God only puts her in this state to inspire her with a holy hatred of herself founded on her detestation of sin. What a beautiful act of contrition is this hatred ! And how it expiates in a manner most pleasing to God not only the actual sins of that soul, but those she might otherwise have committed !

2nd. The love of God is purified by humiliations. This same soul, who a little time before may have passed as a saint in a whole community or a whole town, sees herself suddenly attacked on all sides by calumny. Everyone loses the good opinion they had of her ; she is looked upon as a hypocrite ; her most innocent words have a bad interpretation put upon

them, her most holy actions are considered criminal;
every one abandons her, every one shuns her; her
friends, even her most intimate and confidential friends,
turn against her, and she is condemned by the voice
of authority.   Nevertheless, in the midst of all she
keeps silence, she allows herself to be judged and
condemned.   Thus, to the accusation of her own conscience, which persuades her she is guilty, is joined the
witness of men who treat her as if she were guilty.
She has no idea of feeling hatred or resentment against
them; and although she is innocent of all the things
they accuse her of, she believes that she quite deserves
all the ill-treatment she receives at their hands.   What
becomes of her self-love then?   It finds no more
support, either from the testimony of her own conscience or from the opinion of men.   Everything is
arrayed against it, within and without; the love of
God, which is always growing purer and purer, pursues self-love, drives it out entirely, and leaves it no
place of refuge.

3rd. The last purification of love is caused by God
Himself forsaking the soul.   Persecuted self-love
seemed at least to have this refuge left.   God Himself
takes it away.   At the same time that He delivers the
soul up to the fear of her apparent sins, and to very
real humiliations on the part of men, He treats her
Himself as a severe judge; He seems to reject her
and to leave her to herself.   His justice deals her the
most terrible blows; she thinks she is lost, and lost
without hope.   What a state!   How terrible it is!
how desperate for self-love!   Self-love struggles hard,
and defends itself as well as it can behind its last

rampart. But at last it must give way; it must yield; God is the strongest; and by a last sacrifice, which is the fruit of the purest love, self-love is torn out of the soul even to its smallest root. And by this sacrifice, the love of God is absolutely freed from all admixture, and reigns alone in the heart from which it has banished its enemy.

These are the three degrees by which Divine love attains to its final purification. It is a mistake to say or to think that during all these trials the soul loses the virtue of hope. This virtue is never really lost, even during the most violent temptations to despair : God and the devil may be recognised by their works. The devil begins by temptations to pride, and finishes by enslaving the soul to the sins of the flesh. God attacks the flesh first of all, and finishes by annihilating pride, making use sometimes, for this end, of the temptations of the flesh.

For the state of pure love therefore to exclude hope is quite impossible, and to maintain that it does is a formal heresy.

LIII.

ON THE INTERIOR OF MARY.

" Mary kept all these things in her heart."

THAT we may judge well of the interior of Mary, let us see what God did for her, and what she did for God.

God, Who had predestinated her from all eternity

to be the Mother of Jesus Christ, bestowed on her all these marvellous graces: 1st, He preserved her from the stain of original sin; 2nd, He enriched her with the greatest grace from the moment of her Immaculate Conception; 3rd, He gave her very soon, perhaps even in her mother's womb, the full use of reason; 4th, He raised her to the dignity of the Divine Maternity, and gave her a special and sole share, first in the cross and sufferings, and afterwards in the glory of the Son of God.

Mary corresponded with these graces of God, 1st, by living in such strict watchfulness over herself, so continually maintained, that it was as if she, who was immaculate, had everything to fear from the attacks of the flesh and all the sad consequences of original sin. What then ought to be our watchfulness, we who are born in sin, and have experienced so often the terrible effects of concupiscence!

2nd. By applying herself to follow every motion of Divine grace with so much fidelity that she never committed the slightest actual sin, that she merited every moment of her life a fresh increase of grace, that she never made a single interior act, or performed a single exterior action, which had not for its sole end to unite her more closely to God. What a model for a soul that has given herself entirely to God!

3rd. She corresponded with the grace of God by constantly making the most perfect use of her reason. And what use did she make of it? She submitted it continually to the light of faith; she made of it a perpetual sacrifice to the Supreme Reason, which is

God ; she never allowed herself one single reasoning about the designs of God or His conduct with regard to her, although this conduct was full of mysteries and of apparent contradictions. We shall never make any advance in the spiritual life unless we make the same use of our reason. God often guides souls by ways that are opposed to all human views ; He takes pleasure in upsetting all our judgments, in disconcerting all our foresight, in disappointing all our efforts. We have only one thing to do, which is not to think about ourselves at all, not to reason about what God is doing with us, and being content to walk in blind faith and implicit obedience.

4th. Our Blessed Lady corresponded with the grace of God by preparing herself for the Divine Maternity without knowing it, by the very means, which, humanly speaking, must have deprived her of that honour. All the virgins of Judea were anxious to marry, in hopes of becoming the mother of the Messiah. To be a barren wife was for them the greatest opprobrium. Mary thought herself quite unworthy of aspiring to the dignity of Mother of God. In her most tender years she presented herself in the Temple ; there she consecrated her virginity to God for ever, and by so doing, according to the ideas of her nation, she renounced for ever the highest hope of her sex and her tribe. It is not by aspiring after great things, or having grand ideas and magnificent designs, that we attain to sanctity, or dispose ourselves for the designs of God for us, which are very different to our own. It is by humbling ourselves, by burying ourselves in our own

lowliness and nothingness, by acknowledging ourselves
unworthy of all grace, and dreading all thoughts of
elevation, rejecting them as suggestions from the
spirit of pride.

As to the cross of Jesus Christ, Mary had in it
such a share that, from the birth of her Divine Son
until His death, she felt the very same blows that He
suffered, not only from men but also from God.   To
form some idea of this, it is enough for us to consider
that she loved her Son with a love as great as any
creature could possibly have ; that she loved Him
infinitely more than herself ; that she was closely
united to Him, in such a union that God Himself
could not conceive anything closer ; that she did not
live in herself, but in her Son ; that all the feelings
which the heart of Jesus experienced were communicated to the heart of His Mother with all the strength
and extent of which a pure creature was capable.   Let
us raise ourselves then to the consideration of all that
passed in the soul of Jesus Christ with regard to the
glory of His Father, outraged by men, the holiness
of His Father, dishonoured by sin, the justice of His
Father, of which He Himself was the Victim ; with
regard to so many millions of souls to whom His
Blood and His Sacrifice would be useless, and even
fatal, by the abuse they would make of them.   Let
us consider all this, and think what the sufferings of
Mary must also have been, when we boldly say that
she experienced in proportion the same impressions.

Jesus Christ sacrificed Himself upon the cross by
giving Himself up to all the severity of the Divine
justice.   Mary sacrificed herself, and more than her-

self, by sacrificing Jesus Christ, and consenting to
the accomplishment of the designs of God for the
redemption of the human race, in such a manner
that the greatest sacrifices of the spiritual life are
incomparably less than hers both in extent and in
depth, and on account of the incomprehensible sorrow
which she felt. When we have passed through the
last trials of our love, if God grants us this grace,
we shall have some faint idea of the dolours of Mary.
As for the generality of Christians, they only see in
the passion of Jesus Christ, in His bodily torments,
and in the sorrows of Mary, the compassion she had
for the torments of her Son.

The interior of Mary was then a copy, and the
very closest copy, of the interior of Jesus Christ.
As Jesus sacrificed Himself continually to His Father
during the whole course of His life, Mary also continually sacrificed Jesus in her heart, and herself
with Him, to the Eternal Father in Heaven.

As Jesus humbled Himself and annihilated Himself to such a degree that He looked upon Himself
as loaded with the iniquity of the universe, so
Mary humbled herself and annihilated herself, as the
mother of Him Who bore the sins of the world, and
made Himself the object of the Divine malediction;
and she herself entered, as far as was possible, into
the dispositions of her Son.

As Jesus loved men so much that He gave them
not only the life of His body, but in some sense the
life of His soul, so Mary loved men so much that she
gave them, in Jesus Christ, what was dearer to her
than her own life and her own soul.

Y

What shall I say now of the prayer of Mary? Who can speak of it worthily? Jesus Christ was the sole object of her thoughts, the sole object of her love; after His resurrection and ascension into Heaven it was only her body that remained on earth; her soul followed Him into Heaven. From that time she only languished for her Son, and desired His presence with an intensity which we can neither understand or express. Her only distraction, if we may call it by that name, her only consolation, was to pray for the new-born Church of Christ, and to interest herself in its progress.

With such a high elevation of soul and such exalted feelings, what was the Blessed Virgin in her exterior? A woman of the people, a poor woman, living by the work of her own hands, occupied for thirty years at Nazareth with the cares of her little household, cared for afterwards by Saint John, to whom Jesus had confided her, and who shared with her the offerings of the faithful. What noise did she make in the world? By what great deeds was she distinguished in the eyes of men? What did she do outwardly for the propagation of the Gospel? And yet all the time she was the Mother of God; she was the holiest and purest of creatures; it was she who had the greatest share in the redemption of mankind, and in the establishment of the Christian religion. Oh how different are the ideas of God from our ideas! Oh how far removed from our ways are the ways He takes to attain His ends! How pleasing in His eyes are obscurity, humility, retirement, solitude, and silent prayer! a thousand times greater in His sight are they than all sorts of brilliant exterior works! Oh how true it is that to be anything in the sight of God we must be nothing, we must pretend to nothing; we must only desire to be ignored, forgotten, despised, and considered as the most vile and abject thing in the world. If the life of the Blessed Virgin does not teach us this great truth, if it does not make us love it and embrace it, if it does not stifle in us the desire of appearing as something of importance, if it does not convince us that to find ourselves in God we must first lose ourselves entirely, what more touching example, what more powerful lesson, could ever be able to persuade us? Jesus and Mary demonstrate to every Christian that God finds His greatest glory in this world in our annihilation. And they also demonstrate to us that the more we are annihilated on earth, the greater, the happier, and the more powerful shall we be in Heaven.

How shall we then show our solid devotion to the Blessed Virgin? By striving to imitate her interior life, her lowly opinion of herself, her love of obscurity, of silence, and of retirement; her attraction to little things, her fidelity to grace, the beautiful simplicity of her recollection and prayer, the only object of which was God and His holy will, Jesus Christ and His love, her continual sacrifice of herself and of all she loved most dearly and had the greatest reason to love. Let us ask her every day that she may serve us as our guide and model in the interior life, and let us beg of her to obtain for us the graces which are necessary for us, that we may correspond to the designs of God upon us. And these designs are most certainly our death to ourselves and the destruction of our self-love.

LIV.

THE CRIB OF BETHLEHEM.

THE crib of Bethlehem is as much the school of the spiritual life as the cross is. We begin to learn at the crib, and we finish with the cross; the one contains all the elements of a life of holiness, the other contains its consummation. And as in all sciences it is the elements which are of the greatest importance and necessity, let us devoutly study the crib, and let us try to express in our conduct the truths it teaches. Let us contemplate the Word made flesh, the Son of God Who, for our sakes, became a little child. Let us see what were His interior dispositions at His birth; let us consider what were the exterior circumstances of it, and who those were whom He called to His cradle.

It was His love for His Father and His love for men which attracted Him to earth. The feeling which occupied and filled His Sacred Heart was the desire of offering Himself as a Sacrifice to His Father to repair the glory of God and to save the human race; Saint Paul, speaking as David did, teaches us this. When He came into the world, says this Apostle, Jesus Christ said: " The sacrifices and oblations of the old law did not please Thee, but

Thou hast prepared for Me a body. Then I said, Behold I come, O my God! to fulfil Thy will!" And what was this will of God? It was a will infinitely severe, according to which Jesus Christ was to take upon Himself our sins and to bear the heavy weight of the Divine justice. Therefore, when He was born, He united His will to this will of His Father, and submitted Himself to it with the greatest love. From His very cradle He contemplated the cross, He longed after it, and the first desire of His Sacred Human Heart was to die upon the cross to appease His Father's just anger and to redeem us.

Let us learn from this that the cross must be the chief object of the interior life, that the first thing God presents us with is the cross, and that the first feeling of a heart which gives itself to God is the accepting of the cross. Now, whoever accepts the cross means by that a total forgetfulness of self, a total loss of self in God, and a complete sacrifice of all his own interests, that he may think only of the interests of God. God alone knows how far this sacrifice ought to extend, since it is God Who proposes it to us, Who inspires us with courage to accept it, and Who gives us the strength to accomplish His will. But we on our part must set no bounds to our sacrifice; we must accept it in its fullest extent, and without any restriction, we must contemplate it without ceasing, and must long after its consummation as our Lord and Saviour Jesus Christ did.

But why should He have been born a little child? Why not have come into the world, as Adam did, as a perfect man?

342 Manual for Interior Souls.

No doubt He could have done so, if He would, but He had His reasons for preferring the state of infancy. And the principal of these reasons was, that He wished to teach us that, from the moment we give ourselves to God, we must put aside and trample under foot our own judgment, our own will, and our own strength ; that we must go back to the smallness and the weakness and the foolishness of a little child ; that all our past life must be blotted out, and that we must enter upon a new state of existence, a new life, of which God alone must be the principle. And what is this new life ? It consists in a perfect dependence upon Divine grace, in simplicity and obedience. Let us look upon Jesus Christ in the crib ; He adored His Father as perfectly there as upon the cross. But His adoration was confined in His Sacred Heart; He said nothing, He did nothing, He was as it were annihilated ; and it was in this very annihilation that the perfection of His adoration consisted. Let us imagine this, let us dwell upon this, we who complain continually that we are before God as if we were brutes, without thoughts or words or actions. This passive state, which is death to self-love, is incomparably more pleasing to God than anything, however sublime, which our mind or our heart or our mouth could express to Him. To be silent before God, to humble ourselves, to annihilate ourselves, to be in His presence as though we were not, this is to adore Him perfectly in spirit and in truth. What need has God of our sublime lights, and our exalted sentiments, which only nourish in us a secret pride and a vain complacency in ourselves? The nearer our prayer approaches to the prayer of the Infant Jesus, the more humbling and debasing it seems in our own eyes, the higher and more perfect it is in the eyes of God.

Let us pass on to the exterior circumstances of the birth of Jesus. Repulsed and driven away from one inn after another, Mary was obliged to retire into a poor stable; and it was there that the Son of God was born, in the midst of poverty, humiliation, and suffering.

A manger, strewn with a little straw, served Him for a cradle; He was wrapped in poor swaddling clothes; in the middle of the night, in the most severe season of the year, in a place open to all the winds of heaven, His tender and delicate body was exposed to the cold and inclement air. No one assisted at His birth; no one but His Blessed Mother was there to give Him any aid or any comfort.

What an entrance into the world for the Son of God, for Him Who came to redeem the world, and Who from the very beginning was announced to our first parents as the Deliverer of the human race! Who could ever have believed that He would choose for Himself a birth so poor, so obscure, so suffering?

But how instructive all the circumstances of this birth are for those whom the Holy Spirit brings to a new birth in the interior life! In this Divine Infant they find a perfect model of the three virtues which must be henceforth their inseparable companions: a perfect detachment from all the good things of this earth, to be carried as far as the most rigorous penance, if God wishes it; a sovereign contempt for all the honours of the world, so that they wish not only to be ignored by the world, but to be ridiculed and despised by it; and an absolute renunciation of all earthly pleasures, carried to such an extent that, instead, they devote their bodies to every kind of mortification.

These are the three virtues which the Infant Jesus teaches to His loving spiritual children. And what He chose then at His birth, He loved and practised all His life long. He was always poor, living by the labour of His own hands, not having where to lay His head, He was alway either unknown to the world or a butt for its calumnies, its contempt, and its persecution. He refused Himself every pleasure, and He suffered in His private life and in His public life every privation and every bodily pang that can be imagined. His death on the cross was only in a higher degree the practice of these same virtues. Let us then also embrace them on our entrance upon the spiritual life, and let us never separate ourselves from them.

Finally, who are those whom Jesus admitted to His cradle? It is a very remarkable thing that all those who appeared there had been summoned either by a heavenly voice or a miraculous sign. This teaches us, that if we wish to enter upon the way of perfection, of which the crib pictures to us the beginning, we must have a Divine vocation, and that no one can enter there unless he is called. But we can on our part bring some preparation for this Divine vocation, and for this our dispositions should be the same as those of the shepherds and the Magi.

We must then be simple, poor in spirit, and humble, as the shepherds were; we must have, like them, a great uprightness of heart, and we must either be in a state of innocence or we must have broken for ever with every habit of sin. It is very often persons of low condition, of obscure and retired life, persons unknown and despised by the world, whom God calls to the interior life. More than this, the shepherds watched even in the night over their flocks; which shows us that great watchfulness over ourselves, the fear of God, the flight from all dangerous occasions, and great tenderness of conscience, prepare us for the heavenly vocation. The shepherds lent an attentive ear to the message of the angels—they believed it at once, without reasoning or reflecting upon it; they left all, and set out immediately to adore the new-born Child. Thus the soul ought to listen attentively for the voice of God in her heart, she ought to believe His word with a blind and obedient faith, she ought to leave everything to follow quickly and faithfully the call of Divine grace.

In the person of the Magi, great and learned souls are also called to the cradle of the Son of God; but they must be humble as well as great, they must be detached from all, and ready to sacrifice all to respond to the call of God—learned souls without self-sufficiency, without presumption, obedient to the Divine light, and submitting to it all the reasonings of human wisdom. Such was Saint Louis of France; such was Saint Augustine; such have been many saints of both sexes, distinguished either by the nobility of their birth and dignity or by the greatness of their genius and knowledge.

The character of Herod, of the Pharisees, of the priests and doctors of the law, acquaint us with those whom Jesus rejects, and who on their own part make no use of the ordinary means of grace either to know or to practise the spiritual life.

LV.

ON JESUS CHRIST.

"I am the Way, the Truth, and the Life."

THESE words of our Lord and Master Jesus Christ contain an abridgment of all the motives for our faith, our hope, and our love. The life of the soul, the true life, the eternal life, is the only end of man and the dearest desire of his heart. Jesus Christ has declared to us that He is Himself this life, and that we can only be completely and supremely and eternally happy in the possession of Him. Therefore He alone must be the one sovereign and unchanging object of our love.

The means of attaining to this true life is by knowing and embracing the truth, and by drawing away, in our mind and heart, from all that is false and untrue. Now Jesus Christ tells us that He is the Truth, the infallible Truth, the essential Truth; and therefore everything outside Him must be false-hood and untruth. We ought then to apply ourselves to know Jesus Christ thoroughly, and we ought to employ all the strength of our mind and all the honesty of our heart with that intention; we ought to regulate our judgment of things upon His, our affections upon His, being certain that there is nothing really estimable and lovable but what He esteems and loves.

But by what way shall we attain the Truth? By Jesus Christ, Who assures us that He also is the Way, and the only Way, which can guide us to truth and life. It was on purpose to guide us and instruct us that He was made man, that He gave us in His own human Person united to the Divine Nature a most perfect model, and a model also that was perceptible and proportioned to our weakness, and that to this perfect example He united all the teaching contained in the precepts and the evangelical counsels. Let us see then what Jesus Christ taught. All His doctrine reduced itself to two heads: the love of God and of our neighbour. In the love of God is comprised the legitimate love which we may have for ourselves, in such a manner that the more we love God, the more we love ourselves, because to love God is to love our own true and sovereign and only Good. The love of God must also essentially exclude the love of creatures for their own sake, and looked at as being our good. It excludes in the same manner also all self-love; that is to say, no creature must love itself for its own sake, nor refer to itself the love it ought to have for God only, for this would be to reverse the order which commands us to love God for Himself alone, and ourselves and everything else in God and for God's sake. All our love there-

fore is due to God and to God alone, and He ought
to be the end of all our affections, without any exception. What detachment, what self-abnegation,
what a spirit of disinterestedness, does this love of God
require, if we wish to practise it in all its purity!
Every kind of self-love, whatever its immediate object
may be, is a robbery from God. All self-interest, all
consideration for ourselves, all views of our own advantage, all inordinate desire even of our own perfection, all this stains the infinite purity of Divine
love. Hence it follows that the more a soul is dead
to herself, the more utterly annihilated she is, the
more also she loves God. Hence all the crosses and
trials and deprivations of all kinds, and everything that
tears us from ourselves, are the only steps by which
we can ascend to the true love of God. When this
one truth is well understood it throws a brilliant light
upon all the teaching of Jesus Christ; it makes us
comprehend the conduct of God in the sanctification
of souls, it shows us that the practice of Divine love
consists in sacrifice, and that the more we renounce
ourselves the more truly and sincerely do we love.
That hatred of ourselves which Jesus Christ commands
is then seen to be a true love, and the love of ourselves which Jesus Christ condemns is seen to be a
real hatred. To hate one's soul, in the sense of the
Gospel, is to save it; to love one's soul is to lose it.

As to the love of our neighbour, Jesus Christ
teaches us to look upon all men as our brothers by
creation and redemption; He teaches us that the
whole human race only composes one family, of which
God is the Father, of which His only Son is the

Saviour, of which Heaven is the inheritance, and that all the members of this family would one day possess that inheritance in common, if they would only correspond with the designs of God for them. Thus, we ought to love our neighbour because God loves him, because Jesus Christ loves him, and we ought to put no other bounds to this love than those which Jesus Christ has set, that is to say, we ought to be ready to suffer everything from our neighbour, we ought to forgive him everything, we ought to do him all the good we possibly can, even to give, if necessary, our life for his salvation; for it is thus that Jesus Christ wishes us to love him, following His Divine example.

That which Jesus Christ taught us, He practised Himself first of all in all its perfection; He proposed Himself as our model, but He did infinitely more than ever He asks of us.

He recommends us to be detached from the good things of this world; and He was born, He lived, and died in the greatest poverty. He never possessed anything whatever on earth—neither land, nor house, nor money; and He saw His very clothes divided and torn up before He died.

He recommends to us the renunciation of the pleasures of the world; and from His cradle to the cross His life was only one unbroken tissue of sufferings: He never enjoyed a single moment of rest on earth.

He recommends us to fly from the honours of the world; and He willingly embraced every kind of humiliation. He was born in a stable; He worked in the shop of a poor artisan; he lived on alms dur-

ing the whole time of His.public ministry ; He was
calumniated, outraged, persecuted, betrayed, denied,
condemned to the most shameful punishment as a
blasphemer and deceiver of the people.

Envy, malignity, contempt, derision, and rage were
carried against him to the greatest excess ; never was
any wretched criminal or any public pest treated in a
manner so cruel and so unworthy.

This was the life of Jesus Christ on earth. And
in all these circumstances there was not one that He
had not desired and chosen by preference ; it was He
Himself Who designed the whole course of His life
and arranged all its sufferings. This choice was the
choice of God Himself, and therefore an infinitely wise
choice. This choice had for its end the reparation
of the glory of God ; it is then by poverty, by sufferings, and by humiliations that God wishes to be
glorified. This choice had also for its object the
salvation of the human race ; and Jesus Christ, in
saving us by this way of sorrow, has shown us what
we also must do to save ourselves. Our little crosses,
united to the heavy cross of our Lord and Saviour,
are to be the means of our salvation, and the necessary
and only means. Finally, this choice was for Jesus
Christ at last the source of the greatest happiness
and glory. And it will be the same for all the true
lovers of the cross without exception : the more poor
in heart they are here, the richer they will be in
Heaven ; the more they have suffered here, the
greater will be their consolation there ; the more they
have been humbled here, the greater will be their
glory there ; in fact, the more they have been anni-

hilated in this world, the more will they share in Heaven in the very Being of God.

To believe all this, to practise it, to persevere in it faithfully till death, is, according to the expression of Saint Paul, to be "clothed with Jesus Christ;" it is to follow Him as the *Way*, it is to love Him as the *Truth*, it is to possess Him even in this world as the *Life*.

This Way is one; this Truth is one; this Life is one. Whoever does not walk in this Way draws away from the truth, and will never live with the true life. The contrary way is the way of falsehood, which ends in eternal death. There is no middle course; we must follow one way or the other. Happy are those who have taken Jesus Christ for their guide, and who walk in His light! they will arrive at the same end. Then the Way will pass, but the Truth and the Life will remain for ever.

LVI.

ON THE INTERIOR OF JESUS CHRIST.

"Let this mind be in you ; which was also in Jesus Christ."
—*St. Paul to the Philippians.*

By the "interior" of Jesus Christ, we mean the secret dispositions of His soul, which were the principle and rule of His whole life. It is these interior dispositions which give a value to all actions, in which the holiness of these actions consists, and which make an extreme difference in the very same actions according to the degree of purity of intention and elevation of motive which influence them. If Jesus Christ is the model for all Christians in His exterior conduct, far more is He so in the interior dispositions of His Sacred Heart ; therefore, the most important occupation of our lives should be to study them, to apply them to ourselves, and to endeavour as far as we can to imitate them.

We will now consider the interior dispositions of Jesus Christ, with regard to His Eternal Father, with regard to Himself, and with regard to men.

With regard to His Father, He always looked upon Himself as a Victim, destined to repair His Father's glory, and to appease His justice.   The very instant He came into the world, as Saint Paul says, He offered Himself as a Victim, in place of the victims of the Old Law, which were only the shadows and the types of His one perfect Sacrifice, and every moment of His life He persevered in this oblation of Himself. The cross was the consummation of His Sacrifice, but His cradle was the beginning of it, and the whole course of his life only the continuation of it.   Thus the disposition of Jesus Christ towards His Father was one of continual self-immolation.

Hence came His perfect submission to the will of His Father.   He never wished for anything of Himself, He never desired anything, or wished to follow His own will in anything, incapable as He was of wishing anything that was not good.   He said of Himself, " *My meat is to do the will of My Father.*" And He did it, without interruption, from His birth to His last breath on the cross : He did it in things most painful and fearful to His human nature ; He did it with a joy and an ardour, a generosity and an alacrity, which were inexpressible.

Hence came also that constant dependence upon Divine grace which was always so great in Jesus Christ, so that His soul only acted to second the action of God, and was always in the hands of His Father a most pliable and obedient instrument.

Hence came His great zeal for the glory of His Father—a zeal which dried Him up, which consumed Him, which devoured Him. Hence came His inexpressible love, His continual prayer, the absorption of all the powers of His soul in the Divinity of God, His burning thirst for sufferings, His continual desire for the consummation of His Sacrifice. He said of Himself, ' I am to be baptized with a baptism of blood : and how am I straitened until it be accomplished ? '

Now with regard to Himself : the humility of Jesus Christ, His self-abnegation, were carried to an extent that was prodigious ; the word annihilation is not sufficient to express the state of His soul in this respect. He looked upon Himself as loaded with all the sins of the universe, and as deserving only of all the blows of Divine justice. Nevertheless, His Sacred Humanity was holy with the very holiness of the Word of God, Who was personally united to Him. Who can conceive and who can reconcile the union of a holiness so perfect with those humble ideas of Himself?

Let us judge, after all this, if ever during His mortal life He desired that His Father should glorify Him, if He ever sought after heavenly favours, if He

z

ever wished for the esteem of men, or took glory to Himself for His virtues and His miracles. Jesus Christ never desired anything for Himself worthy of Himself but contempt, humiliation and suffering; He did not think Himself worthy of anything else. He declared by the mouth of His prophet, "*I am a worm and no man; I am the scorn of men, and the outcast of the people.*" He never wished for anything in this world from God but to bear the weight of His anger, and to satisfy His justice by the total destruction of His own being.

Now, with regard to men, the spirit of Jesus Christ was a spirit of love and sweetness, a spirit of peace and union, a spirit of help and condescension, a most tender compassion for sinners, even for those who spoke against Him, who insulted Him, and who wished for His death   He shed His blood, in desire for the salvation of all men, every moment of His life; and, if there had been only one man to redeem, He would have willingly given His life for that one man; and in very truth He did suffer, He did satisfy, He did die for each individual man. He said of Himself, "*Greater love hath no man than this, that a man lay down his life for his friends.*" But He did infinitely more——He laid down His life for His enemies. And not content with giving His life, He gave His soul; He consented, as Saint Paul tells us, to be for them and for their sakes an object of malediction, to be treated by God not only as a sinner, but as if He were sin itself. Such was the extent of the charity of Jesus Christ for us. To die, by the hands of men, in a most cruel and ignominious punishment,

was perhaps not so much ; but to die in His soul, by
the hands of God, to feel in His soul that He was
forsaken by God, to feel the anger of God and the
curse of God inasmuch as He bore the sins of all
men—this was a sacrifice of which only God made
Man was capable.

The interior of Jesus Christ may then be reduced
to three points, which embrace everything : the spirit
of sacrifice, the spirit of humility, the spirit of love ;
but a sacrifice, a humility, and a love carried as far
as it was possible to carry them by a Man enlightened
by all the light, animated by all the feelings, sustained
by all the strength of His Divine nature.   This is
what ravishes with admiration for ever the intelligences of the angels and the souls of the saints !

But how can we possibly venture to express in
ourselves such sublime dispositions ?   We can only
do it in one way, and that a very simple way : by
the union of our whole soul with God.   This union
in Jesus Christ was a hypostatic union : in us it can
only be a moral union, and consequently an incomparably inferior one ; but this union with God,
although so inferior, is capable of producing in us
the fruits of the most eminent holiness.

What must we do, then, to unite ourselves with
God ?   We must desire this union ; we must give
ourselves generously to God ; we must depend
entirely and perfectly upon His grace.   Our only
desire must be precisely and solely what God desires :
which means no less than a total abandonment of
ourselves and all our interests to the care of God.

When this gift of ourselves is once made, there is

nothing more to do but to allow God to act in us, and to correspond faithfully with His action. He will by degrees enlighten our understanding with His heavenly light ; and then we shall see everything as He sees it, and He will teach us to judge all things as He judges them. He will infuse into our will His love, His strength, His ideas. He will dispose as He pleases of all the events of our lives, and will Himself place us in the circumstances which are most proper for the exercise of all the virtues He expects from us and for the accomplishment of His designs for us.

But if we wish to receive in ourselves this light from God, it is quite certain that we must renounce the light of our own mere reason ; and one of our most constant prayers must be to ask of God that He will first blind us and then give us His own light. If we wish to receive His love into our hearts, it is evident that we must banish self-love from them ; for self-love concentrates all our attention upon ourselves, and Divine love makes us come out of ourselves to be concentrated and lost in God. Now self-love is always trying to infect with its venom all our affections, all our most secret desires, even those of eternal happiness. It is therefore necessary that Divine love should purify all our desires, and should take away from them all self-interest, to leave them only concerned with the interests of God.

If we wish to receive the strength of God, we must despoil ourselves of our own strength, or rather of what we imagine to be our strength, for in reality we have no strength at all for the practice of any

supernatural good. Thus we must willingly consent
to feel continually our weakness and want of power,
that so the efficacy of Divine grace may alone
strengthen us. The stronger we are in God, the
weaker we become in ourselves ; and when the feeling
of our own strength is utterly annihilated, the Divine
strength will display itself in us in all its virtue, without finding any obstacle on our part.

If we wish to leave to God the disposal of all the
events of our life, we must wish for nothing, foresee
nothing, make no plans for the future, but remain
calmly and peacefully where God places us, and take
no other measures than those which we feel plainly
are His will.

A perfect union with God embraces all that I
have just said, and it extends to all our free actions
without exception, whether interior or exterior. And
if we are united to God, we shall have all the dispositions of our Lord and Master, Jesus Christ, and
God Himself will guide all the events of our lives as
He guided those of Jesus Christ. Then we shall
resemble our Lord Jesus as much as is possible for
us to resemble Him, and we shall attain in this life
to the degree of sanctity which God wishes for us.
Amen.

LVII.

ON THE EFFECTS OF HOLY COMMUNION.

" He that eateth My flesh, and drinketh My blood, dwelleth in Me, and I in him."

THE meaning of these words of our Lord Jesus Christ, this mutual dwelling of Him in us, and of us in Him, is something so grand and so Divine that it is impossible for us to understand it perfectly. This wonderful effect of Holy Communion takes place more or less in all souls in proportion as their dispositions are more or less perfect; and as these dispositions can always become better and better, the effect which corresponds with them can also become more and more excellent in the same degree. Who shall express to us what is this dwelling of Jesus Christ in us, and of us in Jesus Christ? This is a thing above all created intelligence. Let us not try to comprehend it fully, because we never shall succeed, but let us do all that depends on us to deserve it.

This indwelling is the closest and most intimate that can be conceived; it is a union of Jesus Christ with us, and of us with Him, which is such that nothing in nature can approach to it. His Body is united to our body, His Soul to our soul, His Faculties and all their operations to our faculties, in such a supernatural and transcendent manner that Jesus Christ lives in us, and we in Him: our thoughts, our feelings, and our actions become identified with His thoughts, His feelings, and His actions.

This indwelling is universal ; it includes everything that we can possibly have in common with Jesus Christ, and therefore it must necessarily exclude sin only, and our irregular concupiscence, which is the source of sin.

This indwelling is in its very nature permanent and everlasting ; this is the intention of Jesus Christ, and it is our own fault entirely if, after a good Communion, He ever leaves us again, or if this blessed union, so firm in itself, is ever broken. It is not by a few moments of a sensible devotion and fervour that we can judge of this dwelling of Jesus Christ in us, but it is by the habitual disposition of our souls.

If Holy Communion detaches me more and more from the good things of this world, if it makes them insipid to me, and wearisome, and insupportable— if in all matters of ordinary human life Holy Communion only teaches me what is my duty, and how I ought to practise all Christian virtues—if it teaches me to look upon myself only as a traveller and a pilgrim whose true home is in Heaven, and who must only make use of the things he meets with on his way in such a manner that by them he may reach his home more quickly and surely—if Holy Communion inspires me with a taste for recollection, for prayer, for mortification, for the renunciation of myself and my own judgment—if it reforms my thoughts and my affections on the perfect model of the thoughts and affections of Jesus Christ, so that His doctrine becomes to me familiar, and, as it were, natural to my heart, and I take pleasure in practising it on all occasions —if, like Jesus Christ, I begin to have a horror of the world and its false maxims—if I begin to despise what the world esteems, and to fly from what it most seeks after—if, on the contrary, and still like my Divine Lord and Master, I begin to seek after and embrace all that the world most shuns and abhors— then I have the greatest assurance, and at the same time the only true and solid assurance I can have in this life, of the good effect of my Communions; then I may believe that Jesus Christ dwells in me, and I in Him.

It is principally by the Holy Communion itself that the effects I have been describing are produced, and in their turn, our good dispositions render every day the fruit of our Communions more excellent and abundant.

Thus, little by little, we are transformed into the image of Jesus Christ, and each good Communion adds some more perfect strokes to this transformation.

The whole secret, therefore, of drawing from the Holy Communion all the profit which Jesus Christ wishes for us, is to try, from one Communion to another, to dwell in Him in a manner more and more close and perfect, to suffer ourselves to be animated and guided in all things by His Spirit, and to beg of Him never to allow us to think or say or do anything which He cannot acknowledge as His own. All this requires great attention and a constant watchfulness, but we must do it all quietly and peacefully, and without effort, until it becomes a second nature to us.

Let us persuade ourselves once for all that our own action spoils everything, if we allow it to precede the action of God, instead of following it. But, since it is quite certain that in the Holy Communion Jesus Christ really dwells in us, what can we do better at that time than to place all our conduct in His hands, and to beg of Him to guide us in all things, that we may do simply, and humbly and peacefully, and without reflection, whatever He puts into our heart to do? As long as a soul that is determined to follow Jesus Christ in all things is at peace in her inmost depths, she may be quite certain that Jesus Christ is guiding and directing her. But the moment she begins to be involuntarily troubled, to be agitated and over-eager—the moment she begins to give herself up to uneasy reflections—from that moment she withdraws herself from the guidance of Jesus Christ and assumes the guidance of herself. The best method, therefore, of preparing for Holy Communion, is to leave to Jesus Christ alone the care of preparing us for it He will do it infinitely better than we can; and as we shall have been passive in the matter, we can take credit to ourselves for nothing, but leave all the glory to Him. We shall not be tempted to think that our good dispositions are the effect of our own industry, but we shall acknowledge humbly that He alone has produced them in us. And I will say the same of our thanksgiving after Communion. Can we possibly, by our own efforts, thank Jesus Christ as we ought to do? Are we capable of it? Is it not more glorious for Him, and more advantageous for us, that He should thank Himself for us, and make use for that purpose of the faculties of our soul, then so closely united to His? This simple abandonment of ourselves to Jesus Christ, this simple placing of ourselves in His hands, that He may be the first and only motive of our thoughts, our affections, our words, and our actions, is without contradiction the most excellent disposition we can have, the most conformable to the principles of faith, the most glorious to God, and the most efficacious for our own advancement. It is thus that our life will become the life of Jesus Christ, because He will be the soul and the motive principle of our life, and will never allow us to do anything that is unworthy of Him; instead of which, if we act of ourselves, we live by our own life; we do neither what Jesus Christ wishes, nor in the manner He wishes.

I have not yet said what is the most Divine and ineffable thing in this dwelling of Jesus Christ in us, and of us in Him, which is the fruit of Holy Communion: it is that it is the very image of the union of Jesus Christ with His Father, and of His Father with Him. Our Lord says, *"As I live by My Father, so he that eateth Me shall live by Me."* In like manner, as the Father is the principle of the life of the Son, so is the Son the principle of life to the faithful soul who feeds on His Sacred Body. The Son dwells always in the Father, because He always draws His life from the Father. The Father dwells always in the Son, because He is always communicating His life to His Son by an action which never ceases and will never cease. In the same manner, he who

worthily receives the Body of the Son of God dwells
in Him for ever, because he receives for ever his
supernatural life from the Son of God ; and the Son
of God also dwells in him for ever, because He is
for ever communicating to him His own Divine life.
This effect is continual and permanent in its very
nature ; it can only be hindered or interrupted by
the fault of the creature.

O Christian soul, who now readest these words !
ask of Jesus Christ the grace of always receiving His
life when you receive His Sacred Body ; ask to receive it in all its fulness, each time of Communion,
according to your present capacity, and to preserve
it carefully from one Communion to another, in such
a manner that each time you may receive a fresh
increase of it.

What must you do for that end ? I have already
told you : never do anything of yourselves, nothing of
your own activity, but do everything by the action of
Jesus Christ, and by the principle of life which He
will communicate to you without ceasing. Far from
having any occasion to fear that in this way you will
fall into idleness, you will on the contrary be always
very active, because the Spirit of God will always be
acting within you. The devotion which we produce by
our own efforts exhausts itself all the more quickly as
our efforts have been the more violent. But the devotion that is produced by the Spirit of God is never exhausted, whether we feel it sensibly or not. We must
not even reflect about it, or seek curiously to know
if we have it or have it not. We often have this
devotion most fully when we think the least about it.

LVIII.

ON THE RELATIONSHIP BETWEEN THE HOLY EUCHARIST AND THE CROSS.

OUR Lord Jesus Christ instituted the Sacrament of the Holy Eucharist immediately before His Passion, to show us the connection that there is between this sacrament and the cross. When He instituted it He changed separately, and by two distinct actions, the bread into His Body and the wine into His Blood, to signify that He would pour out His Blood to the very last drop upon the altar of the cross.

When He gave His Body to His disciples, He said to them, *"This is My Body, which is given for you;"* and when He gave them His Blood, he said, *"This is My Blood, which is shed for you, for the remission of sins."*

He wished that His Body in the Holy Eucharist should preserve its character of victim, and His Blood that of a liquor poured out and applied to the soul in expiation of its sins. Finally, when He gave to His disciples the power of consecrating His Body and Blood, He commanded them to perform this action in memory of Him, that is to say, He commanded them always to remember that this sacrament is the memorial of His cruel and bloody death on the cross.

But, on the other hand, He wished also that this sacrament should be the indispensable and necessary food of our souls, in such a manner that we cannot possibly preserve or increase in our souls the life of grace except by this means.

What does all this mean, if not that He intended first that the memory of His cross and passion should ever remain engraven on the heart of His faithful followers; and in the second place, that they should renew this memory in themselves each time they received His Sacred Body; and in the third place, that whenever they were nourished by His flesh, they should also be nourished by His cross, that they should incorporate themselves, as it were, with His cross, that they should burn with love for His glory, and that the increase of their spiritual life by the reception of the Holy Eucharist should be manifested by the increase of their ardour to embrace His cross. This was how the martyrs of the first ages of faith understood His words, when they prepared themselves for their frightful torments by receiving the Holy Eucharist; and then, strengthened by this sacred food, they boldly faced the tyrants and executioners.

Therefore, if we wish to communicate usefully, and to fulfil the intentions of Jesus Christ, let us communicate with the express desire that His adorable Body may produce in us the love of the cross, that is to say, the love of humiliations and sufferings, the desire of dying to ourselves, and of being sacrificed, as Jesus Christ was, to the good pleasure of God. Let us judge by our love of the cross of the fruit of our Communions. Let us not think they are good because we have enjoyed in them many consolations, but only because we come from them filled with a new courage to overcome ourselves, to wage war

against our self-love, to suffer all the pains and sorrows which God may send us, and even to desire
greater ones; let us think our Communions are good
and fruitful when we learn there to seek God no
longer for our own consolation, but to seek Him and
love Him purely and for Himself alone, not to pay
any attention to how He treats us, and to be as content and more content with His severity than with
His sweetness. When our Communions produce these
effects in us, then they are excellent; then they are
in accordance with the designs of Jesus Christ; then
they are glorious to God and profitable to ourselves.
Let us not be alarmed when our Communions are dry
and without devotion, and when God seems to give
us nothing. If this is through no fault of our own,
through no voluntary infidelity, let us take comfort:
it is a sign that the Holy Eucharist is no longer for
us the bread of the weak, but that it begins to become
for us the bread of the strong. For as long as we
require that the Holy Eucharist should be accompanied
for us by a sensible fervour and devotion, we are
weak; but when we communicate without thinking
about ourselves at all, without troubling ourselves
about sensible devotion, without desiring it, and seeing ourselves deprived of it without any regret, then
we are becoming strong; then we are beginning to
live with the true life of the Spirit; then our love for
God begins to be purified, and to be no longer mixed
with love for ourselves. Let us try to understand this,
and let us try to practise it.

As the Body of Jesus Christ is a food, and a food
intended to increase our spiritual strength, we have

only to see in what spiritual strength consists to be able to judge of the good effect of our Communions. It is evident that all our spiritual strength ought to be employed against ourselves, against our own inclinations, against our natural aversions, against our cowardice, our inconstancy, our weakness, against the horror that we have of all that crosses us, of all that restrains us, of all that mortifies us, of all that humiliates us, against our own spirit and our own will, in short, against all in us that resists God and the destroying operations of His grace. If then we find that this strength increases in us every day after Communion, if we acquire more mastery over ourselves, if we are less delicate and sensitive, more generous in undertaking, more patient in suffering, more faithful to our good resolutions, more indifferent to the esteem or contempt of men, more obedient to all the impulses of Divine grace, more ready for all the sacrifices God asks of us, this is an infallible proof of the goodness of our Communions ; and even if we do not so judge it of ourselves, as, in fact, it is not the intention of God that we should so judge of it, we must rely upon the judgment of our director, and by his advice we must go to Holy Communion as often as he thinks it right for us, although sometimes it may seem to us that we derive no profit from our Communions. The devil, who knows quite well how necessary frequent Communion is for interior souls, employs all his malignant ingenuity to deter them from it.

1st. He inspires them with a vague fear of making a sacrilegious Communion. I say a vague fear, because it rests on no foundation, and only exists in the imagination. Our conscience reproaches us with nothing in particular, we have not wilfully failed in anything, and nevertheless we feel troubled and agitated, as if we were going to eat to our judgment and condemnation. We must pass boldly over this fear, and approach the Holy Table without paying any attention to it. The proof that it does not come from God, and consequently that we must despise it, is that almost always, as soon as we have communicated, we find ourselves in peace, and all our vain fears vanish.

2nd. He tries to make them believe that they derive no profit from their Communions, and he particularly makes use of this artifice when the soul, deprived of spiritual sweetness, feels no sensible devotion in communicating. The only way to resist this temptation is to hold fast to obedience, and to make a resolution to go to Holy Communion only for God's sake, and not for our own.

3rd. He suggests to them at the moment of their Communion the most horrible thoughts of impurity, of blasphemy, and of impiety; he inspires them with doubts of the Real Presence; he throws them into every kind of trouble and anxiety, so that they scarcely know what they are doing nor where they are. God even allows the devil to make dreadful impressions sometimes upon our senses, either by himself or by means of our imagination All the masters of the spiritual life, without exception, have decided that we must despise these bad thoughts, and take no notice of them, and that they are rather a reason for communicating more frequently than for abstaining from doing so; for it is quite evident that they are only temptations, having for their object to drive us away from the Holy Table; and consequently we ought to resist them and overcome them by approaching more frequently; for if we give way to them, the devil will have gained just what he wished for.

"But," you may say, "supposing I do make a bad Communion?" I reply that it is not for you to be the judge of that, and that you have no occasion to fear making a bad Communion if you go in obedience to a wise director who knows all that passes in your soul; that if you hold back from Holy Communion every time that the devil makes you believe you are going to communicate badly, he will at last succeed in his aim, which is to prevent you from communicating at all, and so to deprive you of the strength you need so much to support you. Thus, instead of advancing, you will fall back; and if you once give up Holy Communion, you will soon give up all the rest.

Since the effect of Holy Communion is to fasten us to the cross, and to help us to die there, it follows that our dispositions in communicating, and the effects which it produces in us, are always relative and in proportion to the different states of death to ourselves in which we are found; because Holy Communion always operates according to our actual dispositions, and its object is always to lead us on in advance of our present state. Thus it is sometimes accompanied with great sweetness and consolation, sometimes it leaves us cold and insensible, sometimes it crucifies us, sometimes it seems to be dead and null, so to speak, in its apparent effects. It is

2 A

our director who must judge of all this for us; and
the safe rule is that a Communion is as it ought to be
when it is of the same kind as the state in which the
soul actually finds itself.   In short, as our state of
prayer changes as we advance in the way of perfection, so does our state at Holy Communion change
in like manner.   It is at first active—the soul can
produce acts before and after; but at last it becomes
passive—the · soul does not act at this time; it is
Jesus Christ alone Who acts in her, according to the
degree of perfection she has then attained.

LIX.

ON THE CRUCIFIX.

St. Paul said that all religion was contained for
him in the science of the crucifix—"*Jesus Christ,
and Him crucified;*" and most assuredly he was right.
The crucifix is the abridgment of all that a Christian
ought to believe, and all that he ought to practise.
The crucifix makes known to us all the malice of sin,
the excess of our misery, and the still greater excess
of Divine love and mercy.   The crucifix is the
greatest proof that God, God as He is, could give us
of His love, and it is the strongest motive He could
employ to gain our hearts in return.   Every virtue is
included in the crucifix, and it is the consummation
of the way of perfection.   I will say a few words on
each of these subjects, but grace will say many more
to devout souls who wish to devote themselves entirely to the love of God.

The crucifix is the abridgment of all that a Christian ought to believe. The Divine Person Who suffers there, the only Son of God, conceived in the womb of His Immaculate Mother Mary by the operation of the Holy Ghost, proposes to us the two great mysteries of the Trinity and the Incarnation. The object of His sufferings teaches us of the mystery of the redemption, and of original sin. The mystery of predestination, the mystery of grace, the will of God to save all men, are also contained in the crucifix. It is the source of all the sacraments, as it would be easy for me to prove in detail; and all the worship by which the Church honours God springs from the Sacrifice of the cross.

The crucifix is the abridgment of all that a Christian ought to practise. All the morality of the Gospel consists in bearing our cross, in renouncing ourselves, in crucifying our flesh with all its corrupt affections and inclinations, and in sacrificing ourselves to the will of God. Jesus Christ has prescribed no law and has given no counsel that does not find its perfect accomplishment and its perfect model in the cross. It is the most striking and living expression of the whole teaching of the Gospel.

The crucifix makes known to us all the malice of sin. What greater evil can there be, indeed, than that which caused the death of God made Man? Before Jesus Christ came, it was possible to form some idea of what it was to offend God, but it was a very feeble and imperfect idea. The eternal punishment of hell, although it goes beyond all created intelligence, is not even sufficient for the malice of sin, because it can punish sin but cannot expiate it. It required nothing less than a Divine Person to atone worthily, by His sufferings and humiliations, for the injury done to God by the sin of man. Therefore it is at the foot of the cross that we learn what sin really is, and learn to feel all the horror of it which it deserves.

The crucifix makes known to us also the excess of our misery, an excess so great that it was impossible for us to remedy it of ourselves. The whole human race was lost, lost without hope, lost for all eternity, deprived for ever of the possession of the Sovereign Good, if Jesus Christ by His death had not redeemed it, reconciled it with God, and re-established it in its rights and its hopes. Original sin alone is enough to condemn us; but how many actual sins, incomparably more grievous, have we not added to that! Into what an abyss of misery have we not wilfully plunged ourselves !

But the crucifix makes known to us at the same time the still greater excess of the Divine love and mercy. One abyss has attracted another abyss; the abyss of our misery has been absorbed and swallowed up in the infinite abyss of God's mercy. Oh what reason David had to say that the mercies of God are above all His works ! All that God has done in the order of nature is nothing compared to what He has done in the order of grace. The goodness of the All-powerful has infinitely surpassed itself in the work of our redemption. Never, even in Heaven, will our understanding rise to the full comprehension of the greatness of this benefit which faith places before our eyes when we look at our crucifix. God, all God as He is, could not possibly have given us a greater proof of His love. Whatever proof He wished to give us of His love, it must have accorded with all the rights of His justice, which He could not give up. It was necessary that this justice should be appeased ; but by whom ? Who could possibly satisfy it, avenge it, and at the same time, spare the guilty ? Oh admirable invention of Divine love ! God lays upon His own Son all our iniquities ; He punishes them in His Person ; He revenges himself upon Him ; and this adorable Son consents with all His heart to be for us the Victim of His Father's anger. What a love in the Father ! What a love in the Son ! Who can think of it without being ravished with astonishment and admiration, and penetrated with gratitude ! If God had left to us the choice of a remedy for our evil case, should we ever have imagined such a remedy as this ? And even if it had presented itself to our minds, should we ever have dared to propose it ? Such a way of salvation could only have been conceived in the heart of a God who loved us infinitely.

And if our hearts can resist so much love, what hardness on our part ! what malice ! what ingratitude ! God strikes His own Son, to deliver us from hell and to open to us the gates of paradise ; He exhausts His anger upon His Son, and forgives us ; He adopts us as His own children in this Divine Son ; He gives us a right to share in His Son's inheritance, and He showers upon us all the supernatural help we need to attain it. And what does He ask of us in return ? That we should love Him, that we should serve Him,

and that we should obey Him. And we do not love
Him! And we look upon His service as an insupportable yoke! And we violate all His commandments! And all these crimes, all these scandals,
reign to-day, in the midst of a people calling themselves Christians, with as much or even more licence
than they did amongst the heathen of old! And
irreligion is carried to such a degree that Jesus
Christ and His cross have become an object of contempt, and of mockery, and of horror! The very
incomprehensibility and mystery of this love of God
is precisely the reason for which it is rejected. Is it
possible to conceive such an excess of impiety? Is
it possible to conceive how much this love of God,
that is despised, insulted, and outraged, must be
irritated against all these so-called Christians, who
are really apostates, either secret or declared?[1] Ah!
what a powerful motive this is for good and holy
souls to love God with their whole heart, and to try
and atone, by their devotion, for so many outrages.

And what virtue is there of which the crucifix is
not the perfect model?—the love of God, trust in
God, resignation to the will of God, even when it
seems most severe—an invariable patience, charity
for others, forgiveness of injuries, love of enemies,
humility, poverty, utter self-renunciation—and all
these virtues carried to the greatest height of perfection, exercised under the most trying circumstances,
and practised with a courage and generosity worthy
of God made Man. Shall we complain, after all this,
of what virtue costs us? Shall we argue with God

[1] This is said of France at the outbreak of the great Revolution.

about trifles ? Shall we dare to reproach Him with requiring too much from us ? One look upon our crucifix will make us blush for our complaints and our cowardice. What have we ever suffered, what can we ever suffer, for our salvation, which approaches ever so little to the sufferings and humiliations of Jesus Christ for us ? "But," you may say, "He was God, and I am only a weak creature." Certainly He was God, that is quite true, and therefore He suffered everything that it was possible for a human nature united to the Divine nature to suffer. If the hypostatic union communicated to His Sacred Humanity a strength infinite in the Giver, it was only that He might suffer in proportion ; and the justice of God loaded His Sacred Humanity unsparingly with the greatest weight it could possibly bear. It is an article of faith that God will never permit us to be tried beyond our strength. Weak as we are, we can always bear the trials He sends us, because the measure of strength He gives us also equals and surpasses the measure of our sorrows. Thus it is wrong for us to complain of our weakness, and to think that the example of our Saviour is not for us.

Finally, the crucifix is the consummation of the way of perfection. It shows us Jesus Christ as a Priest and a Victim at the same time—Jesus sacrificing Himself for the glory of His Father, sacrificing Himself willingly, and devoting Himself to the justice of God. There are but a very few favoured souls whom God calls to this state of *victim* and this exact resemblance to Jesus crucified. But those who have reason to believe that God has called them to this

honour must take their part in the sufferings and
humiliations of their Saviour; they must plant His
cross in their hearts, or rather they must let Him
plant it and bury it there. Jesus, submissive and
obedient even unto death, must be their model, their
consolation, and their strength.   And if sometimes
their sufferings seem to them excessive, if their
courage begins to fail, if they are tempted to accuse
God of an unjust severity, let them fix their eyes on
the crucifix. Jesus on the cross will be an answer
to everything, and they will leave His presence with
the desire to suffer more.

Let the crucifix then be our chief spiritual book; let
it be a book not for our eyes only, but for our hearts!
Let us beg of Jesus to teach us how to read in it, and
to reveal to us all its secrets, not only that we may contemplate them in the sweetness of prayer, but that we
may practise them faithfully during the whole course of
our life. Let us enter upon the way of perfection with
an absolute and unreserved devotion to the will of
God; let us resign our souls entirely to the workings
of His Spirit and His grace. Let us make with a
generous heart every sacrifice as He asks it of us;
and let us beg of Him to take from us and forcibly
tear from us all that we have not the courage to give
Him of ourselves. In one word, let us try to reduce
ourselves to the state of Jesus Christ dying on the
cross, in agony, with the scorn of men, forsaken
apparently by His Father, uniting in His Soul and
Body all the imaginable sufferings of a Victim to the
Divine justice and to the fury of human passion.

LX.

ON REFLECTIONS DURING PRAYER.

THE wise King Solomon tells us that *"there is a time for all things."* Now in prayer, as in everything else, there is a time to reflect, and a time to reflect no longer. Reflections are very useful, and even necessary, to make us understand the truths of religion, to enter into ourselves and to discover our faults. It is by these salutary reflections that sinners return to God, and that the generality of Christians persevere in the practice of good. As a general rule, as long as a person is being led by the ordinary way, and is able to preserve the free use of his understanding, it is right for him to make reflections, and to apply himself to meditation, without relying on it too much, however, or trying to dig too deeply, because there can very well be an abuse of meditation, as of all good things. And the greatest abuse, undoubtedly, is to think too much about it, and to rely too much on our own judgment and its light. A great deal of distrust of ourselves, a great deal of humility, a continual recourse to God that He may enlighten us, and a certain sobriety of wisdom, which stops the natural curiosity of our mind whenever it is necessary—these are so many efficacious remedies against the rashness of our reflections and the bad effects they might otherwise produce.

But is there not a way of prayer in which reflections become dangerous, and in which we cannot avoid them too much—in which we must allow ourselves to be guided only by the Spirit of God and by obedience? Most assuredly there is, and this way is the dark way of pure faith.

We cannot enter of ourselves upon this way; it is for God alone to lead into it those souls upon whom He has special designs. Neither spiritual books, nor directors, nor our own efforts, can do anything here; we must wait for grace to act, and not allow ourselves to think about such a state of prayer, still less to desire it, for if we do we shall most certainly be exposed to the danger of delusion. But at the same time we must never deny that there is such a way of prayer, and that the chief sign by which we may know that God wishes to lead a soul into it, is when that soul has no longer the same liberty of using her faculties in prayer that she formerly had; when she is able no longer to apply herself to a particular subject, to draw from it reflections and affections; but when she feels within herself, instead, a certain delicious peace which is above all expression, which takes the place of everything else, and which forces her, so to speak, to keep herself in quiet and in silence. When an experienced director is sufficiently convinced of this disposition of a soul, and is quite sure that she is not acting of herself, but that she is only lending herself to the action of God, then there is no longer any occasion to doubt that God wishes this soul to enter upon the way of blind faith. Always supposing, of course, that this soul is simple, upright, and docile, of a clear mind and good sense,

and that she has lived in innocence, or at least that
she has sincerely returned to God, and has led for
some time a Christian and edifying life. For it is a
very rare thing for a sinner to be suddenly raised to
the way of faith, although a few examples of it are
not wanting: for instance, Saint Mary of Egypt and
some others.

Now, it is in this way of pure faith that reflections
are dangerous, and all the masters of the spiritual life
agree that we must neither listen to them nor follow
them. There are several solid reasons for this,
drawn some from the very nature of this way, and
others from the object of the reflections which then
present themselves to the mind, and others again
from the cause which inspires or suggests these reflections.

The way of faith is essentially a dark way, a way
in which the soul can know nothing by the ordinary
light of reason, a way in which the principal intention
of God is to make the soul die to her own spirit. It
is therefore perfectly clear that in such a way it is
no longer by our own reflections that we must be
guided, but by the light of faith, and by the movement of the Holy Spirit. There is no question then
of meditation, for it is impossible to meditate any
longer; nor of following any particular method, for
the Spirit of God blows where He will, and as He
will; nor of exercising our own spirit, for that is
dying; nor of reflecting about what is going on
within us, for we can neither discern it nor have a
correct judgment upon it.

The way of faith is a way in which God, the Sole

Master of the soul and of her liberty, which she has given to Him, takes possession of her, disposes of her as He pleases, works in her according to His will, exercises over her a supreme dominion, and allows nothing to oppose His action. Now, nothing could put more obstacles in the way of God's action than the reflections the soul might make of herself, either to guide herself, or to judge of what is passing within her and act in consequence. It is evident that such reflections must constrain and hinder the Divine operations, and consequently must do harm to the soul, even so as to make her leave this way of prayer altogether.

The way of faith is a way of sacrifice, a way of continual self-immolation, a way which ends in the total loss of the soul in God. This way, which is sweet, and full of Divine favours and lights in the beginning, becomes afterwards a way of obscurity, of nakedness, of despoilment, in which the soul finds herself reduced to the last extremity, without having the slightest perceptible assistance either from God, or from creatures, or from herself. Now, it is quite evident that such a state as this, during the whole course of it, can never admit reflections; it must exclude them absolutely, and the soul must not see, and must not wish to see, where she is going, whither God means to lead her, or in what way He means to lead her; otherwise, she would never be able to make up her mind to all the sacrifices which God will certainly require of her. Especially, she would never make the entire sacrifice of her mind if she could always preserve the use of reflection, and the total immolation of herself, which God expects of her, would never take place.

Finally, the way of faith is a way of temptations, in which God gives the devil a strange power over the soul on purpose to try her. God allows the devil to fill her mind with darkness, her imagination with a thousand wild fancies, and her will with every kind of thought of blasphemy, of despair, of impurity, and of impiety. The soul must bear all this patiently, and she will come by degrees to believe that all these horrors are really a part of herself, that she is consenting to them, and that for that reason she is justly hated by God. This state of extreme temptation, which she could never bear at all except by the most entire abandonment to the will of God and the most complete trust in Him, is not compatible with any reflections to be made upon herself. It is too clear that it cannot possibly be. There is a great deal more to be said on this subject; but I have said enough to make it understood that any reflections can only spoil everything in the life of pure faith, which is only called so because it banishes all reflection.

More than this, the object even of these reflections furnishes us with new reasons to forbid them to those who are in this way of prayer. For their object is, either to know what God is doing in us, and the reasons of His action, and God wishes the soul to know nothing whatever of the secret operations of His grace; or to seek for a feeling of assurance, and God wishes to take away from the soul all assurance; or to examine into the manner in which our director is

guiding us, and God requires no less the blind
obedience of the judgment than of the will. It is
essential to the perfection of this way of prayer that
the soul should walk in it blindly, and that she should
leave to God alone the care of governing her and
guiding her safely to the end, without knowing where
she is, whither she is going, or where she will end.
Thus, all reasoning, all foresight, all examination, all
consideration of self, is strictly forbidden, as an infidelity, a straying from the way, and a temptation of
which the effect will certainly be to withdraw the soul
from the guidance of God.

Finally, it is certain that the soul, in this way of
prayer, must admit no other thoughts than those that
come to her from God. Now, all the reflections
which ever present themselves then to the soul, and
which have for their principle either curiosity, or
uneasiness, or a wish to foresee what is going to
happen to us, or a secret self-complacency, come
always from our own spirit, or are suggested by the
devil. It is easy to recognise this, because such
reflections either inspire the soul with vanity and
presumption, or throw her into trouble and despair.
She must therefore reject them, and never willingly
dwell on them. It is the only means she has of preserving her interior peace in a state so difficult.

Besides, the changes and vicissitudes of this way
are such, and so frequent, that the soul would try to
take note of them, or to keep account of them, or to
remember them; from one day to another, from the
morning to the evening, from one hour to the other,
her state changes; she is like the heavens when they

are charged with storms, or the sea agitated by tempests. How can she possibly reflect in the midst of such agitations? And what foundation could she possibly make on thoughts suggested either by nature reduced to its last extremity or by the spirit of darkness? When the storm is over, and a blessed peace and calm has succeeded it, she will enjoy that calm and think no more of the torments she has just been suffering.

"But," you will say, "is it not very ill-advised to forbid the soul to make any reflections upon her state, when this is precisely the matter which interests her most to know, and in fact is the only thing that is of interest to her?"

I reply, no: it is not ill-advised, when once we have all the necessary proofs of the reality of this state. The less the soul reflects the more she will advance, the stronger she will be against the devil and against herself, the more generosity she will have to accomplish all the sacrifices which God asks of her.

And I may add that she will thus considerably shorten her time of trial, and will spare herself many troubles and anxieties of which her own reflections are the source, and also that she will be much less difficult a charge to him who has the care of her direction.

LXI.

ON SIMPLICITY.

It is more easy to feel what simplicity is than to define it. To understand what it is, let us contemplate it first as it is in God; afterwards we will consider it as it is displayed in an interior soul; and we shall come to the conclusion that in God, as in His favoured creature, simplicity is the source, the principle, and the crown of all perfection.

God is infinitely perfect, with every kind of perfection, because He is a Being infinitely simple. He is eternal, because His existence, having neither beginning, nor end, nor succession of time, is simple and indivisible in its duration. There is in God neither past nor future, but an unchanging present.

We cannot say of God, as we can of a creature, *He was, He will be;* but we must always say, *He is;* and in this *He is* is comprehended in an ineffable manner all time, either real or imaginary, without having, however, with time, any common measure.

God is immense, because His existence is infinitely simple as to His omnipresence. He is everywhere, and yet He is not bounded or contained anywhere. No other body, and no other spirit can be nowhere, because every body is necessarily bounded by the space it occupies, and every created spirit only exists and acts where God wishes it to exist and act.

The science of God is infinite, because it is simple;

there is in Him no reasoning, or multiplicity of ideas, as there is in created intelligences. He has only one single idea, which embraces the perfect knowledge of all things in itself. It is the same with all the Divine perfections : simplicity is the character of them, and they are infinite just because they are simple.

His exterior actions are varied, and can be infinitely so ; the operations of His grace, of His justice, and of His mercy are varied, in like manner, if we consider them in creatures, who are the end of them. But when we consider these actions and operations in God Himself, they are nothing else but His one, continued, and infinitely simple action—an action which, in its Divine simplicity, extends to everything in the physical and moral order.

The end which God proposes to Himself in all He does, in all He commands or forbids or permits, is infinitely simple, and has only one sole object in view, which is His own glory. It is to His glory that everything that happens in this world must necessarily tend, as well as the happiness of the good in another life and the misery of the wicked. Thus, under whatever aspect we contemplate God, He is simple, and His simplicity is the root of His infinity. Our intelligence, when it is enlightened by the Divine light, can understand a little of this great and sublime truth ; it can contemplate it, but it can never fathom the depth of it, or perfectly comprehend it. God alone can comprehend His own infinite simplicity. The little I have just said is enough to give us a just idea of it, although a very imperfect one.

It is evident that simplicity can never be the same

2 B

in a mere creature as it is in God; but it is none
the less evident that the perfection of the creature
consists in his resemblance to God, and that the more
simple he becomes, after the manner of God, the more
perfect he is. Everything therefore that God does
to a soul to make it holy, has for its first object to
make it simple; and all the co-operation He requires
from that soul is that it should allow itself to be torn
from every kind of multiplicity, to pass on to a state
of simplicity which shall be a participation in the
simplicity of God.   .

When, therefore, a soul has given herself entirely
to God, that He may do as He pleases with her in
time and in eternity, He simplifies her first of all in
the very depths of her nature by placing there a
principle of infused and supernatural love which
becomes the simple and only motive of her whole
conduct. She begins to love God without any other
motive than because He is God; she loves Him for
Himself, and not for her own sake; she refers everything to this love, without even thinking expressly
about it or paying attention to it: love is the simple
and sole object of this soul; she is always out of
herself, as it were—always tending to despoil herself
of self and to be transformed into the beloved object.
God makes her simple in her understanding. The
multitude of thoughts which formerly embarrassed her
ceases; during this time she can no longer meditate, or
reason, or speak. A light that is simple, though
indistinct, enlightens her; she walks by the guidance
of this dim light, without perceiving anything very
clearly. Her prayer, which before was full of con-

sideration, affections, and good resolutions, becomes quite simple; she is occupied, and nevertheless she does not feel that she is occupied with anything; she feels and enjoys without being able to say what she enjoys. It is no longer a particular feeling; it is a confused and general feeling which she cannot explain. Do not ask of her upon what subject she is making her prayer; she cannot tell you, she does not know; no ideas present themselves to her mind, and she cannot seize any of those that are offered to her. All that she knows is that she is in prayer, and that she is there as it pleases God, sometimes dry, sometimes in consolation, sometimes sensibly recollected, sometimes involuntarily distracted, but always in peace, and united to God in the depths of her being. She passes whole hours in this state without fatigue or disgust, empty apparently of thoughts or affections: it is because her thoughts and affections have become quite simple, and have for their only end God, the Being Who is infinitely simple. This soul is almost always the same, even when she is not actually in prayer, if she is reading, or speaking, or occupied with work and domestic cares, she feels that she is less taken up with what she is doing than with God, for Whom she is doing everything, and that He is really the secret occupation of her spirit, in such a manner that in this respect her prayer and her attention to God are continual, and are not distracted by any exterior object whatever. This simplicity of spirit is perfected from day to day, and the great care of the soul is to drive away everything which could bring her back to multiplicity.

God makes her will simple by reducing it to one sole aim, one sole object, one sole desire, which is the accomplishment of His Divine will. The soul is no longer wearied, as formerly, by a thousand desires, a thousand cares, a thousand anxieties. Her affections are all concentrated on One alone. She loves all she ought to love—parents, relations, husband, children, and friends—but she loves them only in God, and because of the love she has for God. She knows no longer whether she wishes for anything, because her will is lost in the will of God, and He wills for her from one moment to another whatever is most suitable for her. It is thus that her simplified will finds its rest and its centre in the will of God.

God makes her simple by detaching her little by little from herself, and from all regard for her own interests, even from all care about her actual situation. All the things she liked formerly—play, or conversation, or reading, or sight-seeing—all these become insipid to her; the society of creatures is only annoying to her; she only associates with them as a matter of duty, and from courtesy and kindness; God draws her incessantly within herself, and separates her from all exterior things. He takes away from her by degrees all considerations about herself, or about what is going on within her, because if her thoughts were thus divided, and fixed sometimes upon God, and sometimes upon herself, she would never become perfectly simple, until at last she comes to know no longer how she is never to think of herself at all, never to be troubled about herself, and carefully to suppress every thought as far as is lawful of which she herself is the object, that God alone may occupy her entirely. He takes away from her, for the same reason, all care for her own interest, because her intention would not be perfectly simple and pure if she united a seeking for her own interest to her care for the interests of God. Therefore she never looks at her actions, or her good works, or her progress in perfection, as if they had anything to do with her, or as if they were things that interested her personally, but she looks at everything with regard to God alone, as things which come from Him, which belong to Him, and of which He can dispose as He pleases.

God makes her simple in all her exterior conduct. There is in her no evasion, no pretence, no dissimulation, no intrigue, no self-seeking, no affectation, no human respect. She goes simply as God leads her; she says and does what she thinks to be her duty, without troubling herself about what any one will say or think of her. Her conversation is simple, true, and natural; she prepares nothing beforehand, she says what the Spirit of God suggests to her without fear of the consequences. Even if it were in a matter concerning her honour, or her possessions, or her life, she would never say a word or take a step of herself, but she would leave to God the arrangement of all things, and she would never see anything but His hand in whatever might happen to her from creatures.

This is a brief picture of true Christian simplicity, as it is found in a soul which suffers herself to be led entirely by God. And it is easy to see that this virtue embraces the whole perfection of the interior life—that it is the beginning, the middle, and the end of it—and that the soul has attained the highest degree of sanctity when, becoming perfectly simple, she only sees God in all things, she only loves God in all things, and when she has no other interests but the interests of God—that is to say, His glory and the accomplishment of His will.

We can understand now why interior souls are so despised by the world, which is, as Saint John says, given up to wickedness and to the multiplicity of created things, whilst interior souls, on their side, are all innocence, candour, and simplicity. These are two most opposite spirits, each of which condemns and reproves the other. The world is nothing but pretence, dissimulation, deceit, and self-love; it refers everything to itself and to its temporal interests. Interior souls are just the contrary; and for this reason they pass in the eyes of the world as fools and madmen.

We can understand also why these interior souls are hated and detested by mercenary and self-interested souls, although they may be otherwise virtuous and devout: it is because they are both travelling on such very different roads; it is that the one kind are serving God for His own sake, without any thought of their own interest, which is the necessary fruit of their simplicity; while the other kind are seeking themselves in the service of God, appropriating all to themselves, greedy for sensible fervour and consolation, wishing always to be certain about their state, and never consenting to lose sight of themselves for a moment. It is impossible that these two kinds of devotion can ever be sympathetic, and the simple souls, who have abandoned themselves entirely to God, must always have a great deal to suffer from the others, who see in them a silent condemnation of their principles and their conduct.

Finally, we can understand now why the sanctity of simple and interior souls is unknown on earth, unless God manifests it Himself. It is because their very simplicity makes them walk in a way that is quite common and ordinary as to the exterior; because they affect no singularity; because they have few exterior practices of devotion; because everything passes within them secretly, and is only seen by the eye of God, and because they hide themselves not only from others, but also from themselves. God wishes them to belong to Him only; He hides them in the secret of His Presence; and to make the singular graces He gives them more safe and sure, He almost always allows them to be humbled, calumniated, and persecuted. In like manner Jesus Christ was misunderstood, despised, and rejected by the Jews, and was only glorified after His death on the cross.

LXII.

ON THE WORDS OF PSALM VIII:

"Ex ore infantium et lactentium perfecisti laudem."

"Out of the mouths of babes and sucklings Thou hast perfected praise."

JESUS CHRIST applied these words to Himself, and made use of them to confound the Pharisees, who were offended at the homage the people paid Him on His entry into Jerusalem, a triumphal entry which exalted His littleness and His humility. The people then recognised Him, saluted Him, and blessed Him as the Messiah, the Son of David, the King of Israel. And in so doing the people rendered to their God and Saviour a perfect homage, because they honoured His poverty, His humiliation, and His annihilation of Himself. On the contrary, the proud Pharisees, led away by their false reasoning, saw nothing in this triumph but what shocked all their ideas, nothing but what seemed to them contemptible, ridiculous, and extravagant; and their false lights, their low and human prejudices, and their wrong ideas of real greatness, blinded them and confirmed them in their unbelief.

Not only does our natural reason not understand the things of God, but it is naturally disposed to despise them and treat them as folly. This disposition is more common than we should ever think for amongst Christians, even amongst those who imagine themselves devout; these are often great enemies of an interior life, just as the Pharisees, who were the devout people of Judaism, were the greatest enemies of Jesus Christ.

We can never begin to enjoy the things of God, or even to understand them, until we enter upon a state of spiritual infancy. And what is this infancy? A spiritual child is one who feels himself incapable of reasoning or speaking about the things of God; one, who, feeling all his weakness and ignorance, allows himself to be guided by the grace of God and by those who hold the place. of God towards him; who is humble, obedient, and dependent in all things; who believes without examination whatever is told him as to his spiritual state; who accomplishes blindly whatever he is commanded, without knowing, so to speak, what he is doing. He is one who, reduced to a blind instinct, which is none the less Divine, and to a spirit of pure faith, which is superior to all reasoning, walks all the more securely that he knows neither the way by which he is being led nor the end towards which he is travelling. He is in the same state as Saint Paul when, blinded by the heavenly light, his companions led him by the hand to Damascus without his seeing at all of himself where he planted his footsteps.

I repeat it once more: we either cannot discern anything at all about our interior state, or we see badly, and make mistakes, as long as we are guided by our own spirit. The total loss of our own spirit is what introduces us into the secrets of God; and the more we advance the more this loss increases, until at last it becomes complete and irrevocable. Those who think their advancement consists in having great light of the understanding, or sublime ideas, or profound reasonings, are very much deceived. The devil has more intelligence, more knowledge, more exalted ideas, than all men put together. When he lost his happiness for ever he did not lose his natural intelligence; it even serves to torment him still more.

Therefore, all our spiritual progress consists in the annihilation of our own spirit and of our own judgment, so that we have absolutely no reliance whatever on ourselves, that we see nothing with our own sight, that we judge of nothing and reason upon nothing of ourselves.

This state is quite incomprehensible to any one who has had no experience of it. The enemies of the interior life treat it as a vision and a fancy. But it is very real, and is confirmed by the experience of many saints; Holy Scripture speaks of it in a thousand places; and we shall never thoroughly understand the teaching of the Gospel and the life of Jesus Christ unless we are in this blessed state of spiritual infancy. Yes, happy, thrice happy is he who, having given his whole mind and heart to God, knows no longer whether he has a mind or a heart; who does not even know what God is doing with him; who practises virtue without thinking that he practises it; who prays always, without knowing how he prays, or even that he is praying at all; who loves without reflecting upon his love; who walks on calmly, without knowing his way, or seeing the progress he makes; who, in a word, perfectly forgets himself, and, without care or anxiety, without reflection or thought of the future, reposes in peace upon the bosom of God as a little infant sleeps upon his mother's breast.

This is the state from which God derives the most perfect homage, because in it God is everything and the creature is nothing, because God does with this creature just what He wishes, as He wishes, and as much as He wishes, without finding the slightest obstacle to His designs. What is it that most honours God? Is it our great actions, our magnificent projects? Is it our great austerities, our long prayers, our multiplied practices of devotion? Is it even our crosses, and sufferings of all kinds? No: nothing of all that can in itself honour God. Pride can poison all that, self-love and our own will can be the motive principle of it, and with a semblance of holiness we may be all the time rejected of God. What really honours God is our destruction, our self-annihilation, the entire consuming of the victim!

Now, it does not belong to us to destroy and annihilate ourselves. If we could do so by any principle that is in ourselves, this principle would draw its life and strength from the death of all the rest. The work of our destruction belongs only to God. The destroying principle must be from outside, and must attack our whole being. The fire that consumes the victim must come from on high; and all that the victim has to do is to remain quietly upon the altar, fully consenting to be consumed, and offering no resistance to his total destruction.

During this operation the victim must be purely passive; it is God who must move his soul to act; he must not pay any attention to what the Divine fire

is doing to him ; he must not even look at it, for if
he looks at all, it is an act of life, and as long as he
looks or is able to look he is not dead.

Thus, that state of spiritual infancy which despoils
us of our own spirit, of our own will, and of our own
life, to make way for the Spirit and the will and the
life of God, is the beginning of the mystical death ;
it is the creation of the new man and the destruction
of the old man.   And in proportion as the old man
is destroyed the new man grows and thrives, and
when the new man is perfectly formed the other is
perfectly annihilated.

We see clearly now that the spiritual life, like the
natural life, must begin by infancy—that infancy is
the entrance to it and the first step in it ; the foundation of the man, and all that constitutes his state as
a perfect man, both in body and soul, is in the little
child.   Time, and food, and education, and exercise,
and experience, may develop his spiritual and cor-
poreal faculties.   But from his earliest infancy all
those faculties are already there in miniature.   And
it is the same with the spiritual man.   When God
wishes to form that in us, He produces it by His
grace in the state of a little child : afterwards, by the
continual operation of this same grace, with which
the soul co-operates by a full consent and an inviolable fidelity, God gives her, little by little, and
by almost insensible degrees of progress, increase
and perfection.   God always does first the most
essential part, which is the formation of this spiritual
child ; He does it alone, and the child contributes
nothing to his own formation, but when he is once

formed he must second the action of God, not by acting of himself, but by doing all that God wishes him to do and by suffering all that God wishes him to suffer.

It is quite right that God should give this child a director to guide him, for how can he guide himself in this state ? And the child and his guide must both be perfectly submissive to all the movements of Divine grace. And God requires of the child an un-bounded confidence and an entire obedience to him who is given as his guide. This confidence must go so far that the child must communicate without reserve to his guide everything that passes in the most secret and closest depths of his soul, and this obedience must be such that the child has no longer any will of his own or any judgment upon anything whatso-ever.

LXIII.

ON ENTIRE ABANDONMENT.

" Father, into Thy hands I commend My Spirit."

OUR Lord and Saviour Jesus Christ made this act of entire abandonment when He was forsaken by His Father, treated by Him as a Victim loaded with all the sins of the universe, and as if He were an object of malediction—when He was experiencing at the same time in His Soul all the severity of God's justice, and in His Sacred Body all the torments and igno-minies which the rage of his cruel enemies could invent—when His holiness, His miracles, His prophecies, His mission as King and Messiah, were all turned into derision—when of His own apostles one had betrayed Him, one had denied Him, all had forsaken Him—when, naked and poor, having absolutely nothing on this earth, not even His immaculate and broken-hearted Mother, whom He had given away to Saint John, He was about to breathe out His last sigh upon the cross. It was then that, collecting all His strength and all His love, accepting fully and with a generous heart all that He suffered in Soul and Body from God and man, deprived of all exterior aid and all consolation—it was then that He pronounced those great words, " *Father, into Thy hands I commend My Spirit.*"

This soul of mine, which has exhausted all the bitter scourging of Your anger—this soul of mine, which is the reproach of men and the outcast of the people, I commend it, I sacrifice it, I lose it in Your hands !

We must not doubt that this act of entire resignation was also the expression of the most pure and disinterested love. Pure love is not separated, in the faithful soul, from faith and hope ; on the contrary, it perfects them both. We may not have the feeling of them, nor even the perception, but we have the reality of them in the most sublime degree. And it is an error to think that love, when it attains its greatest height in this world, weakens or destroys the other two theological virtues ; and it is a gross calumny upon the followers of the interior life to accuse them of this error, and to impute to them the abominable heresy of Quietism, when they teach that the height of perfection is to serve God for His own sake alone, without any thought as a rule of self-interest, either for time or for eternity.

But it is quite certain, by the doctrine and experience of the saints, that man, assisted by Divine grace, can in some degree imitate Jesus Christ in this supreme abandonment. It is quite certain that God can place a soul, and has placed many souls, in such a state of trial as this, and that He has led them by degrees to make to Him the sacrifice of their dearest interests. I grant that we cannot make such a sacrifice with only ordinary grace, and that we must have passed beforehand through very high and very purifying states of prayer, into which no one must dare to venture of himself, and of which this supreme sacrifice is only the consummation. God alone, by an extraordinary grace, can bring a soul into this state, and lead her by the hand to the end of it. There is nothing to fear from delusion in this state, because nature has a horror of it, as it is infinitely painful to nature, and only tends to its destruction ; and it is impossible to imagine or to feign this state. For those who are really in it do not generally know that they are in it ; they walk, feeling their way in the darkness of pure and blind faith ; they accept this state in the superior part of their soul, but the inferior part suffers the most violent conflicts ; it would gladly avoid all this intense suffering, and is far from taking any pleasure in it. If it ever happens that such souls are persecuted and misunderstood, it can only be by those who have had no experience whatever and no knowledge of this state ; and we cannot take too many precautions, we cannot distrust our own judgment too much, we cannot call upon God too humbly and earnestly, when we have to pronounce upon such matters as these.

When God wishes to lead a soul by this way, He inspires her first of all to give herself up entirely to Him. Then He calls her to a state of passive re-collection and continual prayer. He gives her a taste for those books only which treat of the interior life, and gives her an infused knowledge of it in proportion to His designs for her. Often also He enlightens her Himself without the aid of books. Above all things, He takes care to give her a wise and experienced guide who can help her to make progress in the way of perfection, and He inspires her with a docility and a spirit of obedience above the common.

Then He tries her by degrees; He makes her pass from one renunciation to another, from one trial to another, all becoming more and more interior and spiritual. He joins to this various kinds of tempta-tions, either from the devil or from men. At the same time He blinds her as to herself and her interior state; she has no certainty where she is or how she stands, whether she loves God or whether God loves her; she fears to offend Him by her every action; she thinks her incapacity of feeling is hardness of heart; she thinks that the apparent estrangement of God from her is the beginning of His rejecting her altogether; all which causes her inexpressible torment and anguish. It is in vain that her director and superiors try to reassure her and to calm her; all their reasonings make no impression upon her. God leads her thus from precipice to precipice, until at last He brings her to the edge of the great abyss, and commands her to cast herself down there by an utter and generous resignation of her whole self into His hands. He leaves her some time in this abyss, after which He draws her out of it, and gives her a new and glorious life in Him.

All this is an enigma and a mystery for any one who is not enlightened by a supernatural light. But it is not right to treat such states as these as mere fancies, and those whom God leads by them as if their brains were deranged; we must respect what we are ignorant of, or at least we must not venture to decide upon it.

As to those favoured souls who have some reason to believe that God is calling them to this state of entire abandonment, let them not be frightened under the pretext that all this is quite beyond their present strength, that such a sacrifice inspires them with horror, and that they cannot even bear the thought of it. It is truly here that we may say that the things which are impossible to men are possible and easy to God. He Himself will prepare the soul, she need only leave it to Him; He will change all her interior dispositions; He will purify her and detach her little by little from self-love; He will inspire her with a holy hatred of herself, until He convinces her that she is indeed worthy of condemnation.

All this is true; there is no delusion or Quietism in believing it, still less in experiencing it. This state is the height of perfection for the creature. It

2 C

is quite clear that we must refuse absolutely nothing
to God, if we wish Him to lead us by this way; that
we must give all, detach ourselves from all, allow all
to be torn from us.   What danger can there possibly
be in a way so perfect?

APPENDIX.

WE may have remarked, in several of these sketches of
Father Grou, that he lays great stress upon the importance
of making interior souls understand how very necessary it
is for them to repress their natural activity, and to accustom
themselves by degrees to be very simple before God in the
practice of prayer, to repose sweetly in God, and to fix in
Him all the agitation of their minds and hearts. "It is
in vain," he says, "that we seek for rest outside of God;
it is only and can only be found in God alone. It is not
by agitating ourselves, or exciting ourselves, or making
many acts, that we succeed in finding rest in God; it is by
putting a stop to all agitation, to all over-eagerness, and all
restless activity, that we may give free scope to the action of
God: God is always acting, and always perfectly tranquil.
The soul united to God shares equally in His action, and in
His repose; she is always acting, even when she does not
perceive it, but she acts then in the greatest peace; she
does not outrun the action of God, but she waits until God
pushes her forward; she moves under the Divine impulse,
as the hand of a child, who is learning to write, moves
under the impulse of his master's hand. . . The soul that
is under the action of God is never for one moment idle,
as those imagine who have no true idea of what rest in
God really means. . ."

"Activity," he says again, "engenders multiplicity, and repose conduces to unity and simplicity, even to that simplicity of which Jesus Christ declares the necessity. Activity multiplies practices of piety; it embraces every kind of new devotion; it passes incessantly from one act to another; it agitates itself, it torments itself, it thinks it has never done enough. Repose concentrates us in God, and fixes us on one thing only—to listen for the voice of God in prayer; and when we are not in prayer, to accomplish His Divine will in the moment that is passing, without troubling ourselves about the past or the future, in such a manner that the soul has never but one single object in view, and that she is never drawn away by exterior things, being less occupied with what she is actually doing, than with the will of God, which is its motive and its end."

This is the same doctrine as all the masters of the spiritual life teach, and especially one of the most celebrated of all, Saint Francis de Sales. "We place ourselves," he says, "in the presence of God for two special reasons ; the first is, to render to God the honour and homage we owe Him, and *this can be done without God speaking to us or our speaking to Him.* This duty is done by acknowledging that He is our God, and that we are His vile creatures, and by remaining before Him, prostrate in spirit, waiting for His commands. How many courtiers there are who go a hundred times into the presence of the King, not to speak to Him, or to hear Him speak, but simply to be seen by Him, and to show, by this attention, that they are his faithful servants ! *And this simple end of presenting ourselves before God solely to show to Him our gratitude, and our goodwill, acknowledging that we are His faithful servants, is most excellent, most holy, and consequently of the greatest perfection.*

" The second reason for our presenting ourselves before God is to speak to Him, and to hear Him speak to us by His inspirations and the interior movements of His grace. And one of these two benefits can never fail us in prayer. If we can speak to our Lord, let us speak, let us praise Him, let us listen to Him; *if we cannot speak to Him because we are hoarse, let us stay nevertheless in His presence and do Him reverence : He will see us there ; He will be pleased with our patience, and He will look with favour on our loving silence.* Another time we may be quite amazed and overwhelmed when He takes us by the hand, and converses with us, and makes with us a hundred turns in the fragrant walks of His sweet garden of prayer ; but even if He never does this, let us be content that it is our duty to be among His followers, and that it is a great favour and a greater honour that He allows us to be in His presence. In this manner, we shall not be in a hurry to speak to Him, since the other way of being near Him is not less useful for us, although it may be a little less agreeable to our taste. Whenever, then, you come near our Lord, speak to Him if you can. If you cannot, remain there, let Him see you, and do not trouble yourself about anything else."

It is nevertheless too true that many good and pious souls who give themselves to prayer regard their silence before God as a sort of idleness which is disrespectful to His Divine Majesty, and even go so far as to confound it with Quietism. This is why it has seemed useful to us to terminate this Manual by a little treatise of Bossuet, the most celebrated adversary of Quietism, which is very little known.

*A Short and Simple Manner of making our Prayer in the
Spirit of Faith, and in the Simple Presence of God.*

I. We must accustom ourselves to nourish our souls
with a simple and loving look at God and at Jesus Christ
our Lord; and to do this we must withdraw our souls
gently from all reasoning, from all arguments, and from a
multiplicity of affections, to keep them in simplicity, respect,
and attention, and thus to draw nearer and nearer to God,
our only Sovereign Good, our first beginning, and our
last end.

II. The perfection of this life consists in union with our
Sovereign Good, and the greater our simplicity is, the closer
and more perfect will this union be. This is why Divine
grace interiorly persuades those who wish to be perfect to
make themselves simple, that they may thus be capable of
the enjoyment of the *One* Who alone is necessary—that is
to say, of the Eternal Unity: let us then say from our
hearts, *O unum necessarium, unum volo, unum quæro, unum
desidero, unum mihi est necessarium, Deus meus et omnia!*
O One Who only art necessary! It is Thee alone Whom
I wish for, Thee alone Whom I seek after, Thee alone
Whom I desire! Thou art my sole necessity, O my God
and my All!

III. Meditation is very good in its proper time, and very
useful in the beginning of the spiritual life; but we must
not stop there, when the soul, by her fidelity to mortification and recollection, generally receives the gift of a purer
and higher state of prayer, which we may call the prayer of
simplicity, because it consists in one simple look of ours,

one loving attention on our part, towards some Divine object—either God in some of His infinite perfections, or Jesus Christ in some of His mysteries, or some of the Christian virtues. The soul, then, leaving all reasoning, makes use of a sweet contemplation, which keeps her in peace, attentive and susceptible to all the Divine operations and impressions which the Holy Spirit communicates to her. She does little, and receives much; her labour is sweet, and nevertheless it is very fruitful; and as she now approaches nearer to the Source of all light, of all grace, and of all virtue, these blessings also increase in her more and more.

IV. The practice of this kind of prayer must begin on our first awaking, by our making an act of faith in the presence of God, Who is everywhere, and of Jesus Christ, Whose looks never leave us, even if we were to be swallowed up in the depths of the earth. This act may be produced either in a sensible and ordinary manner, by saying in our hearts: " I believe that my God is present ;" or it may be produced by a simple memory of pure faith, which sees God always present in a manner that is purer and more spiritual.

V. After this, we need not try to produce several other acts or different dispositions, but we may remain simply and peacefully attentive to this presence of God, knowing that His Divine looks are fixed upon us, and continuing this devout attention as long as our Lord gives us the grace to do so, without troubling ourselves to do anything else than attend quietly to what is happening to us; for this prayer is a prayer with God alone, and a union which pre-eminently includes all other special dispositions and which forces the soul to be passive, because God is then the sole Master of her, and is acting in her in a more particular manner than usual; so that the less the creature labours, the more powerfully God works in her. And since the work of God is always also a rest and a deep peace, the soul becomes in this kind of prayer in a manner like unto Him, and receives also most wonderful effects from His Divine goodness. And as the rays of the sun make the plants of the earth grow and flower and bear fruit, so the soul that is thus exposed and peacefully attentive to these rays of the Divine Sun of Justice will receive from It an outpouring of the Divine influence which will enrich her with every kind of virtue.

VI. The continuation of the soul in this prayer of faith will help her to thank God for all the graces and blessings received from Him during the past night and the whole course of her life, to offer herself to Him, as well as all her actions, sufferings, and intentions for the coming day, to pray for others, and so on.

VII. The soul might imagine at first that she is losing a great deal for omitting formal acts, but experience will teach her that, on the contrary, she is gaining very much, because the greater her knowledge of God is, the purer will be her love, the more upright her intentions, the stronger her hatred of sin, the more continual her recollection, her mortification, and her humility.

VIII. All this does not prevent her from producing acts of virtue, either interior or exterior, whenever she feels herself drawn to do so, by the impulse of grace; but her ordinary state ought to be this loving attention of faith and union with God, which keeps her entirely abandoned into His hands and given up to His Divine love, that He may do with her as He wills.

IX. When the time for actual prayer has come, the soul must begin it with great respect by the simple remembrance of God, invoking His Holy Spirit and uniting herself closely to Jesus Christ; she may then continue it in the same manner, and also all her vocal prayers, her office in choir, the Holy Mass, either said or heard, and even her examination of conscience, for this same light of faith which keeps us attentive to God will also discover to us our least imperfections, and lead us to conceive the greatest sorrow and regret for them. We must also go to our meals in the same spirit of holy simplicity, paying more attention to God than to what we are eating, and thus being free to listen better to the reading that is going on. This practice makes us think of nothing but keeping our soul detached from all imperfections and attached only to God, being united closely to Him, in which consists all our happiness.

X. We must go to recreation in the same disposition, to give our body and mind some little distraction, but without allowing ourselves to become dissipated, or curious about news, or giving way to immoderate laughter or any indiscreet words; but we must keep ourselves pure and free in our interior, without being a restraint upon others; uniting ourselves frequently to God by a simple and loving look at Him, remembering that we are in His presence, and that He does not wish us ever to be separated from Him and from His holy will. It is the most ordinary rule of this state of simplicity, and the supreme disposition of such a soul, to wish to do the will of God in all things. To see everything come from God, and to pass on from everything to God, is what sustains and strengthens the soul in all events and occupations, and keeps us also in possession of simplicity. Let us then always follow the will of God, after the example of Jesus Christ, and united to Him as our

Head; and this is a most excellent means of increasing in us this kind of prayer, and attaining by it a more solid virtue and a more perfect holiness.

XI. We ought to behave in the same way, and with the same spirit, and preserve ourselves in this simple and close union with God, in all our actions and conduct, whether in the parlour or in our own cell, in the refectory or at recreation; and I may also add, that in all our conversations we must try to edify our neighbour, making use of every occasion to exercise ourselves in piety and the love of God, and in the practice of good works, that we may be the sweet odour of Jesus Christ. "*If any one speaks,*" St. Peter says, "*let him speak the words of God*"—that is, as if God were speaking by him. It is sufficient for this to give ourselves simply to the guidance of the Spirit of God; He will suggest to us on all occasions the right words to say, without allowing us to fall into affectation.

Finally, we will finish the day still in the presence of God; we will thus make our examination of conscience, our evening prayer, and we will lay ourselves down to rest and fall asleep in peace still with this loving attention, interrupting our repose with a few fervent and loving words if we happen to awake during the night, and send them as so many swift arrows and tender aspirations straight from our heart to the heart of God. Such cries as these, for instance: "My God, be Thou all things to me! I desire only Thee, for time and for eternity! Lord, who is like unto Thee? My Lord and my God! My God and my All! My God, and nothing else!"

XII. We must also observe that this true simplicity makes us live in a continual state of death to ourselves, and in a perfect detachment, because we must go to God with a perfectly pure heart, without being held back by any created thing. But it is not by speculating about it that we obtain this grace of simplicity; it is by keeping our heart in great purity, and by a true mortification and contempt of ourselves. Any one who shuns suffering, humiliation, and dying to himself will never enter there. And this is also the reason that so few persons really advance, because so few really wish to renounce themselves, and thus they suffer an immense loss, and deprive themselves of inexpressible benefits. Happy are those faithful souls who spare themselves in nothing that they may belong entirely to God! happy are those religious persons who faithfully practise all the rules of their holy institute! This fidelity makes them die continually to themselves, to their own judgment, their own will, and all their natural inclinations and aversions, and thus disposes them in an admirable though unknown manner for this excellent kind of prayer. For what is there more hidden from the world than a religious man or a religious woman who does nothing but follow his or her rule in all things, showing nothing extraordinary as to the exterior, but living all the time in a continual and wonderful state of total death to self? It is by this way of prayer that the Kingdom of God is established in our hearts, and everything else is given to us.

XIII. We must not neglect the reading of spiritual books; but we must read them simply and in a spirit of prayer, and not from curiosity. I call it to read in a spirit of prayer when we allow our soul to be impressed by the light from God and the pious feelings which the reading brings to us, and when this impression is made more by the thought of God than by our own industry.

XIV. We must also be acquainted with two or three wise maxims: the first, that a devout person without prayer is a body without a soul; the second, that we cannot have a true and solid spirit of prayer without mortification, recollection, and humility; and the third, that we have great need of perseverance, never to be discouraged by the difficulties which meet us on our way.

XV. We must not forget that one of the greatest secrets of the spiritual life is that the Holy Spirit leads us in it not only by light and sweetness, by consolations, tendernesses, and facility of prayer, but also by obscurities and blindness, by insensibility, troubles, anguish of soul, sorrow and desolation, and often the rebellion of all our evil passions and tempers. And I will say more, and that is that this crucified state is necessary for us, that it is good, that it is the best and safest, and will bring us much sooner to the height of perfection. A soul that is really enlightened thinks very highly of this conduct of God with regard to her when He permits her to be tried by creatures and overwhelmed with temptations and desolations; and she understands quite well that these are favours rather than hardships, and she would rather die upon the cross of Calvary than live in the sweetnesses of Thabor. Experience will teach her in time the truth of those beautiful words: *Et nox illuminatio mea in deliciis meis, et mea nox obscuram non habet, sed omnia in luce clarescunt.* Even the night shall be a light to me in my happiness, and my night has no obscurity, but all things shine forth in clear light.

After the passive purgation of the soul in this purgatory of suffering through which she must of necessity pass, will come light and rest and joy, through her close union with God, Who makes even this world, place of exile as it is, a little paradise to her. The best prayer of all is that in which we abandon ourselves most to the feelings and dispositions which God Himself implants in the soul, and in which we study with the greatest simplicity, humility, and fidelity to conform ourselves to the will and example of our Lord and Saviour Jesus Christ.

Great God! Who by a wonderful concurrence of very special circumstances hast decreed from all eternity the composition of this little book, permit not that certain spirits, of which some will be wise and some spiritual, should ever be accused before Thy dread tribunal of having contributed in any way to hinder Thy Divine entrance into many hearts, because Thou didst wish to enter there in a manner whose very simplicity shocked them, and by a door which, open as it has been to Thy saints in all ages of the Church, they have wished to close because they knew it not! Grant to us rather that, becoming all as little children, as Jesus Christ commanded us, we may enter ourselves once for all by this little door, and then may be able to show others the way more surely and more efficaciously. Amen.

THE END.

PRINTED BY BALLANTYNE, HANSON AND CO.
EDINBURGH AND LONDON

CPSIA information can be obtained
at www.ICGtesting.com
Printed in the USA
LVHW082352201019
634794LV00002B/24/P